Rhetorical Ethics and
Internetworked Writing

New Directions in
Computers and Composition Studies

Gail E. Hawisher and Cynthia L. Selfe, Series Editors

in preparation:

Rhetorical Ethics and Internetworked Writing

by

James E. Porter
Purdue University

Ablex Publishing Corporation
Greenwich, Connecticut
London, England

Printed in the United States of America

Library of Congress Cataloging-in-Publication Data

Porter, James E., 1954–
    Rhetorical ethics and internetworked writing / James E. Porter.
      p. cm. —(New directions in computers and composition studies)
    Includes bibliographical references and indexes.
    ISBN 1-56750-322-5. — ISBN 1-56750-323-3 (pbk.)
    1. English language—Rhetoric—Study and teaching—Moral and ethical aspects. 2. English language—Computer-assisted instruction—Moral and ethical aspects. 3. World Wide Web (Information retrieval system)—Moral and ethical aspects. 4. Report writing—Study and teaching (Higher)—Moral and ethical aspects. 5. Report writing—Data processing—Moral and ethical aspects. 6. Electronic discussion groups—Moral and ethical aspects. 7. Internet (Computer network)—Moral and ethical aspects. 8. Electronic mail systems—Moral and ethical aspects. 9. College teaching—Moral and ethical aspects. 10. Rhetoric—Moral and ethical aspects. I. Title. II. Series.
PE1404.P614 1998
808'.042'07—dc21   97-43391
                                              CIP

Ablex Publishing Corporation
55 Old Post Road #2
P.O. Box 5297
Greenwich, CT 06830

P

Published in the U.K. and Europe by:
JAI Press Ltd.
38 Tavistock Street
Covent Garden
London WC2E 7PB
England

To Uncle Tom

Contents

Acknowledgments

Portions of Chapter 1 based on:

> Porter, James E. (1994). Electronic writing. In Alan C. Purves (Ed.), *Encyclopedia of English studies and language arts* (pp. 420-424). New York: Scholastic Press.

> Porter, James E. (1995). Rev. of *Computer Ethics. Technical Communication Quarterly, 4*, 96–100.

Portions of Chapters 2 and 3 based on:

> Porter, James E. (1993). Developing a postmodern ethics of rhetoric and composition. In Theresa Enos & Stuart C. Brown (Eds.), *Defining the new rhetorics* (pp. 207–226). Newbury Park, CA: Sage.

Portions of Chapter 5 based on:

> Porter, James E. (1997). Legal realities and ethical hyperrealities: A critical approach toward cyberwriting. In Stuart A. Selber (Ed.), *Computers and technical communication: Pedagogical and programmatic perspectives.* (45–73) Norwood, NJ: Ablex.

> Porter, James E. (1994). Ethics and computers. In Alan C. Purves (Ed.), *Encyclopedia of English studies and language arts* (pp. 456–461). New York: Scholastic Press.

Several grants have provided support for this project. Two grants (in 1992 and 1994) from the School of Liberal Arts Faculty Development Fund at Purdue University provided funds for travel and project expenses. A summer grant in 1992 from the Purdue Research Foundation enabled me to do much of the necessary background reading and preliminary writing. A semester's research leave granted by the Department of English (in Fall 1992) allowed me to devote a large block of time to work on the book.

Special thanks go to Gail Hawisher and Cynthia Selfe for their editorial encouragement and commitment; to Anne Trowbridge and Lisa Barnett at Ablex for their thorough editorial help; and to Anne Wysocki for her cover design. I am especially grateful to several colleagues who provided helpful feedback on all or part of the manuscript at various points in its development: Nancy Allen, Gary Beason, Marilyn Cooper, Ellen Cushman, Janet Carey Eldred, Lester Faigley, Johndan Johnson-Eilola, Tharon Howard, Janice Lauer, Charles Moran, Thomas E. Porter, James

Sosnoski, Patricia Sullivan, and Lisa Toner. I also want to thank the rhetoric/composition Ph.D. students in two courses taught at Purdue University (Ethics, Rhetoric, and Writing in Spring 1995; and Postmodernism and Issues in Composition in Spring 1996) for their helpful responses.

Preface

If you like definite answers, you won't like this book. This book raises a lot of questions, considers a lot of tough cases, and mainly situates itself in the gray areas between certainties. It courts ambiguity and complexity and revels in diffi-culty in its examination of ethical issues in the realm of the Internet, the World Wide Web, electronic mail, and the networked classroom, in the rapidly expand-ing writing space that I refer to as the terrain of *internetworked writing*.

The World Wide Web is probably the fastest growing piece of this terrain. As of March 1995, there were reported to be over 27,000 sites on the World Wide Web, holding some 5 million documents (*Business Week*, February 27, 1995, p. 78). Even more amazing than this figure is an accompanying statistic: The num-ber of sites doubles every 53 days, and the number of documents stored on the Web doubles every six months to a year. According to one study, 72,000 users browsed the World Wide Web in January 1995 (*New York Times*, March 1, 1995). In short, the Web has seen incredible growth and expanding use. This year, 1996, marks the beginning of common usage of URLs in television and magazine advertising, a clear sign of the dominating presence of the World Wide Web on mass consciousness in the United States.

With this rapid growth come predictable problems: misuse of resources, theft of documents, electronic flaming and harassment, and innumerable misunder-standings about how we are to behave in this new medium and how we are to treat one another. (See Chapter 5 for a discussion of ethical issues and cases in the electronic realm.) In 1994 and 1995, the popular media in the United States discovered how fascinating problems in this realm were and began reporting on cases of network pornography, cyberspace harassment and even rape, electronic censorship, as well as "theft" and other misuse of electronic text. One by one, the major news publications—*Time, Newsweek, The New York Times*—have begun publishing "amazing stories" about the Internet. Often cases seem to be chosen for their technological novelty or for their legal ramifications. For instance, in 1994, a student at Texas A&M University broke into a professor's computer account and used it to send racist electronic messages to perhaps 25,000 people (*The Chronicle of Higher Education*, October 26, 1994, p. A24). Although this case might be interesting for its initial novelty, I contend that it is less interesting ethically. First, the break-in itself is unethical (constituting a computer crime, a clear misuse of computer facilities). Second, the "spamming" of a racist message (i.e., its indiscriminate mass distribution on the networks) is also unethical—although its legal status is less clear.

Not all popular treatments of Internet problems eschew the complexities: *Time* magazine's discussion of the problem of "Censoring Cyberspace" (November 21, 1994) examined a genuine dilemma in determining whether universities should restrict access to "pornographic" electronic databases. *Business Week*'s article "Flamed with a Lawsuit" (February 6, 1995) examined the issue of electronic libel. Even so, the emphasis in the popular media has been on the legalities, rather than the ethics, of cyberspace—and on telling the public about the shocking incidents—"Look! Teenagers are downloading pornography off the Internet!"—rather than exploring the complexities.

My focus in this volume is mainly on the ethical complexities and only secondarily on the legalities of various uses of electronic discourse. My interest is cases not of clear computer crime but of ambiguous and day-to-day electronic ethics. (Not that I'm above telling a few shocking stories myself—but only if they are instances of an ethical confusion.) My contention is that when we enter the Internet, we bring expectations and ethics from the print world and from the face-to-face conversational world, ethics that do not quite correspond to the new medium we find ourselves in, a medium that is not print nor conversation, not the library nor the telephone, but some new ecology, some new space for which we have not yet developed an ethical paradigm.

This book attempts to develop such an ethical paradigm, what I call a *rhetorical ethics for internetworked writing.* You will notice that this ethic begins with a basic disciplinary assumption that I hope to demonstrate through the course of the study: that computer-networked activity is a type of *writing*, and that a writing/rhetoric frame (and not the more common computer-mediated communication, or CMC, frame) is the most helpful one for understanding the dynamic of network activity. The disciplinary perspective I develop borrows from the fields of rhetoric, ethics (particularly postmodern ethics), and computers and composition—and merges the three into a framework that I think is helpful for critiquing writing activities on the network. *Rhetorical ethics* is a frame that can provide *help* in answering some of the questions that have been arising on the Net, although in most cases it does not directly answer those questions.

I think there are *some* definite answers to some questions regarding the ethics of internetworked writing—and when I get to those kinds of questions, I do try to provide a clear answer (where I am most certain readers should be most skeptical). However, I am not that interested in the easy cases or the clear answers because I believe that the clearer the answer the less interesting the question. The interesting facet of human relations lies in the tougher issues, in the matters we struggle with and disagree over as we write or talk to one another. That is the realm of rhetorical ethics.

Rhetorical ethics does not often provide definite answers to content questions. It is a realm of sophistry and casuistry and maybes and it depends. However, it does provide guidance in the form of some general principles (respect for audience being one) as well as in the form of procedural strategies. Rhetorical ethics will not tell us directly, yes or no, whether a particular email note is actually harassment, but it will suggest some strategies to help us decide how to decide. Rhetorical ethics is procedural, it is case specific, it provides some principles (although it does not trust them very much, as it is sensitive to the mandates of particular situations), and it privileges the specific and concrete over the general and abstract. For these reasons, and because of its flexibility and adaptability in the face of tough cases, it offers an extremely powerful paradigmatic perspective. Neither mass culture nor academic culture has yet appreciated the role that rhetoric can play in everyday life.

When problems arise in the electronic realm, arguers often appeal to "the law" as the instrument that can provide guidance. This book argues that the law is insufficient, that we need an *ethic* for electronic writing because (a) the law as written and practiced does not always support or promote ethical practice; (b) the law drags slowly behind what people are actually doing, especially in the realm of new technologies; (c) the law seldom addresses the day-to-day activities, the strange occurrences, or the new circumstances; and (d) despite what many arguers think, "the law" is not a single, well-defined entity that can provide us with clear answers in every instance—the law itself is often murky. In the realm of day-to-day electronic writing, we need an ethic that will help us in our mundane decisions about writing. Laws that were developed for print materials (e.g., the Fair Use statute in copyright law) may or may not apply for electronic discourse. Although some general principles regarding respect for intellectual property no doubt do carry over, it is not always clear in particular cases exactly how the print principles really apply in each particular electronic case. If I find an article posted on a newsgroup that ends with the designation "Copyright 1995 Janet Jackson," can I repost that article on a LISTSERV group that I am a member of? If I do not know the answer to that question, how do I find out? (Here is a tentative answer: A developing common law ethic seems to be emerging that would permit such a practice, as long as the author's copyright notice remains attached to the reposted message.)

How can *rhetoric*, a despised art, possibly help this process? Popularly, *rhetoric* is the term for political manipulation, deceit, and lying. ("Of course, *our* side always tells the truth, the *other* side uses rhetoric.") I cannot fault the public or the press too much for this misconception of rhetoric, as it is not far from young Plato's view in *Gorgias*, which opposed rhetoric (as a knack like cookery) over and against truth. However, there is another view of rhetoric, the largely unrecognized disciplinary view that sees rhetoric as a noble art: Rhetoric is the art of constructing discourse—which includes figuring out what to say or write, where, when, how, and to whom. The "to whom" part—a.k.a. the audience—makes rhetoric an art of human relations, and here is where we can see the point of overlap with ethics, and here is where we should be able to see its wide applicability and usefulness in human affairs.

Ethics refers to the relations of humans to one another (and also to their God, or gods, and to their environment). Ethics is the practical art of determining the *should*, the action we should take. How we should act with one another is the central focus of ethics, and how that interaction with one another is established through acts of discourse delineates the province of rhetorical ethics—a pretty vast province as it turns out. Rhetorical ethics, as I define it, has to do with questions about human relations as they are constructed and maintained through acts of discourse. (The question of the historical and disciplinary relationship between rhetoric and ethics is discussed in more detail in Chapter 2.) This book focuses in particular on the rhetorical ethics of internetworked writing: How should our relations with one another be constructed through the realm of networked computer communications?

The concept that ties rhetoric and ethics together is *action*. It is not unusual to see ethics discussed in terms of moral action and moral decision making, but rhetoric is usually thought of as the art of producing an oral or written artifact, a piece of writing, or a speech. Rhetoric is typically viewed as the productive art of *making* something instead of *doing* something, and so the common view understands writing either as *the process of inscription* or as *the inscribed text itself*.

However, there is a sense in which rhetoric (and writing) is also a doing. It is an action in the sense that it establishes a relationship with an assumed audience and pushes forward a "should," a picture of how things ought to be for "us." I argue, in Chapter 2 and elsewhere, that all acts of writing are also ethical actions (as well as products), in that they always inevitably assume a "should" for some "we." Figuring how we might determine and negotiate this *should* and define this *we* in our internetworked writing—on the Web, on the Internet, and in our electronic classrooms—is the purpose of this book.

1

Ethics in Internetworked Writing Classrooms and Communities

> Everything we do, then, as teachers, has moral overtones.
> —Noddings, 1984, p. 179

> Moral judgment is what we "always already" exercise in virtue of being immersed in a network of human relationships that constitute our life together.
> —Benhabib, 1992, p. 125

Most notions of ethical rhetoric or ethical writing, even in contemporary postmodern critical theory, derive from print assumptions. For instance, the legal and ethical understandings of copyright and Fair Use derive from a world of paper and ink, they apply to a world of books and journal articles and magazines and newspapers and academic papers, and for the most part they do not apply (and certainly not in the same way) to technologies like the World Wide Web and hypermedia and electronic mail.

Overall, this project examines what it means to write *electronic* discourse ethically. How do the rules change (and did we know what they were for print?) when we move from the world of print to the world of virtual discourse, to the realm of what I term *internetworked writing*? Such a question should be of special importance to two groups: cyberwriters (that is, network participants, users who post messages to electronic groups or who use texts from electronic archives or who themselves maintain such sites) and teachers using network technology as a way to teach writing (Hawisher & Selfe, 1991b; Porter, 1992b, 1993b, 1993c, 1994a, 1994b; Rezmierski, 1992; Schwartz, 1990; Stager, 1992; Webster, 1992).

Writing teachers in networked computer classrooms especially need to take heed of the issue of Internet ethics. Many of us teaching in professional writing and rhetoric at Purdue University, and many writing teachers at other universities and secondary schools, regularly have students using electronic mail, joining LISTSERV groups, using gopher and FTP to access remote archives, browsing remote World Wide Web archives using tools like Netscape and Mosaic, constructing their own web sites, engaging in newsgroup discussions, and interacting in MUD sessions with people not on the class rosters. For instance, in my Spring 1995 graduate course on Ethics, Rhetoric, and Writing, the students contributed to an "electronic community journal" by publically posting responses to class topics to a LISTSERV group called PURWCLAS (for PURdue Writing Class). This discussion was not limited to class members, however, as we invited colleagues from rhetoric programs across the United States to participate in our virtual journal.

As students move around the nets, pulling in files and interacting with people around the globe, the parameters of the writing class get incredibly stretched. What and where is "my" class when my business writing students are doing collaborative assignments with communication students in Ecuador? Or when my graduate students can have electronic interactions with the people whose works they are reading in a course?

This project raises questions about the ethics of *internetworked writing*—by which I mean computer-based electronic writing that makes synchronous or asynchronous links to remote participants or databases. Internetworked writing refers to the creation, design, organization, storage, and distribution of electronic information via wide-area networks. (Electronic information includes not only verbal text, but also audio, visual, and cinematic "text" distributed via the Internet and World Wide Web.) Internetworked writing includes activities such as posting email messages to groups or individuals, browsing and collecting documents from electronic archives, developing electronic text for and maintaining electronic archives and web sites, and synchronous conferencing. *Inter*networked writing differs from networked writing in that it involves writing for and on the Internet. It refers to more than simply closed, local-area classroom or corporate systems, but refers more broadly to what we might consider a wider *public* space (although the exact notion of "public" may vary from technology to technology). It refers to wide-area and public uses of electronic text (as opposed to, for instance, using word processing to create a print document). In the sense I am using the term, internetworked writing also refers to more than simply *posting* text: It includes reading, browsing, and collecting electronic text, as *research* activities that are also types of *writing* activities.

In the writing class which employs some form of internetworked writing, traditional roles for teachers and for students are being challenged and modified. The chief significance of this change is that the dynamic mix of the writing classroom is changed. Teachers and students are not the only characters involved, and the individual teacher's authority in the classroom might need to be negotiated with a larger set of participants. If I decide to have my writing class use email or Netscape to scan the World Wide Web for research sources, the first thing I will have to do is enter a process of negotiating my use of resources with the Purdue University Computing Center (PUCC). Charles Moran (1990) sees this kind of development as bringing writing teachers some institutional power (through the process of gaining technological expertise), but also maybe some headaches, as it raises the possibility of "turf wars" with institutional computing centers.

Published accounts of electronic communities in computers and composition research have tended to focus on the dynamics of the synchronous classroom as a closed community—that is, mainly or exclusively on the students and teacher who appear on the class roster, a fairly well-defined community in terms of its participants and geographical location (e.g., Romano, 1993). However, the internetworked classroom is a much more crowded and ill-defined place. As Figure 1.1 illustrates, when the writing classroom employs internetworked electronic communications, classroom borders are opened and new parties admitted into the rhetorical and social mix: computing center personnel, students and teachers from other universities, professionals from all walks of life, members of the public, government officials, and so on.

As we open the borders of the writing classroom, our formerly well-established conventions for classroom ethics are disturbed. Now we are in a realm where "our" classroom practices have to be negotiated with campus computing policy, Internet policy, and the diverse conventions and contentions of different electronic communities and technologies. There are obvious advantages to involving our students in this rich rhetorical stew. There are also some troubling ethical and legal implications.

As classroom borders formerly defined by building space begin to change, new ethical issues arise. With the internetworked writing class come added responsibilities for teachers and students, a bevy of new social relations, and the possibility of new ethical dilemmas involving a broad range of interested parties, sometimes providing competing guidelines and policies. At Purdue we are certainly aware of how PUCC can change our writing environment, and it seems to do so almost daily. We are aware of how technical changes always represent ethical choices (about access for instance), but technological developments *always* have ethical and legal ramifications. As a writing teacher you may have one set of expectations about what constitutes appropriate writing within your class— and in the traditional classroom you had a fair amount of autonomy in determining the standards for appropriateness. However, what happens when your students' electronic writing is deemed inappropriate according to guidelines instituted by campus computing? For instance, what if a synchronous chat session in "your" class is deemed by campus policy to be "offensive speech"? Further complications arise when campus computing policy abridges students' rights as citizens to practice free speech. If your students post aggressive and critical

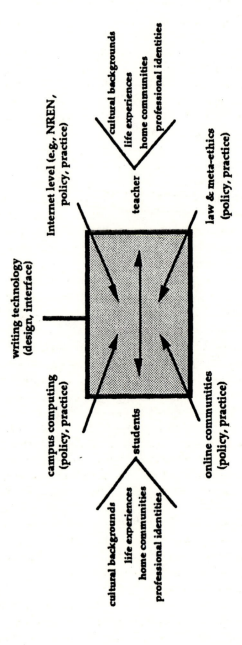

FIGURE 1.1.   Social/ethical relations in the internetworked writing class.

4

messages to newsgroups, can campus computing revoke their computer accounts? (The response to this question has to do with the issue of the status of newsgroups as public forums. Is a newsgroup a restricted or unrestricted public forum, and what difference might this make to teachers and students doing course work in such forums?)

By no means do I think the traditional classroom is a closed and private place. It has its institutional and political connections as well: The outside world does get in, but usually in ways that are so familiar we may not think about them very much. There are more established patterns, expectations, and ethical norms. Teacher and student roles are relatively well defined; in fact, we may have to struggle to free ourselves *from* these roles.

Acceptable behaviors, roles, and ethical norms are not nearly so clear in the internetworked classroom, which is a writing class that both moves out into the Internet to disperse and at the same time allows the Internet into the classroom. In fact, the differences between "inside" and "outside," and between public and private space, blur. The notion of "our classroom" becomes obsolete as the space of the classroom dissolves and as teachers' presumed stewardship over it disappears. The electronic network is a new geographical region where our old trustworthy borders (classroom vs. workplace, speech vs. writing, industry vs. academy) are no longer viable. The network is a place where our favorite divisions are challenged, breached, and eliminated. We are now in the process of creating new borders, new divisions, new categories for this realm, but these new conventions are by no means established. It is not clear that they ever will be.

It is time to make an important point: I do not want to suggest that, because of the legal and ethical complications involved, writing teachers should not use electronic writing in their classes—just the opposite. The internetworked classroom has the *potential* (not yet realized) to empower students by giving their work potential for broad distribution, a development that I strongly want to promote and a development that the field of computers and composition has for some time been actively promoting (see Hawisher & LeBlanc, 1992; Hawisher & Selfe, 1989, 1991a; Selfe & Hilligoss, 1994). I would like to see us overturn the traditional hierarchies and norms and reconstruct social relations in the classroom, and I believe that the electronic network can potentially enable that. By joining network discussion groups students can engage other students across the country, even across the world. They can access government documents *as* they are published. They can interact with professionals in business and industry and with government officials. They can become, and not just pretend to become, active professionals and citizens in the writing classroom.

Networked electronic communications—in particular, email postings to public newsgroups and professional LISTSERV lists—allow for the rapid and frequent exchange of ideas across conventional institutional, disciplinary, and international boundaries. LISTSERV groups like HUMANIST and H-RHETOR, for instance, have helped to bridge the distance gap between scholars across the globe and between the various humanities disciplines. The TECHWR-L (Technical Writing) list is helping to break down the long-standing division between academics who teach technical writing and professionals who do it; now the two groups can speak to one another directly via the network (see Sullivan & Dautermann, 1996). The PURWCLAS list (Purdue Writing Class, of which I am listowner) was established to promote "long-distance class discussion" about international business communication, linking Purdue students with students and teachers in Rhode Island, France, Germany, Latin America, Indiana, and other exotic places. The technology enables new rhetorical arrangements and promotes more frequent communication between formerly separate groups.

Unlike television, the electronic network is a medium that calls for the active participation of students, *who must write or read in order to participate*. In this medium, the publication decision often belongs solely to the writer, and publication can be instantaneous. (In some online conferences, for instance, the gap between writing and publishing is no more than a keystroke.) Although there are some drawbacks to having such open borders to the classroom (e.g., are student writers *ready* to publish their work?), overall the advantages are exciting as students will have even greater opportunity to engage diverse audiences with their writing.

I am definitely in favor of using electronic networking technologies in writing classes. I think it is where we should be teaching writing, in part precisely *because* of the ethical and political dissonances that do get played out there. Networking offers a way to break through the borders of the classroom, to teach writing in live public forums. I see the opening of these classroom borders as a good thing, promoting broader interchange, better research, more purposeful writing. In general, I see it supporting the aims of writing instruction, but we do need to be alert to the ethical implications of going out on the net. The tremendous potential I am imagining here has by no means been realized—and there is no guarantee that it will be.

Writing teachers working within these new spaces had better be prepared to make some tough ethical decisions regarding issues such as access, privacy, electronic harassment, and intellectual property. We have relatively well-defined conventions that govern student and teacher behaviors and interactions in the traditional classroom of desks and chairs, of rows and brick walls, of books and articles. However, when "the classroom"—now in quotation marks and up for renegotiation—becomes electronic, what happens? The walls and desks and chairs and books that help us define our positions and relations with one another disappear. Those conventional architectural and spatial configurations dissolve, to be replaced by electronic configurations for which we do not yet have a map.

Electronic networking changes the very nature of the "classroom," multiplying the number of rhetorical and social relations possible (with many of those being unfamiliar and complicated relations), and raising new questions about the ethics and etiquette of computer use. What rights can the composition teacher exercise in maintaining control over network usage by his or her class? How should instructors proceed if their students use the computer network to harass or insult others, or if others outside the class harass students in it? How do the principles and conventions that apply to conventional classroom discussion change in the environment of electronic conferencing? (That is, do the rules change just because the medium is different? I argue that they certainly do.) What happens when the student's right to free expression in the classroom—which includes the network—and the instructor's responsibility for instruction in the classroom conflict? What constitutes fair use, or ethical redistribution, of others' electronic texts? Teachers need to be aware that the conventional policies and practices governing traditional classroom settings (e.g., print copyright guidelines) may be inadequate, even illegal or unethical, for handling the distinct dynamic of internetworked writing.

It is clear to those who participate in internetworked exchanges, and to those who study them, that conventional notions of rhetoric (that is, the notions of appropriateness, of authority, of agency, of audience, etc., derived from speech or print paradigms) are radically changed in the medium of electronic networked communication. What are the rules or guidelines for holding "discussions"—if we can even call them that—in an IRC (Internet Relay Chat) session? (IRC is a multiuser system that allows for real-time conversation between a number of participants.) What are the turn-taking conventions for a MUD conversation that proceeds without the visual cues that you would get with face-to-face visual contact (that tells you when there are openings in the conversation), but which is nonetheless a real-time "conversation" held via written messages?

My interest in these issues is partly motivated by my feeling that there is a decided gap between the principles espoused by various network advocates (like the Electronic Frontier Foundation) and ethical problems arising on the nets. For instance, the various ways electronic text tends to be produced, distributed, and reproduced (especially via wide-area networks, or WANS) are raising a serious challenge both to the conventional notions of intellectual property rights (i.e., authorship and ownership of text) and to the publishing industry. Who owns electronic text? Who has the right to borrow it, and for what uses? The ethical/ political principles people frequently invoke do not help them address such problems. *Free speech* and *pluralism* (or *diversity*) are the most common god terms. Like *democracy*, everybody believes in *free speech*, which makes such a term useful as a rallying cry and strong as a principle, but nearly useless in terms of mediating differences about the limits of free speech (Fish, 1994). In short, it functions well as a prayer, a rallying cry, or as a starting point for inquiry. It does not function so well as a heuristic or guide to addressing ethical dilemmas facing cyberwriters.

Conventional legal guidelines are not much help either. Who is responsible for the content of pornographic electronic text that may be in transit through various network sites or that may be deposited at a site without prior approval or knowledge of the site manager? Can teachers and administrators be held ethically responsible or even legally liable for offensive materials stored on their computer systems or posted on their online conferences? The question of legal liability on the networks is a complicated one, as Henry Perrit (1992) points out: "The legal system is struggling to adapt traditional doctrines to new market structures and technologies of information production and distribution" (p. 29). Anne Wells Branscomb (1991) refers to the Internet as an "electronic frontier." Law, acceptable use policies, and other conventions are in the process of developing, but they are not yet firmly developed. Their status is much contested, and the result is numerous questions and complications regarding users' rights and responsibilities on electronic networks.

It is important at this point to distinguish between *ethical* and *legal*. *Legal* describes what is allowable to do; *ethical* describes what one *should* do, whether or not it is legal. Ethics extends to specific situations and, further, to questions of what is right, what is preferable, and how one should act in any given case. Law by itself is inadequate as an ethical system. Not all legally permissible choices are ethical ones, not all ethical choices are legal (Branscum, 1991).

Obviously, the legal has a strong bearing on the ethical. Ethics as a decision-making activity should certainly be guided by, although not completely determined or replaced by, what is legal. Legal issues in electronic networking are in the process of being sorted out right now. Yet what people do on the networks will shape what comes to be legal—that is, what the norms and conventions will be for electronic discourse, and to what extent the law will specify or constrain those norms. In short, we are in an ethically sensitive and important time right now because what we as users (and as teachers of users) do on the networks will help constitute the norms for such discourse as they become stabilized and legally sanctioned (or not) in the future.

Although ethics has been dismissed by some as simply no more than formalized personal and subjective opinion, as religious belief, or as critically unjustifiable foundationalism, it is impossible to function in social contexts without making ethical choices on a daily basis. Ethics is critical and also inevitable. As Seyla Benhabib (1992) points out, by "virtue of being immersed in a network of human relationships" (p. 125) we are already in a space where moral judgment is required. If we engage in any act of communication, we cannot avoid making decisions that constitute our relations with others. At this point, we are in the realm of ethics. The difficulty of making ethical choices on a social scale is that ethical standards are subject to a wide range of variation and to debate. Thus, sometimes law is the final arbiter, the last if not best means for mediating some irreconcilable ethical differences in a society.

All these complexities make the Internet, as well as the internetworked writing classroom, a very promising site for problems—and so also for ethical study.

INTERNETWORKED WRITING

Do we think we know what *writing* is? In many contexts the term is ambiguous. Writing sometimes refers to *any* inscribed document; sometimes it refers only to *published* documents. Writing can refer to the *process* by which documents are produced. Sometimes writing means *handwriting*, as opposed to print. Where are the limits of writing? Is a hypertext application produced in STORYSPACE "writing"? Sure, but it is certainly not conventional writing, as a STORYSPACE document appears in the visual form of notecards (representing nodes) with connecting arrows between them (links). However, what about a multimedia hypertext that is predominantly music and animation, with some written captions here and there? Is *that* writing?

Computer technology is blurring the boundaries between the print paradigm notion of writing-as-inscribed-text (what people usually think of as writing: words in sentences and paragraphs presented on paper) and writing-as-publishing or writing in new visual manifestations (like hypertext and CD-ROM). Before we can talk about the ethics of internetworked writing, we have to have some sense of what we mean by that complicated term *writing*.

Writing is produced through a variety of technological forms ranging from the simple (the pencil) to the advanced (the word processor) to the highly complex (the networked multimedia publishing workstation). Theory on the rhetoric of writing technology argues that these forms of technology are not neutral tools. Although these tools do not determine the writer's behavior (because they always offer some degree of choice), they do channel the writer's consciousness, enabling and encouraging some types of communication and discouraging others (Bolter, 1991; Heim, 1987; Ong, 1982; Sullivan, 1991).

As a form of writing technology, the computer is more than simply an expensive device for making writing look better, for making editing and revision easier, or, through networking, for sending messages more conveniently (Porter, 1994c). The computer, in its variety of technological forms, influences the consciousness of the writer and shapes both the production and reception of the message, allowing for (and restricting) social relations, influencing the writer's view of communication and writing, enabling (and constraining) certain writing practices. Writing, both as a textual product and as a process of composition, is dramatically altered in the electronic environment of the computer.

This discussion occupies a terrain in which rhetoric/composition theories of "writing" merge with a concept not typically treated in rhetoric/composition—publishing (Amiran, Unsworth, & Chaski, 1992). "Publishing" as a concept is distinct from "composing" because "publishing" foregrounds the question of distribution as well as the economic and proprietary facets of writing (the term *composing*, as it is understood in rhetoric/composition, does not imply these concerns). However, conceived as a process, publishing is certainly intertwined with composing—and what is happening is that the growth of the Internet and the free-wheeling approach to distributing text over the Internet are breaking down the old conceptual and institutional boundaries between writing-as-publishing and writing-as-composing, raising new issues for scholars, publishers, and librarians, as well as writing teachers.

The networked computer is a tool both for composing (or producing) documents and for publishing (or distributing) them. In one sense, what we might call "electronic writing" (see Bolter, 1991; Heim, 1987; Moulthrop, 1991) refers to a mode of *production*: to writing created in whole or in part with a computer, in whatever format (e.g., print, digital) and with whatever form of writing technology (e.g., word processing, desktop publishing, email, synchronous discussion, hypermedia authoring). From this perspective, all documents produced with a computer are electronic writing, and, like the word *writing* itself, electronic writing can refer to the created document or to the process of creation. Also, electronic writing in this sense can include more than merely verbal text, as multimedia technologies allow writers to complement the verbal with sound, icons, and both static and animated visual graphics.

In another sense, however, electronic writing refers to a specific mode of *distribution*: to the transmittal of electronic documents (or e-texts) intended to be read online (although, of course, they can always be printed out) and distributed to readers electronically via local or wide-area networks. This second notion of electronic writing is further complicated by its connections with the term *electronic publishing*.

In the print paradigm, amateurs and professionals both "write," but what distinguishes them is that professionals "publish" their writing. In the conventional print realm, the term *published* carries several connotations: (a) that a document will be widely distributed, if not for commercial sale than usually for professional recognition or promotional purposes by an *author* (although the text is usually owned and distributed by someone other than the author); (b) that a document has met some editorial standard of quality (published writing has a special authority because readers assume that it has been reviewed, screened, and edited); and (c) that a document will *look* professional in terms of its layout, design, and packaging (the appearance of the document itself carries some weight in convincing readers of its authority).

Developments in electronic publishing are challenging these common criteria and upsetting conventional expectations. Writing used to mean preparing a paper manuscript (consisting of words in sentences and paragraphs) that would then be handed over to an editor, who in turn would screen the manuscript before passing it on to the commercial publisher. The process was mainly linear, usually slow, and different facets of the publishing process were handled by different specialists. Writers did not have to worry about matters such as type font and page design. However, electronic publishing now provides any writer with the means for creating laser-printed documents that *look* like published quality and the means for distributing documents instantly via computer networks. Electronic publishing—on the World Wide Web, for instance—makes the publication process potentially much more dynamic and interactive. As Patricia Sullivan (1991) pointed out, it places more responsibility in the hands of the individual writer, who can now do tasks formerly the purview of the layout editor, printer, and typesetter. The technology has narrowed the gap between *writing* a document and *publishing* it, and it is in fact changing the very notion of writing.

The sense of electronic publishing that seems to have emerged as the consensus understanding is in reference to documents distributed via computer networks for the expressed purpose of being read online (Hawkins, Smith, Dietlein, Joseph, & Rindfuss, 1992). This notion of electronic publishing is networked based, viewing the computer network as the place of publication for electronic texts (i.e., documents existing in digital format). This perspective focuses on *how documents are distributed* and views electronic publishing as offering an alternative to print publications, not simply as a more efficient method of producing print publications.

Published online electronic writing exists in many forms, ranging from the formal to the informal and from local to wide distribution: electronic academic publications (like *EJournal*, *DEOS [Distance Education Online Symposium] NEWS*, and *POSTMODERN CULTURE*); online conferences or discussion groups (like HUMANIST and PURTOPOI); bulletin boards and newsgroups; World-Wide Web sites, as typically browsed with Netscape or Mosaic; hypertext; and networked education systems (such as the Texas Education Network [TENET]). The NII, or National Information Infrastructure (an offshoot of the National Research and Education Network, or NREN), funded by the federal government, links libraries, schools, companies, and universities in an immense network that provides wide access to electronically published documents. Online information is catalogued at various sites and can be accessed by users through remote login via FTP (file transfer protocol) or through use of HTTP (hypertext transfer protocol) using an interface like Netscape. Through the technology of Internet Relay Chat and with programs like DAEDALUS and ASPECTS, writers can engage in synchronous (i.e., real-time, or nearly simultaneous) "dialogue" or "chat."

The use of network technology as a tool for electronic publishing raises questions about the status of documents. Is any email message distributed to a newsgroup, bulletin board, or discussion list or any entry on a MOO or MUD synchronous discussion an electronic *publication*? Some discussion groups permit instantaneous publication: Whenever anyone posts an email message to the group it is distributed to all members—and is thus "published." Other groups exercise more editorial restraint, screening messages for appropriateness or bundling messages into packets according to topic (called "digesting"). On many discussion lists messages are stored and indexed and are retrievable. Thus the technology makes publishing more accessible to the individual writer who has access to a computer and a modem—and yet the editorial constraint that often (but not always) characterizes print publishing is often (but not always) missing in networked publishing.

One significant feature of writing created and distributed via the computer and intended to be read online is that it brings closer together the activities of writing and publishing. In the era of online publications and wide-area networks, the once vast split between writing (as composing the text) and publishing (as printing and distributing the text) has narrowed. In online conferences, for instance, the gap between writing and publishing has been reduced to a keystroke (Poster, 1990), and control of that keystroke is now in the hands of the writer, not, as formerly, the editor or publisher (Sullivan, 1991). Many applaud this development, seeing electronic publishing as signaling the end of writers' and readers' reliance on commercial publishers (and on other editorial intermediaries) and as a means for providing wider public access to a large number of online and unrestricted (and perhaps even free) documents. Others caution that this ideal will be realized only when such technology is made available on a wide scale—for example, to the urban and rural poor, who currently do not have access to this technology. Still others worry that such capabilities will lead to an explosion of bad information, more clutter, and more noise rather than useful information—that is, we might have a more vocal citizenry, but not necessarily a wiser or better informed one.

When does the electronically *written* word become the *published* word? In the traditional writing classroom the teacher usually does not need to worry about publishing issues because in the traditional composition classroom, writing activities usually remain within the relatively secure confines of the course, shared only with the teacher and perhaps with classmates. It is decidedly *not* published. However, in the realm of internetworked writing, student text can be quickly distributed over a wide territory. In fact, it can be quickly and easily published—and this gives it a social, ethical, and legal status unlike student writing in the traditional classroom.

My use of the term *internetworked writing* is intended to obscure the conventional distinction between *writing* and *publishing* and to reflect my view that the act of writing in internetworked space is often also an act of publishing. In electronic discourse the once separate acts of *writing* and *publishing* become merged. The significance of this change for writing teachers should not be underestimated. I suspect many writing teachers in computer classrooms still hold to a print-paradigm view of the writing process, but when their students' writing on electronic networks actually achieves the status of "publication," its ethical and legal status as text changes as well.

So why not use a readymade term like *computer-mediated communication*, or CMC? Because I see an important disciplinary distinction between research that views the computer as a writing technology and research that views the computer as a communication medium—in other words, CMC research. The former sort of research focuses on writing in or with the medium, whereas the latter research focuses on general usage of the medium. CMC researchers (e.g., Hartman et al., 1991; Komsky, 1991; Mackay, 1988; Rice & Shook, 1988; Sproull & Kiesler, 1991; Steinfield, 1992) typically focus on patterns of usage (e.g., frequency of use, attitude toward use, types of interactions), usually in terms of a general communication theory and sometimes based on instrumentalist and/or management assumptions about the communication dynamic (see DiMatteo, 1991). Although that research provides information about user habits, it does not predominantly address *writing* issues: How is the medium used as a writing tool? What happens to writers and writing within the medium? How is the writing process changed by the medium? Because I am working in different research paradigms (rhetoric and composition, computers and composition, professional writing), which view the computer very specifically as a *writing* technology, I prefer the distinguishing term *internetworked writing*.

Why not *desktop publishing*? Desktop publishing is an older (and perhaps now obsolete) term that refers to the creation of publication-quality *paper* documents, usually from a single site ("the desktop"), through the use of multiple technologies available at that site (e.g., scanner, laser printer, graphics and layout software). Internetworked writing refers exclusively to the publication of electronic texts—that is, texts that are (a) written for the expressed purpose of being read online (although, of course, they can always be printed out); and (b) distributed electronically, through wide-area networks. This can be distinguished from desktop publishing—or what has also been called "electronic-*aided* publishing" (see Hawkin, Smith, Dietlein, Joseph, & Rindfuss, 1992; Tovey, 1995), which refers to the use of computer technology to produce more conventional print documents.

It is, of course, possible for various forms of computer writing technology to be combined and entangled. Any text written for any purpose can be distributed and read electronically or in paper form, whether or not the text was designed for that medium. However, printing out and reading a paper copy of a synchronous chat discussion or a hypertext database certainly changes the rhetorical nature of the text. Being *in* a synchronous chat discussion is being involved in an internetworked writing activity. Reading the transcript of the event is a dramatically different kind of rhetorical experience—actually, not the same experience at all. The ethics of the one situation is quite different from the ethics of the other.

TREATMENTS OF COMPUTER ETHICS

The people doing work on ethics and rhetoric have not said enough about computers, and the people doing work in computers and composition have not said enough about ethics. So this study attempts to bridge a gap between two groups whose respective areas of expertise have much to offer one another.

You will find numerous comprehensive and systematic discussions of rhetorical ethics in philosophy and postmodern critical theory (Benhabib, 1992; Fish, 1994; Foucault, 1984b, 1984c, 1984e, 1987; Habermas, 1990; Jonsen & Toulmin, 1988; Lyotard & Thébaud, 1985), as well as in rhetoric/composition (Cooper, 1991; Katz, 1992, 1993; Miller, 1993; Phelps, 1988). Yet such discussions rarely mention the specific realm of internetworked writing, and the theorists not in rhetoric/composition seldom focus on writing issues per se. Although most rhetorical ethicists agree that ethics has to be situated in particular events, particular communities, and particular technologies, none has yet moved to treat ethical issues in the situated realm of internetworked writing.

You typically find very little discussion of ethics in how-to guides to Internet use. Guides such as Hahn and Stout's *The Internet Complete Reference* (1994), Eager's *Using the World Wide Web* (1994), and Krol's *The Whole Internet* (1992) provide very little discussion, if any, of ethical considerations involved in network use. (Handbooks will give you 400+ pages of information on the *how-to*, but maybe no more than a page or two on the *whether-to*.) Hahn and Stout's *The Internet Complete Reference* (1994) is not so complete. It has one chapter that focuses on browsing, or navigating, the World Wide Web, but does not offer advice on how to write for the web, nor does it focus on ethical and legal problems that may arise. The first edition of Krol's *The Whole Internet* (1992) has half a page on "network ethics" (p. 35). The dominant focus of the book is on listing resources and instructions for browsing and navigating through the network, but it has very little to say about legal and ethical matters. The second edition (1994) shows only slight improvement: It includes an entire chapter on "What's Allowed on the Internet?", but only three generalized paragraphs on the legalities and ethics of intellectual property in cyberspace. Eager's (1994) book tells you how to use HTML markup language in order to make a hyperlink to another web site, but it does not consider the ethics of such a link, nor does it consider possible legal problems with random linking to sites whose documents may have a protected status. Angell and Heslop's handbook, *The Elements of E-Mail Style* (1994), does provide some generic advice about netiquette and about avoiding involvement in flame wars. It provides pithy advice, such as "Don't use abusive or obscene language in e-mail" (p. 5), but it does not handle borderline difficult cases, and it does not develop a comprehensive discussion of email ethics. Such handbooks provide hundreds of pages on *how* to do the Internet, but hardly anything on *whether we should*.

The excuse that the legal and ethical considerations have not yet been sorted out, that such considerations will come "later," is a lame one. The law is never totally, finally, and definitively "sorted out," but that does not mean that legal and ethical considerations cannot be introduced into the discussion. Handbooks that do not consider the legal/ethical issues of cyberwriting are irresponsible in separating the *how-to* from the *whether-to*. They represent what Feenberg (1991) calls an instrumental approach to technology: that technology is assumed to be neutrally "good," to be operating on behalf of human progress, and that ethical considerations are separate from technical knowledge. This kind of "systems rationalization"—this division between technical knowledge and social/political consciousness, between abstracted systems design and situated use by people—is all too common in the computer industry (it is probably the dominant paradigm), and it is the paradigm that a *critical* approach to the design of computer systems opposes.

It is surprising to me that computers and composition researchers and theorists have not said more about ethical issues in the use of computers for writing—except that indirectly they have said a lot. Numerous commentators have discussed the *political* implications of the use of the computer in writing classrooms and in society at large (Cooper & Selfe, 1990; Janangelo, 1991; Ohmann, 1985; Poster, 1990; Romano, 1993; Selfe, 1994; Shields, 1996). Occasionally—or perhaps, inevitably—these discussions touch on ethical concerns. For example, an article by Pamela Takayoshi (1994) in *Computers and Composition* considers whether computer networks are really hospitable places for women. Such a discussion does have ethical implications concerning how gender intersects with notions of community, justice, fairness, and ethics, although Takayoshi does not directly discuss those issues from an ethics framework. Some have considered the ethics of teacher surveillance (Janangelo, 1991; Provenzo, 1992), the issue of whether networks do or do not support egalitarianism, and gender and ethnic identity on the networks. The issue of power, especially as it pertains to gender and ethnic relations, has been addressed frequently in journal articles and in chapters in collections. Cynthia Selfe (1994; see also Selfe & Selfe, 1994) perhaps comes closest to any within the computers and composition community to recognizing the ethical implications of internetworked writing. Her treatment focuses mainly on the economics and politics of technology, but ties those factors to ethical issues such as access. Janangelo (1991) considers the issue of teacher responsibility to students (both collectively and as individuals). Jobst (1987) is one of few studies that directly examines the ethics of computer use in the writing classroom, although his discussion does not consider network use.

A few book-length treatments have taken up issues involving the politics and ethics of electronic networking. In *The Mode of Information*, Mark Poster (1990) treats political issues involved in computer use, although he eschews issues pertaining explicitly to ethics. Lester Faigley's *Fragments of Rationality* (1992), which has one chapter on synchronous interchanges in a networked writing class, comes closest perhaps to considering explicitly the ethical dilemmas of writing and to situating those dilemmas in the electronic realm. Tharon Howard's dissertation, *The Rhetoric of Electronic Communities* (1992), examines political and ethical issues in the formation of an electronic community (the PURTOPOI LISTSERV group) and takes up the issue of freedom versus constraint on electronic networks (see also Gurak, 1995, 1997).

Although not in the field of computers and composition per se, authors such as Howard Rheingold, Mitchell Kapor, Pamela Samuelson, and Anne Wells Branscomb publish frequently on legal and ethical problems involved in computer-mediated communication (CMC). Rheingold's *Virtual Community* (1993) considers a number of legal and ethical issues involved in CMC. However, these discussions do not focus very much on *writing* issues, and they tend to equate ethics with "legal rights," a position I find limiting and problematic (it is a position that simply does not address some of the tough cases we are seeing on the network—for more on this, see Chapter 4).

Numerous sources address computer ethics in general (Dejoie, Fowler, & Paradice, 1991; Forester & Morrison, 1994; Johnson, 1991, 1992; Johnson & Snapper, 1985; Mason, 1991; Mason, Mason, & Culnan, 1995; Parker, Swope, & Baker, 1990). Computer ethicists generally agree that the key computer ethics issues involve equity (or access), privacy, property, and accuracy (e.g., Mason, 1991). Accuracy refers to the care taken with information: Is the writer careful in reporting facts, or careful in preserving stored information on computer systems? Deborah Johnson (1991) adds to this list personal identity as an important issue. Personal identity pertains to the treatment of others, those a writer writes about as well as those a writer writes to: Does the writer treat others fairly? Is the writer respectful of his or her audience?

Computer ethicists such as Johnson apply general ethical and professional ethics to develop specific standards for computer use. Typically such ethicists distinguish ethical responsibilities by role or professional identity, for instance, cataloguing the different kinds of ethical issues facing computer system administrators, teachers, and students. The important point here is to notice that their ethical perspective emphasizes the importance of one's professional role in any given situation (a point I return to in Chapter 6). The specific role to a great extent determines one's ethical obligations, and in different roles people will face different kinds of issues and perhaps be obliged to apply principles in different ways. For instance, computing center administrators will make ethical decisions in drafting campus computer policy and then in applying it to particular cases; teachers will decide the ethical and legal limits of their authority in establishing a moderating role for themselves in online class conferences.

Mainly these sources are geared for computer designers and systems administrators: They say very little specifically about ethical issues pertaining to writers or writing contexts, and they seldom provide a systematic or comprehensive discussion of ethical issues (Mason, Mason, & Culnan, 1995, is an exception in this regard). Ian Barbour (1993), for instance, considers the general impact of computers on society at large, but does not focus specifically on their uses as a writing technology. A collection by Ermann, Williams, and Gutierrez (1990) considers diverse ethical and legal issues involving computers, but also does not focus on writing issues per se. The most comprehensive discussion of legal and ethical issues in computing is Effy Oz's *Ethics for the Information Age* (1994).

Oz does attempt to provide a systematic although brief overview of differences between ethical systems (in Chapter 1, "What Is Ethics?"), but in the main the book treats the issue of computer ethics in terms of the broad effect on society in general and uses a "dramatic case" approach similar to that employed by Forester and Morrison (1994). (Oz's book is probably the most comprehensive and helpful of those just mentioned in terms of providing basic information about computer-related law and policy: It provides samples and a comparative analysis of numerous professional codes of conduct and university computer center policies, includes survey results of professionals' attitudes toward computer ethics, and cites the basic legal background, such as the current status of copyright law, for the reader new to the area.)

Forester and Morrison's book *Computer Ethics* (1994) is worth considering in some detail (see Porter, 1995) because it is fairly typical of ethics treatments in the fields of information management and computer technology. *Computer Ethics* does not address very many ethical issues pertaining directly to writing or communication per se, for example, issues pertaining to readability or usability; netiquette for different electronic media (e.g., email vs. MOO); electronic harassment, stalking, and even rape on the Internet; or plagiarism (or other misuse) of electronic text. Other issues of possible importance to writing teachers that are *not* discussed include access to computers and computer literacy (who can afford them? who can use them?); race, gender, and ethnicity; and acceptable use policies pertaining to network problems such as offensive or obscene speech, virtual harassment, and "spamming" (i.e., excessive posting of political or commercial messages inappropriate to a group's defined focus). Rather, *Computer Ethics* takes an "amazing stories" approach to defining computer ethics and does not address so much the day-to-day ethics of computer design and use. Forester and Morrison cite examples that show that unreliability of computer systems is a problem in society, but they do not suggest guidelines, practices, or heuristic procedures that systems developers might apply to ensure greater reliability. We can wring our hands, express dismay or moral outrage, and hope that future computer professionals will be more responsible than current ones, but the book does not suggest specific ways to ensure more responsible and ethical use of computers, other than the general advice that teachers should teach ethics in the computer science curriculum. (But *how*, other than by telling stories?)

In many ways I think *Computer Ethics* is problematic as a book on ethics. It reinforces the attitude that ethics is a private or indeterminate affair, that there are no systematic procedures or principles to be applied to determine responsible action. The only procedure the authors suggest is the examination and discussion of cases. Out of general discussion in the classroom will arise, somehow, a sense of what should be done in any given case. The authors dismiss ethical relativism because "it offers no guidance as to what is correct behavior" (p. 15), yet their own methodological approach in the book is relativistic to an extent, except when it shifts to a reductive utilitarianism in the discussion of specific cases. The

authors congratulate themselves on avoiding "lengthy discussion of philosophical and ethical theory" (p. x). However, this avoidance is, I think, a serious mistake for a book that claims to provide guidance about computer ethics.

Forester and Morrison's book is an example of how the popular media use a
case approach to handle ethics: The media take an "amazing stories" approach,
telling tales that frighten us, shock us, entertain us, and make us love or hate electronic discourse, but which are likely to have very little propaedeutic effect in
terms of developing an understanding of how we should make ethical decisions
as writers (or writing teachers) in internetworked writing space.

In the field of computers and composition, and in related fields, numerous theorists mention ethical issues, but none of these discussions develops a comprehensive or systematic rhetorical-ethical position on the issues. None of these
works develops a comprehensive or systematic discussion of ethics as it pertains
to writing. Few of them consider the range of tough cases one is likely to encounter in electronic writing/publishing. Hardly any develop *rhetorical heuristics*,
guidelines or strategies useful to ethical decision making in writing situations. I
am not above telling a few amazing stories myself, as you will see, but I want to
move beyond merely listing cases to constructing a systematic postmodern rhetorical ethic that will help us negotiate some of the ethical dilemmas arising on
the network.

HOW THIS PROJECT WORKS: FOCUS, METHODOLOGY, AND ORGANIZATION

Three main questions guide my inquiry:

- How should we constitute and situate ourselves ethically in these four roles: as
  writers/publishers of electronic discourse; as listowners, managers, or developers of network groups, web sites, and electronic archives; as participants in
  electronic communities; and as teachers in internetworked writing classrooms?
- What ethical problems can writers and writing teachers expect to face in internetworked writing classrooms and communities?
- What principles should we invoke or stances adopt for assistance in guiding
  our ethical choices or in doing ethical electronic writing, especially when the
  traditional sources of ethics have been challenged by the postmodern critique
  of Western metaphysics, rationality, and masculine logocentrism? How can
  writers and writing teachers exercise sound rhetorical/ethical judgment in the
  face of postmodernism's radical critique of ethics (MacIntyre, 1984, 1988)?

One issue this book addresses has to do with what posture, or *ethos*, we
develop as writers or as writing teachers participating in the networked environment. I see most academic discussions of network ethics embracing one of two

positions: either (a) a liberal-individualist position (such as advocated by Howard Rheingold) based on an Enlightenment trust in the sanctity of the individual *man*, or (b) an extremely ironic postmodern position that leaves the ethical issues unaddressed, more or less. I do not believe that either position is adequate. Neither responds sufficiently to the kinds of problems writing teachers face on the network. Neither supports the kind of situated commitment and judgment writing teachers, indeed any network participants, need.

It is even more clear that traditional notions of ethics (discourse ethics particularly) do not carry much weight in the electronic medium. Most ethical systems and approaches assume or arise from a print paradigm. My position is that problems are best worked out in terms of a situated and kairotic rhetorical ethics, which grants ethical authority to local practice and the conventions of particular communities, which accounts for the specific technological nature of the electronic medium, and which invokes a discourse ethic that is essentially pluralistic in its constitution and heuristic and rhetorical in its methodology.

The sources of this situated ethic can be found in various postmodern ethical systems: feminist ethics (Benhabib, 1992; Cahill, 1990; Jaggar, 1992; Noddings, 1984), communitarian ethics (D'Entrèves, 1992; Villa-Vicencio, 1992), neocasuistic rhetorical ethics (Jonsen & Toulmin, 1988; Lyotard & Thébaud, 1985), and neopragmatic liberation ethics (Bourdieu, 1977; Dussel, 1988; Freire, 1970/1993). This approach differs sharply from that advocated by many groups, such as the Electronic Frontier Foundation, who are promoting network policies based on legal principles of Enlightenment liberalism. Attempts to settle issues invoking some grand metanarrative of ethics or rhetoric do not address the pluralistic nature of global electronic communities and so will be unlikely to settle the sorts of practical problems that are now arising. Some language philosophers (like Habermas) have attempted to describe the fundamental ethical conventions of all discourse situations. Without getting into the argument in this chapter about whether it is possible (or how helpful it is) to establish universal ethical discourse conventions (I think it is possible, but I do not think it helpful), I examine specific and situated ethical problems involved in electronic communication.

Rhetorical Ethics and Internetworked Writing is a theoretical study built on a case approach, although it is not a case study, and it does not employ the amazing stories case approach typically used in the media. I have collected cases of ethical problems involved in electronic networking, some arising directly from writers' and writing teachers' experiences and others anticipating problems writers and writing teachers can expect to face. Through discussion of the cases (throughout the project, but especially in Chapter 5), I identify several kinds of ethical dilemmas—involving, for instance, copyright and distribution of electronic text, privacy and freedom of speech, and electronic harassment. The approach taken here is partly what might be called "neocasuistic," that is, it relies predominantly, although not exclusively, on a case-based approach that uses particular instances to challenge general ethical and theoretical principles.

In *The Abuse of Casuistry* (1988), Albert Jonsen and Stephen Toulmin attempt to revive the casuistic approach as a way to develop ethical positions in a pluralistic climate. They define *casuistry* as

> the analysis of moral issues, using procedures of reasoning based on paradigms and analogies, leading to the formulation of expert opinions about the existence and stringency of particular moral obligations, framed in terms of rules or maxims that are general but not universal or invariable, since they hold good with certainty only in the typical conditions of the agent and circumstances of action. (p. 257)

The casuistic approach to ethics takes general and conventional principles and then looks at cases (or develops them) that challenge the parameters of those principles. The aim of this process is to develop analytically and analogically more flexible ethical principles capable of addressing the complexity of human action. Principles derived in such a way do not hold "universal or invariable" status, but they do have a heuristic power in guiding ethical determinations.

Chapters 2 and 3 explain the connections between ethics, rhetoric, and writing (as composing act), laying the foundations for the postmodern ethics I advocate overall in the book. Chapters 2 and 3 do a certain amount of theoretical groundwork necessary to understanding the conception of rhetoric/writing that informs this study. From the postmodern perspective of rhetoric-as-composing, writing is both a product and an action, an action with political and ethical consequences. Every act of writing attempts to establish relations with some audience—and the ethical question that intersects that attempt pertains to the ultimate goal of the action. What *telos* drives the action? What sense of "good" warrants the effort? My position is that all acts of writing are ethical insofar as (a) they aim at some kind of change, presumably for "the good" (or the better); and (b) they presuppose roles for, and relations between, writers and readers.

Chapter 3 also defines what I mean by *rhetorical ethics*. Ethics in this sense is not an answer to a question, but is rather a mode of critical inquiry into how writers determine what is good or desirable in any given case. Ethics in this postmodern sense does not refer to a static body of foundational principles, laws, and procedures; it is not to be confused with particular moral codes. A postmodern ethics refers to a mode of situated, historicized questioning—in a sense, a heuristic for writing—rather than a set of static principles to be "applied" to situations (Porter, 1993a; Scott, 1990).

I do not want to suggest by this theoretical discussion that I think rhetorical/ ethical theory should *discipline* the practice of internetworked writing or provide determining or explanatory metanarrative for it. Rather, just as much the opposite; what I see happening is that networking practices are challenging ethical theories, provoking them in interesting ways and necessitating their revision. What people are doing in electronic discourse—and especially what writing teachers are doing in computer classrooms—should be of considerable interest to the Big-T Theory people because it challenges their very conception of ethics. Unfortunately, few of them are paying attention yet.

In Chapter 4, I configure various rhetorical-ethical positions by applying a postmodern mapping methodology that Patricia Sullivan and I have used in several publications (Porter & Sullivan, 1996; Sullivan & Porter, 1993a, 1993b). This methodology is useful for identifying and critiquing a broad range of rhetorical-ethical positions. My purpose is to expand the range of ethical options available for writers and writing teachers and to identify the strengths and weaknesses of various positions. The mapping procedure also helps to identify a space for the nomadic, kairotic, and situated ethics that I advocate. Starting with a discussion of what I see as the dominant liberal-individual view of Howard Rheingold and Mitchell Kapor, I identify various positions and discuss their implications for internetworked writing. The chapter defines a space for a practical and flexible (although not pluralist) postmodern rhetorical ethics that is sensitive both to particular electronic writing technologies and to the ways that "virtual communities" develop their identities in the electronic realm.

Chapter 5 examines particular legal and ethical issues in internetworked writing, as well as cases that either provide precedent-setting examples or challenge and problematize existing norms and categories. This chapter considers ethical issues involving access to computers; ownership and distribution of electronic text; privacy, constraint, and freedom of speech; netiquette; and electronic harassment. Chapter 5 also discusses examples of acceptable use policies and other conventions that are now emerging to provide ethical and legal guidance to writers on the networks; it provides basic information about constitutional law as well as case law. For instance, I consider how the Fair Use doctrine might apply to use of electronic text. I identify sources for teachers to consult when making ethical decisions, both in the chapter itself and in an Appendix.

Chapter 6 demonstrates how this rhetorical ethical approach works in practice by examining three cases representative of the type that might face writers or teachers working in an electronic environment. Chapter 7 concludes by listing criteria and rhetorical guidelines for doing and teaching internetworked writing. It offers these principles as heuristics guides for writers and writing teachers, articulating how a postmodern rhetorical ethic might help guide interworked writing activity.

We need to examine the ethical issues involved in internetworked writing—particularly in *doing* and in *teaching* such writing in writing classes and communities. I agree with Noddings's (1984) point: Every act of teaching is a political stance that also establishes a value, that is, it says "here is something we should be doing" (as opposed to something else). That "should" is an unavoidable facet of any rhetorical action according to Kenneth Burke (1966); the "should" (the "thou shalt" and the "thou shalt not") is built into the nature of language. Ethics, in the broad sense that it is used here, means the process of determining the "should" and, if necessary, of justifying it.

Any use of the computer as a writing instrument entails both ethical and legal obligations. It is deceptively easy to articulate the general principles of computer ethics for writers and writing teachers: Writers who use and produce electronic text should adhere to ethical and legal guidelines for the use of computing facilities and resources. Writing teachers who use computers for instructional purposes are responsible for guiding their students toward (and themselves to adhering to) ethical and legal use of computing facilities and resources (see Porter, 1994d). The principle is easy (it being an abstraction bordering on a tautology). What is difficult is determining ethical action in any particular instance. Much of the available research and commentary pertains to general use of educational computer resources; much of it occupies the terrain of abstraction; very little specifically addresses writing applications.

Rhetoric is absolutely necessary to this process. Of course, in public and philosophical discourse *rhetoric* is a maligned term, traditionally associated with manipulation, deceit, and lying. Rhetoric is the negative second term opposed to *truth*. In this study, however, rhetoric refers to the reliance of *all* discourse—including all pronouncements on ethics, law, and "truth"—on situated discursive interaction. A key argument in this book is that rhetoric has a vital role to play in the development of any cyberspace ethic.

2

Recovering an Ethics for Rhetoric and Writing: Classical and Modern Views

> In my opinion, however, the best course is to have some acquaintance with both practice and theory. It is a fine thing to have a tincture of philosophy, just so much as makes an educated person, and there is no disgrace in a lad philosophizing. . . . But when I see an older man still at philosophy and refusing to abandon it, that man seems to me . . . to need a whipping.
> — Plato, Callicles in *Gorgias* 485

This chapter and the next reexamine the classical question about the relationship between ethics and rhetoric, adds a third, usually neglected, component to the issue—writing—and investigates the three-way relationship from the perspective of postmodern critical and ethical theory. The purpose of this discussion is to argue the necessity of keeping ethics, rhetoric, and writing together as an intertwined set. Ethics and rhetoric do have their distinct domains of concern, but they are also inevitably entangled. I see value in maintaining that entanglement—imbrication, if you like—and I discuss here how I would like to see ethics, rhetoric, and writing work together as a complementary set.

Is all this historical review and theoretical contortion really necessary? Well, maybe I need a whipping, but yes, I think so. The exercise is vital in the formation of a rhetorical ethics for internetworked writing, as it addresses several positions that theorists espouse when arguing about writing on networks or about teaching electronic writing. You cannot neatly separate out rhetoric as a neutral art or as an abstract set of principles or as an instrumental technology, as some in rhetoric/composition have attempted. Nor can you teach rhetoric as politically imbricated *without* also addressing the ethical implications, as some in cultural studies have tried. Nor can you make rhetoric the handmaiden of philosophy and ethics, as the Great Western Tradition has done. Nor can you ignore technology considerations, assume them as neutral, transparent, or incidental to the operation of ethics. My examination considers how developments in postmodern ethics—and yes, there is such a thing—contribute to developing a productive way to perceive ethics/rhetoric/writing.

What follows in this chapter is a brief and decidedly uncomprehensive overview of some of the treatments of the rhetoric-ethics relationship in recent rhetoric/composition theory, in classical rhetoric, and in some modern discussions that have had significant influence on the conception of that relationship (e.g., Perelman, 1982). To do justice to the theoretical aspects of this discussion, this chapter should probably be a book—and perhaps one day it will be. For now, though, the discussion serves to establish: (a) that examining the rhetoric-ethics relationship is by no means a new idea—it has always been a critical issue in rhetorical history; and (b) that there are different configurations of the rhetoric-ethics relationship, not all of which are compatible with the postmodern critical position this book is advocating. It is important to my construction of rhetorical ethics to establish which configurations I am drawing on and which I am rejecting. The construction I am adopting might be called the messy view—one that views rhetoric and ethics as, in a sense, indivisible arts, or at least thoroughly entangled ones. This view must be distinguished from other calls for a return to ethics that view rhetoric as an inferior and derivative art—at best, as the necessary evil means by which true ethics is promoted.

RECOVERING THE ETHICAL IN RHETORIC/COMPOSITION

We can view the vigorous—often vitriolic—discussion about the role of cultural studies in the composition classroom as a debate about the connections between, on the one hand, rhetoric/composition and, on the other, politics, power, and ideology (see Hairston, 1992; Trimbur et al., 1993). In the 1980s, rhetoric/composition scholarship (if not pedagogy) had a predominantly epistemic focus, viewing writing in its function as a knowledge-making activity. In the 1990s, the emphasis, in both scholarship and pedagogy, shifted to writing as a political activity, as a form of critique, as a way to resist oppressive structures and effect social change (see Berlin, 1996). Interestingly, this development within rhetoric/composition parallels that of the critical analytic of Michel Foucault from archaeology (the examination of systems of knowledge) in his earlier works to genealogy (the analytic examining the power-knowledge connection) in his later ones.

The third and lesser known facet of Foucault's critical development is the ethical axis—an analytic that examines the relationship between language use, power relations, and the ways that individuals and groups establish their identities, determine conventions or norms of behavior, and "constitute themselves as moral agents" (Foucault, 1984c, p. 351; see Davidson, 1986). My intention in this chapter is to demonstrate how the ethical axis is an important—indeed, necessary—concern of rhetoric. The ethical axis pertains in crucial ways to questions about the writer's relationship with various audiences and about the loci of authority for rhetorical acts, and provides rhetoric with a means of discussing motives—the reasons people communicate in the first place, the driving force of rhetorical activity.

In the 1980s and early 1990s, some in rhetoric/composition had already begun what I consider the revival of interest in the role of ethics—in particular, Carolyn Miller (1989, 1993), Steven Katz (1992, 1993), James Kinneavy (1987), Louise Wetherbee Phelps (1988, 1992), Lester Faigley (1992), Thomas Farrell (1993), and Gregory Clark (1987, 1994), all of whom called attention to rhetoric itself as necessarily involving ethical action (see also Bizzell, 1992; Couture, 1993; Friend, 1994; Fulkerson, 1990; Hansen, 1994; Porter, 1993a; Schilb, 1990; Dale Sullivan, 1990; Toner, 1996; Zappen, 1987, 1991). As early as 1980, Michael McGuire attempted to articulate an "ethic for rhetoric" (p. 134) that did not begin with the assumption that ethical truth precedes rhetorical action. McGuire notes that traditionally ethics of rhetoric have "been of the rationalist sort" (p. 134); his statement is one of the earliest calls for a postmodern rhetoric of ethics (although he did not, in 1980, invoke the term *postmodernism*). Lester Faigley (1992) calls for us to do something about "a missing ethics throughout the activities of composing" (p. 239). Steven Katz (1992) urges us to recognize "the essentially ethical character of all rhetoric, including our writing theory, pedagogy, and practice" (p. 272). He points to the dangers of divorcing rhetoric from ethics: Such a split can lead to promoting an "ethic of expediency," whereby we can judge a document as "good writing," even though it is a report arguing "for technical improvements to the vans being used in the early Nazi program of exterminating the Jews" (p. 256).

Such discussions in rhetoric/composition are characterized by their effort to develop an integrated view of the ethics–rhetoric relationship. Such efforts have to be distinguished from efforts to insist on the superiority and priority of ethics over rhetoric. Kurt Spellmeyer (1993), for instance, invokes Socrates and Plato in urging a focus on *wisdom* as the proper basis for sound writing. Spellmeyer's version of wisdom/truth is not a rhetorical one; rather, he subscribes to an attenuated view of rhetoric—he sees truth as preliminary to the operation of rhetoric and the process of writing as the presentation or expression of a wisdom discovered through some means prior to writing. This is *not* what I mean.

This theoretical work from the 1990s integrating ethics and rhetoric differs from the treatments by earlier rhetoricians in one particularly important way: These more recent discussions view ethics not from the rationalist paradigm as a set of fundamental and abstract and a priori principles to be applied to situations, but rather as a process of inquiry necessarily intertwined with rhetoric, with the activity of composing a written text, and with the construction of writer (and perhaps reader) identity. Here we can track a shift from conventional conceptions of rhetoric as a subfield of philosophy to an emerging notion of "rhetoric/composition" as something distinct. Rhetoric/composition focuses on a particular form of communication technology—writing.

ETHICS ON THE RIGHT AND THE LEFT

There are several ways to think about the relation of ethics to rhetoric and writing. The cultural right (in rhetoric theory, represented most clearly by Richard Weaver) perceives ethics as a set of static principles or moral dicta (Truths, capital T) located someplace outside the field of rhetoric, discovered through some kind of prior dialectic or analytic procedure, and preexisting any particular act of writing. This is the Truth that exists outside the situated use of language but that language use must recognize. This view despises rhetoric and regrets its necessity, and it is the dominant public view of rhetoric (as politically manipulative use of language, if not blatant lying). This is the notion of ethics that antifoundationalists in rhetoric despise as traditional, Western, logocentric, deontological, metaphysical, masculine/phallogocentric, rationalist, foundationalist, and conservative (if not "right wing").

The left in rhetoric/composition is decidedly suspicious about ethics, seeing it as incompatible with politics, or at least threatening to it, and seeing ethics as the rallying cry only of the radical right. (Their suspicions are warranted in terms of most public invocations of "ethics"; however, they are wrong to reject all ethics on this basis.) According to Andrew Feenberg (1991), "Marx conceived of ethical values as, at worst, mere ideological veils for exploitation; at best they represent utopian demands that cannot appear as the interest of any significant social group" (p. 144). To the extent that ethics stays "above the fray" (p. 143), then ethics ends up being inadequate to change social structures. In its abstract impracticality it leaves the status quo intact.

What Feenberg and others seem to overlook is the integration of Marxism and ethics in developments like liberation theology (see Dussel, 1988; Freire, 1970/1993; West, 1991). Stanley Fish (1994) tends to dismiss the ethical, associating the term exclusively with right-wing male apologists for traditional values: Allan Bloom, Charles Sykes, John Silber, Dinesh D'Souza, and Robert Bork. Fish's critique of such authors is that they appeal to a transcendental ethic as a way to control (and obscure) the operation of the political. (Fish's list is woefully incomplete. He does not consider a range of works by postmodern ethicists who have a very different agenda and who do not at all shirk from the political, but fully embrace it. Fish faults the right for obscuring politics in their focus on ethics. Meanwhile, Fish, from the standpoint of the theoretical left, obscures ethics in his focus on politics.) Zavarzadeh and Morton (1994) view ethics, whether the traditional or postmodern variety, as a threat to the political efforts to change the structure of the university (and, indirectly, society). They see the focus on ethics as rendering "invisible the structure of exploitation and oppression" (p. 4) that underlies classed societies.

James Berlin (1990) places ethics as separate from, and a malformation of, politics. According to Berlin, ethics is a threat to politics because ethics cannot help but to view things in universal terms, neglect material conditions, and create an "invidious distinction" between the self and the community:

> The consideration of any topic under the heading of "ethics," however, creates an immediate stumbling block. . . . To dwell on ethics is to risk elevating an histori- cally specific mode of thought to a universal standard. A central feature of this ges- ture today is the assertion of the bourgeois individual of liberal humanism, the autonomous self who freely adjudicates competing moral claims. This self is then situated in opposition to suspect, self-threatening material conditions and the dan- gers of communal encounters. Recent discussions of ethics thus tend to fall com- fortably into the privileging of the subjective and the personal, relying on an invidious distinction between the individual and the social, the private and the pub- lic, the solitary and the communal. (p. 170)

Similarly, Victor Vitanza (1990) despises the totalizing tendencies of tradi- tional ethics:

> In previously discussing the issue of "ethics"—specifically ethics in Revisionary Historiographies—I have concluded that "Revisionary" ethics, like "Traditional" ethics, is irresponsible and (in another word) *unethical-because-molarpolitical*; that is to say, at least, *as I define it,* "Revisionary" ethics is *unethical* because of its inev- itable penchant for "totality" . . . and "Revisionary" ethics is unethical because of its inevitable reliance on a narrative of victimage; that is, in its attempt to redeem the past, it must have a scapegoat, victim, to punish, which only perpetuates victim- age. (p. 241; italics in original)

Vitanza goes on to suggest a "counterethic" based on "resistance and disrup- tion."

Berlin's critique raises an important warning about traditional deontological ethics and about Enlightenment ethics, but his overall condemnation of ethics confuses some ethical systems with all of them. Likewise, Vitanza condemns both traditional and revisionary ethics for their "penchant for totality," but Vitanza is careful to limit his critique. Not *all* ethical systems share this pen- chant—such as his own. Numerous postmodern theorists have attempted to build a postmodern ethics. Indeed, some argue that pluralism—the celebration of diver- sity itself (in opposition against efforts to totalize or homogenize) along with the complication of subjectivity—is one of the chief features of postmodern ethics. In cultural studies work, ethics plays an important role. However, to many people in this side of the field *ethics* is a dirty word, recalling a suspect appeal to universal or transcendental or masculine values, a foundationalist gesture that works against the goals of freedom and justice and radical democracy and that is inconsistent with their preferred pedagogical models. What they are objecting to is ethics as framed by the cultural right.

One preferred cultural studies model is the "democratic free-for-all," the town-hall meeting in which all citizens have a right to be heard and a role to play in forming government. Another model is "critique" (see Berlin, 1996; Harkin & Schilb, 1991). In such a model students are encouraged to be critical of the ways in which existing cultural practices, institutions, and hierarchies block freedom for some and the ways in which they exclude or otherwise abridge freedoms for others. They are taught to express "their opinion," and, if all opinions are heard, truth is guaranteed (the word *truth* is avoided). Justice will out in the end. What guarantees freedom is the right and the ability to express an opinion, and the assumption is that all opinions are of equal value (although perhaps all are not expressed in an equally capable way—it is the civic responsibility of writing teachers to provide students with the tools to express their viewpoints).

. Such an approach in the composition class does teach a model of social responsibility: It teaches students to recognize, first, the problems of society, which are, after all, the substance of writing. It teaches students techniques for uncovering the underlying—or, in some cases, blatantly obvious—acts of injustice: prejudice, sexism, racism, or oppressive moves of various sorts. It teaches students to critique the presumptions, the binaries on which social institutions often reside—and, often, from which they take their power. This model, then, is based on a vision of rhetoric as critique, on a vision of the teacher as having a civic responsibility to students, and on the students as having a civic responsibility. The whole operation is often warranted by the belief in democracy (or radical democracy) as ultimately the ideal form of social exercise. Certainly the agenda has ethical implications—as all teaching agendas do.

Some cultural studies theorists' rejection of ethics is based on a limited understanding of ethics: a view that sees ethics as the procedure of applying general norms of behavior to specific situations and rendering judgment about them. However, not all ethics are the traditional sort, based on classical virtues or Kantian deontologism. The complaint about traditional ethics is its reliance on foundational principles derived from philosophical inquiry and supported by rigorous institutions and principles (the Church, the State, Man) now suspect in the postmodern era.

The use of the term *ethics* is just as problematic, just as fraught with troublesome baggage, as the term *rhetoric*—but no more problematic. Both invoke a distant and shady past, although perhaps *ethics* was more conventionally the term held by the religious powerbrokers (the Church). We can also look to a revival of ethics and to the emergence of a postmodern ethics that embraces and is consistent with some of the positions taken by cultural studies' theorists.

In this study, ethics is viewed as a necessary complement to rhetoric. Rhetoric as a process of communicating involves making decisions—that is, exercising *phronesis*, the art of considering divergent norms, principles, and conventions in light of particular circumstances that require action. Does my family leave my grandmother on a life support system or not? In such a situation it is not possible to avoid an ethical response of some kind, if one considers failure to respond as itself an ethical response. Yet ethics does not pertain only to the hard cases, to life-threatening situations, or to special circumstances. My investigation considers practical problems that intersect with writing situations, to show how and that writing itself is an activity fraught with ethical decisions, which is a normal, not an unusual, part of the activity.

The very act of writing etches a space, a territory—it positions itself. Berlin and Vitanza embrace the *political* implications of such an etching, but distance themselves from the *ethical* implications—that any act of etching establishes a value—because of their association of ethics with totalizing systems. (Traditionally, "politics" has been the rallying cry of the left, "ethics" the banner of the right, although there are signs of that changing as feminist and postmodern theorists of various sorts take up the issue of ethics.) Vitanza will say that he is fleeing from ethics—he will dance, weave away from, and resist positions—and that becomes his position. He will remind us of the very elusiveness, and illusionness, of positionality, and in so doing he establishes a value: Listen to me, he says, take the position of nonseriousness seriously. Okay, I will, as long as he does not try to persuade me that he is not practicing an ethic (or perhaps, a counterethic).

There are numerous kinds of ethical systems and numerous ways to view the relationship between ethics and rhetoric. The following are some possibilities to be pursued in this study:

1. Ethics pertains to a *process of inquiry* by which we determine what is right, just, or desirable in any given case. This sense of ethics requires rhetoric as a co-equal partner in the pursuit of a position—this is not ethics as a Final Truth, but as a standpoint, a contingent commitment.

2. Ethics pertains to the *subjectivities of writers and readers*, to the way that roles are defined in written texts and through the processes of writing and reading. This view very much relates to the classical sense of *ethos*, in the sense of ethically you are what you write—although it is important to recognize that from a postmodern standpoint the writing "you" is never a single or unified subject. Your symbolic actions, including your discursive actions, create who you are ethically—but this process operates socially, not autonomously, and can generate multiple you's. Similarly, ethics pertains as well to the subjectivity of the writing teacher—the *ethos* of the teacher, the stance he or she takes vis-à-vis the students, how he or she constructs authority and exercises it. (Lisa Toner's [1996] work identifies a range of ethical roles for

writing teachers implicit, mostly, in rhetoric/composition research and scholarship.)

The views of ethics that Berlin and Vitanza critique represent only a few of the numerous views; in fact, the versions they critique (deontological ethics, Enlightenment liberal ethics) have suffered a good deal of bashing already, even within ethics, philosophy, and theology. There are other sorts of ethical theories—postmodern ethics, feminist ethics, situational ethics, liberation ethics, neocasuistic ethics, and rhetorical ethics—all of them decidedly alternative approaches that are particularly compatible with rhetoric because (a) they are all in some sense contingent, situational, pragmatic, or kairotic; and (b) they focus more on ethics as a mode of inquiry rather than a set of answers.

We see some evidence of such ethical models being explored within rhetoric theory. Neosophistic rhetoricians like Kenneth Burke and Susan Jarratt have recognized the messy and multiple connections possible between ethics and rhetoric; feminist theorists especially have acknowledged the integral role ethics plays in political/rhetorical action and in subjectivity. In *A Rhetoric of Motives* (1969), Burke says that his project of describing rhetoric is concerned with "the underlying ethical assumptions on which the entire tactics of persuasion are based" (p. 54). For Burke, ethics and rhetoric are interdependent because the truth arises out of the "synthesis" of rhetorical dialectic. Burke's (1970) dramatistic perspective sees language as action, and all action "involves character, which involves choice—and the form of choice attains its perfection in the distinction between Yes and No (between *thou shalt* and *thou shalt not*)" (p. 41 italics in original). For Burke, symbolic action "implies the ethical" (p. 41).

In *Rereading the Sophists* (1991), Susan Jarratt talks about the role of rhetoric in establishing *nomoi*, the habits or customs of any particular community. All rhetorical texts—that is, all writing—contribute toward constructing and establishing some sort of provisional code (see Kerferd, 1981). In Chapter 8 of *Audience and Rhetoric* (Porter, 1992a), I argue that all writing entails ethical obligations because writing always involves social relations between readers and writers, which presuppose some understandings about how those social relations are to be constituted.

Within this general sophistic discussion, ethics refers to *nomoi*: to the policies, conventions, and practices governing social relations; to the developed understandings about how people are to speak to, write to, and act toward one another; and to the process of negotiating and constructing conventions. Rhetoric contributes to this process, first, because it is the means by which conventions are constructed. In turn, rhetoric becomes constrained by those conventions. Rhetoric is both the means of consent and dissent.

Many in rhetoric/composition and computers and composition have talked about the politically committed nature of writing, but more frequently using the terms *politics* or *ideology* instead of *ethics*, concluding that no act of writing (or

teaching writing) is ever neutral. Many have talked about rhetoric and social relations, but often without explicit reference to ethics. Most notably, Jim Berlin
(1988) and Nancy Kaplan (1991) refer to *ideology*, concluding that any act of
writing (or teaching writing) represents a value. Numerous researchers in computers and composition have also called attention to the political implications of
writing and teaching writing with computers (Cooper & Selfe, 1990; Janangelo,
1991; LeBlanc, 1990; Ohmann, 1985; Ray & Barton, 1991; Selfe, 1994)—and to
the relations between computers and power and authority.

If there is some difference in invoking the term *ethics*, it might be this: Ethics
accepts the presence of ideology, power, and politics, but then also goes on to
address the problem of *practical judgment*. How do we arrive at a standpoint, recognizing that any act of writing requires taking one? How do we decide what to
do, what action to take in situations involving competing ideologies? How do we
determine what is just to write?

PLATO AND THE PRIVILEGING OF ETHICS

Plato, Aristotle, and Cicero present us with contrasting views about the relationship between ethics and rhetoric. It is helpful to go back and track these classical
views because they are often invoked as authoritative in discussions of rhetoric-
ethics, and because they help us understand the variation in approaches to the
rhetoric-ethics configuration (see Johnstone, 1976, 1980; Olian, 1965). Not all
types of rhetorical ethics are the same.

The Platonic view sees rhetoric as the indispensable tool of ethics. Rhetoric is
implicated with the moral. In *Gorgias*, Plato considers the problem of bad rhetoric; in *Phaedrus*, he describes the value of good rhetoric. In *The Republic*, he
defines the role of rhetoric in politics: Rhetoric should be used only in support of
the good and the true; and the good and the true are discovered through the process of dialectic by wise philosophers, properly trained thinkers, whose job is,
first, to discover the good and the true, and then, second, to persuade the masses
to act in a manner according to the good and the true. Later, in rhetoric history,
we see Augustine taking a similar position in *De doctrina Christiana*—in his
examination of how rhetoric should be used to persuade the laity to act in accor-
dance with the truth of the Christian message. (In Augustine's system, the truth
and knowledge of the truth are antecedent to the action of doing good and to the
rhetorical action of persuading others to do the good.)

Plato describes for us a view of the ethics–rhetoric relationship that has per-
sisted within the tradition of philosophical ethics. In short, knowledge of the
good inevitably results in virtue (i.e., doing the good), and this knowledge precedes rhetorical activity. In short, ethics is tied to knowledge, but both necessarily
precede rhetoric. It is in the *Gorgias* that we see Plato draw a marked line separating rhetoric as the art of persuasion from arts having to do with truth and

knowledge and pursuit of the good. Socrates builds the argument and gets a passive Gorgias to agree with him, that rhetoric is the art of securing conviction (belief) but has nothing to do with true knowledge (454). Rhetoric's aim is gratification of audience; the determination of truth or falsity lies in other arts. Socrates calls rhetoric a knack, an art like cookery (if an art at all), and a subdivision of pandering (462)—and so mostly dishonorable (463). In response, Gorgias offers a complex view: that rhetoric is interwined with other arts and in fact it "embraces and controls almost all other spheres of human activity" (456). If that is the case, Socrates asks, then does that not mean the rhetor must know all things about all subjects in order to discourse properly on them? That response ends that line of thinking. (Grimaldi, 1980, points out that Aristotle's response to Plato on this point lies in the first line of the *Rhetoric*: by referring to rhetoric as the counterpart [*antistrophos*] of dialectic, Aristotle begins his argument for a responsible rhetoric [p. 2].)

In *Phaedrus* (1973), Plato does allow for the possibility of a "good rhetoric," but it is good only to the extent that it is built on knowledge and truth (as determined through a rigorous dialectic method), not merely on opinions (262). The ethical is determined by groups of right-thinking experts (trained lovers of wisdom, philosophers). Rhetoric comes second, as the tool necessary for persuading the public to accept the ethical. Rhetoric in this view is the handmaiden of philosophy. The disadvantage of this view, according to its detractors, is that it is an elitist view that places authority in the hands of a few individuals—and by what virtue should *they* be in charge?

In *Phaedrus*, Socrates entertains a thought that challenges this linear view of philosophy preceding ethics. He tells Phaedrus of the importance of dialectic methodology, based on the principle of careful division and unification, skillful analysis, arguing that this is the basis on which a "good rhetoric" must be founded:

> Well, Phaedrus, I am a great lover of these methods of division and collection as instruments which enable me to speak and to think, and when I believe that I have found in anyone else the ability to discuss unity and plurality as they exist in the nature of things, I follow in his footsteps "like the footsteps of god." Hitherto I have given those who possess this ability the title of dialecticians. (266)

Socrates then raises the question I pursue here, as to whether these methods actually belong exclusively to dialectic or whether they are part and parcel of the art of rhetoric: "Can it be that what I have been describing is precisely that art of rhetoric?" Phaedrus—playing straight man for Plato—assures Socrates that no, dialectic must be the correct term, but Socrates does not seem so sure.

The exchange between Socrates and Phaedrus in section 266, one well known to rhetoric, raises a significant question this chapter addresses: Is dialectic a separate art, prior to the art of rhetoric? Or are dialectic and rhetoric entertwined in some other relationship? Although admittedly complex, the main thrust of Plato's comments on rhetoric, and the main conclusion of the *Phaedrus*, is that dialectic (and, by extension, ethical inquiry) precedes rhetoric. However, this single question of Socrates—a question that Plato does not seriously take up—is worth pushing. Should we assume that ethics is prior to rhetoric?

ARISTOTLE AND THE ENTANGLEMENT OF ARTS

What kind of relationship should there be between ethics and rhetoric? Do the two areas overlap or coincide—or are they simply separate arts? Traditionally, anyone attempting to answer that question has begun with Aristotle, who issued the definitive and, historically, the dominant word on the matter (see Katz, 1992; MacIntyre, 1984). In Aristotle's canon, rhetoric is an art of production (*techne*), and for Aristotle arts of production (like poetry and rhetoric) were distinct from practical arts (like ethics and politics).

The most common interpretation of the Aristotelian view, at least in rhetoric theory, sees the art of rhetoric as ethically neutral. Rhetoric as productive art is simply an examination of the available means of persuasion, the art of determining what is the best argument in any given case. Now the art itself can be used for good or for ill; it can generate good or it can generate bad—but, *as an art,* rhetoric is amoral because it can argue both sides of a case (Aristotle, 1991, 1.1.1355a). Through the process of judicial and deliberative rhetoric, the good and the true will emerge because in the long run the moral arguments will win out over the immoral. Justice will prevail, and rhetoric can be the means to assist justice in its efforts. Taking this view of rhetoric as amoral art actually serves our best interests, some rhetoric theorists argue, because it protects us from the elite despotism implied by the Platonic view.

Aristotle's view eschews moral certitude. Ethics is not and never can be an epistemic science; there will never be moral certainty. However, we can have moral probability. Aristotle's view is sometimes cited by advocates of cultural studies as the view of rhetoric promoting participatory democracy: What we should teach in composition classrooms is not what is good and true because the art of rhetoric does not provide direct commentary on that. Rather, we should encourage our students to enter the public discussion, arm them with the tools of rhetoric, and help them make their arguments, whatever they may be. (Note that this description of the cultural studies position is almost exactly the opposite of what its detractors say it is. The cultural studies approach to teaching composition—as described by Jim Berlin, Linda Brodkey, John Trimbur, and others—does not teach students *what* to think, as some critics have claimed. It focuses on the practice of critique, using rhetoric as a tool for critiquing language use.)

In any cultural studies view one important principle is keeping the public forum open, to allow for rhetoric to do its work, and not to close off discussion and participation. This view is represented on the Internet by the activities of the Electronic Frontier Foundation (EFF), a group devoted to maintaining individual rights and freedoms on the network. The EFF stands opposed to any government or bureaucratic efforts to abridge free speech on the network. Their electronic newsletters and publications keep electronic citizens abreast of threats, usually from the government, to individual network rights. EFF'ers represent a position of absolute individual rights, and they see their job as maintaining the freedom of the network (for more discussion on the EFF position, see Chapter 4).

The problem with this view of rhetoric serving the ends of participatory democracy, from the Platonic position, is that it places authority in the hands of the unruly mob. This view encourages discussion—but if everybody's view has validity, how do we address the tough decisions? By what means do we make ethical decisions? How do we arbitrate conflict? *Who* decides? Both Plato and Lyotard, for different reasons, are uncomfortable with the prospect of letting the mob decide.

So we have here two extreme versions of the role of rhetoric. In the Platonic view, rhetoric has a secondary status and serves the interests of a ruling elite, who use rhetoric as a tool to persuade the unruly mob to accept the Good and Right that has been discovered through some prior process of thought or analysis (dialectic). This is perhaps an efficient process, but has its implicit dangers. In the Aristotelian view, rhetoric has a primary status in enabling free democratic participation: Rhetoric assists the process, but as an art does not itself determine what is good and right. From this perspective, everybody could be heard, but it looks like a pretty inefficient process. Sometimes we do have to make decisions, and how do we decide? *Who* decides?

I have, of course, stacked the deck in this portrayal of the Platonic and Aristotelian views. There are, of course, other versions of their views, versions that sketch out alternative positions—not necessarily compromise positions, but alternatives.

The view of Aristotle's theory that I have described is valid if we accept Aristotle's distinction between practical and productive arts—and only if we are willing to grant the productive arts (rhetoric and poetics) a status as neutral techniques. That is a distinction that Aristotle makes, but not one he is consistent with. Sophistic rhetorics, both new and old, get caught in the middle of this dilemma. On the one hand, they want rhetoric to be a master field, to play an important role in public life, to include an expansive notion of invention. On the other hand, if they take the view of rhetoric as a set of neutral techniques, they then risk being caught in the handbook problem: Rhetoric becomes no more than a set of stylistic tactics.

The key to the problem is, of course, the art of invention: What role does rhetoric play in the construction of positions (that is, the construction of knowledge as well as of ethical stances)? Is invention simply the art of discovering the available means of persuasion (what Aristotle says in *Rhetoric*)? Or does rhetoric also involve exploring the available positions in the first place—that is, determining what is ethical (what Aristotle perhaps should have said)?

What I attempt to show in the argument that follows is that we can take—I go so far as to say *should* take—another view toward Aristotle's theory. Those who advocate rhetoric as neutral art stress the distinction between the practical and the productive arts. I review here the deconstruction of that binary, showing that the distinction between the practical and the productive is not airtight, and that Aristotle himself is inconsistent on this point (although in *Nicomachean Ethics* [1976], he clearly distinguishes between "making" and "doing" [*praxis*]).

Aside from which, whatever Aristotle's position may be, why do we have to pay any attention to it? I try to demonstrate how the practical–productive split is indefensible in terms of the warrants of postmodern theory. To wit, if you accept that any method is ideological, then rhetoric is implicated with the ethical. If you accept that rhetoric includes the art of invention (in the sense of knowledge formation), then you are opening the door, necessarily, to admit the question of ethics. If you view writing as an action (and not just a product)—that is, if you question the presumed split between "product" and "act"—then you are viewing rhetoric as to some extent a practical art and not strictly a productive one. You are talking about a *phronesis* for rhetoric—that is, a practical judgment in the art itself.

However, his argument will by no means beat a shameful retreat back to Plato, rather, my critique is intended to expose a rhetoric theory that I believe emerges from Aristotle, although it is a decidedly different reading of Aristotle. It is a path that recognizes as valid and as inevitable the rhetoric–ethics relationship, without embracing either the moral idealism and authoritarianism represented by Plato or the moral relativism embraced by some sophists (and later by postmodern ironists). This path starts with Aristotle, who shows us the way in the notion of probability, and it is a path that leads as well to Cicero and Quintilian, who offer us, I think, a more integrated vision of the relationship between ethics and rhetoric and practical action.

It is a position that says, finally, we cannot know with certainty what is right, but we can make intelligent guesses. We can establish contingent moral truths based on probability. Those truths do not, will never, have the status of certainty. Yet to even hold up that criterion (i.e., certainty) is to cater shamefully to the scientific paradigm's view of knowledge as epistemic only, which is simply not a viable criterion in the social realm of political and rhetorical action. In the rhetorical and ethical realm, however, we can have truth. Furthermore, rhetoric is not simply the tool we use to persuade others to accept the truth we have found through other means. Rather, rhetoric provides the inventional method that we use to construct new truths that can become probable ones, and it provides us with procedures for critiquing truths.

However, is Aristotle's theory so tainted by its distressing social context—chiefly, classical Athens' institution of slavery and the failure to recognize women or slaves as citizens—that to borrow from Aristotle is to risk buying into a system that will lead to audience management and manipulation or, on a larger scale, totalitarianism, as Steven Katz (1992) suggests? Does Aristotle's sexism render his system unusable in any form?

There are good cultural reasons for not accepting Aristotle's divisions as the only possible ones, or embracing them as our own. Although Aristotle provides us with a powerful and elaborate rhetoric, that rhetoric is culturally situated: It suits the needs of a particular time and place, a particular political setting (both the abstract notion of the *polis* and the actual Athenian legislature) within a particular social system (which privileged male citizens over slaves and females). Aristotle's *Rhetoric* provides us with a significant and comprehensive model of rhetoric, but we know that his configurations and classifications are not the only possibilities.

As Enos and Lauer (1992) point out, we have to follow Aristotle's process, his manner of inquiry, rather than the particulars (which are products of his historical context and which are not transferable to ours). Obviously we are not going to share Aristotle's views about the appropriateness of slavery (and his views of the master–slave relationship generally), nor his views about the "natural" superiority of men over women, nor the immorality of charging interest on loans. Nonetheless, we can still see that Aristotle's manner of exploring the issues of his time does provide a strategy for us to explore our own. For one thing, unlike most rhetorics since, Aristotle's rhetoric recognizes the importance of difference between audience types and the variations of human emotions and "frames of mind." We are not likely to make much use of his particular audience distinctions—e.g., the characters of young men, old men, and men in their prime; or the variations of "gifts of fortune." However, what we should take from these strange (to us) distinctions is the importance of distinction: Rhetoric must consider *difference*, variations among audience types, emotions, attitudes, or backgrounds. The principle of "difference," as discussed later, emerges as perhaps the key feature of postmodern ethics.

There is also a textual argument for not accepting Aristotle's system as totally binding: Aristotle himself does not maintain as strict a distinction between rhetoric, ethics, and politics as some commentators suggest. In their attempts to render Aristotle's system coherent and consistent, some have made a neat and clean system of classification out of what may be a more complicated structure. In Aristotle's canon, the arts overlap and bleed into one another in crucial ways. In fact, I argue, the way that Aristotle frames his rhetoric specifically includes questions of the good life, questions of the right and the true, questions of justice, questions of knowledge, and so on—these concerns are all a part of the art as he constructs it.

We see this in Book 1, especially sections 1.2 through 1.7. Aristotle identifies rhetoric as "an offshoot of dialectic and also of ethical studies" (Book 1.2, 1356a). Each type of rhetoric has an ethical component: deliberative rhetoric aims at social good, judicial rhetoric aims at justice, and epideictic rhetoric aims at determining the worth or value (of someone) (Book 1.3, 1358b). The goal of all rhetorical activity is happiness (*eudaimonia*) (Book 1.5.1, 1360b).

There are frequent connections between Book 2 of the *Rhetoric* and *Nicomachean Ethics* (Aristotle, 1976). The points of overlap have to do with the pursuit of the good (*agathon*) and the moral character of the speaker or citizen (*ethos*). Grimaldi also makes the argument that *ethos* refers both to the speaker's character and the character of the auditors. That is, "the speaker . . . must attend and adjust to the *ethos* of varied types of auditor if he is to address them successfully" (1988, p. 186). To be an effective rhetor, you have to know what is good, be able to move toward it yourself, and be able to have the persuasive capacity to move others toward it as well; you have to have goodwill toward others; you have to be attuned to differences of character and of emotional state; and you have to have virtuous qualities.

One explicit connection is found in Book 2 of the *Rhetoric*, where Aristotle describes "three reasons why speakers themselves are persuasive" (2.1.1378). Effective speakers have practical wisdom (*phronesis*), virtue (*arete*), and good will (*eunoia*). Here Aristotle is referring to the qualities of character the speaker should have. *Ethos* is one of three means of securing persuasion in Aristotle's rhetoric: "Ethos refers to the need for rhetors to portray themselves in their speeches as having a good moral character, 'practical wisdom,' and a concern for the audience in order to achieve credibility and thereby secure persuasion" (Cherry, 1988, p. 253). As Cherry points out, the connection between ethics (εθos) as moral habit and ethos (ηθos) as moral character are linguistically close, sharing the same stem in Greek. Who you are and what you do, ethically speaking, are very close, although not precisely the same (see Grimaldi, 1980, p. 247; 1988, pp. 183–189).

In Aristotle's *Rhetoric*, the common aim for both rhetor and audience was the good of the *polis*. Thus, the act of composing a speech was situated within a political as well as ethical framework. Aristotle's *Rhetoric* leans heavily on his description of "the good" in *Nicomachean Ethics*; because the rhetor must have "the good of the *polis*" as the ultimate aim, determining what is good is involved in the rhetorical enterprise. In Book 1.5 of *Rhetoric*, one of the most neglected sections of the *Rhetoric*, Aristotle considers the components of happiness (*eudaimonia*). What does happiness have to do with rhetoric, the art of production? The answer lies in *Nicomachean Ethics*:

> Every art and every investigation, and similarly every action and pursuit, is considered to aim at some good. . . . Since all knowledge and every pursuit aims at some good, what do we take to be the end of political science—what is the highest of all practical goods? Well, so far as the name goes there is pretty general agreement. "It is happiness," say both ordinary and cultured people; and they identify happiness with living well or doing well. But when it comes to saying in what happiness con-

sists, opinions differ, and the account given by the generality of mankind is not at all like that of the wise. (1094a1-22; 1095a7-28)

The aim of any art, including rhetoric, is "some good" (*agathon*). The aim of politics is "the social good"—of which happiness is a vital component:

> Observation tells us that every state is an association, and that every association is formed with a view to some good purpose. I say "good," because in all their actions all men do in fact aim at what they think good. Clearly then, as all associations aim at some good, that association which is the most sovereign among them all and embraces all others will aim highest, i.e., at the most sovereign of all goods. This is the association which we call the state, the association which is "political." (Aristotle, 1962, 1252a1-6)

In *The Politics*, Aristotle raises the key questions that guide the interchange between ethics and politics: How should I live? How should we live together? What is often not recognized, though, is the role language plays in answering this question. (Aristotle does not have much to say about the role of rhetoric or language in political life in *The Politics*, although he certainly does in *Rhetoric*.) In the state, "the good" aimed at is justice, which is defined as that which benefits the whole community (Aristotle, 1962, 3.12.1282b14). Language plays an integral, not just an incidental, role. Language is not merely the instrumental means by which we adjudicate our differences. Language is how we constitute the "I" and the "we"—our individual, social, and political identities—in the first place. At this point, it might seem like we are up against the chicken and egg question: Which came first? However, the argument I am making is that it is not an either-or question. My point is to urge us to see the arts as imbricated.

Examined in conjunction, these passages in Aristotle's corpus suggest an important point about the intersection between ethics, rhetoric, and politics (see Cherry, 1988, for additional discussion). The three arts can be seen to have a mutually reinforcing function: Ethics is the practical art of determining the social (as well as personal) good; politics is the practical art of implementing the social good; rhetoric is the productive art enabling ethical and political action. They are tied together by virtue of their common aim—happiness for all.

To arrive at this position, you have to read against what the Western tradition has constructed as Aristotle's classification system and be willing to view rhetoric, politics, and ethics as not necessarily having a fixed, determinable relationship. The three areas do not have to be viewed in any strictly static, hierarchical, or linear way. As texts, *Rhetoric*, *The Politics*, and *Nicomachean Ethics* can be read hypertextually. They can be accessed according to different readings. They can be seen to mutually relate to and reinforce one another. They can operate interactively and recursively. The Venn diagram (see Figure 2.1), rather than the genealogical tree (the traditional graphic for representing Aristotle's system),

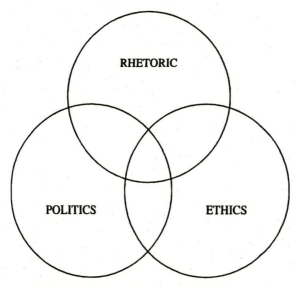

FIGURE 2.1.   The overlap of ethics, rhetoric, and politics.

might be a more helpful way to envision the interrelationship between ethics, rhetoric, and politics.

The three Aristotelian texts and three arts can be configured in different ways, even according to different cultural needs. As James Murphy (1974) points out, medieval scholars tended to publish or collect Aristotle's *Rhetoric* with ethics and political science texts more often than with other "rhetoric" texts: "Aristotle's *Rhetorica* became for the middle ages not a rhetorical or dialectical work, but a treatise useful in the study of moral philosophy" (p. 101). Jonsen and Toulmin (1988) also indicate that in the Middle Ages "ethics remained associated with rhetoric" (p. 123). The issue of the relationship between ethics and prudence was particularly important during the Renaissance, according to Victoria Kahn (1985). During the Renaissance the subjects of theology, philosophy, rhetoric, reflection and learning, and writing and speaking were not divided as disciplines or activities to the extent they are today. Renaissance humanists took a more unified view of what we now treat as separate disciplines. Humanists like Coluccio Salutati, Giovanni Pontano, and Lorenzo Valla recognized "the inseparability of ethical and linguistic practice" (Kahn, 1985, p. 68). Lanham (1993) sees the Renaissance as a critical historical juncture for considering the relationship of ethics and rhetoric.

Jonsen and Toulmin (1988) sum up the case for connecting rhetoric and ethics in Aristotle:

Aristotle presents rhetoric as a combination of logic and ethics—the chief aim of which is to persuade people about the right and the good. It is concerned with recommendations about actions to be pursued or avoided, with the justification or condemnation of actions already performed, and with the allocation of praise or blame to past actions, with an eye to the future. Rhetoric thus deals with questions about benefit or harm, justice or injustice, and human worth, and in one respect its methodology is similar to that of ethics: both subjects finally rest on appeals to "ultimate particulars" or "paradigm cases." Given this convergence of ethics and rhetoric, he concludes, his treatment of rhetoric must refer to ethics, at least in a summary fashion; so he inserts into the argument of the *Rhetoric* a digest of books I–IV of the *Nicomachean Ethics*. (p. 73)

CICERO AND THE OBLIGATIONS OF THE RHETOR

In Cicero's *De Oratore* (1942), ethics and rhetoric are even more intertwined than they are in Aristotle's *Rhetoric*. According to Kahn (1985), "in Cicero's view, even more than in Aristotle's, the faculty of prudence is inseparable from the ideal practice of the orator" (p. 35). Cicero decries the separation of morals from rhetoric, and in *De Oratore* argues for a holistic, multidisciplinary view of rhetoric. He blames Socrates for dividing things unnecessarily:

For, as I said before, the older masters down to Socrates used to combine with their theory of rhetoric the whole of the study and the science of everything that concerns morals and conduct and ethics and politics; it was subsequently, as I have explained, that the two groups of students were separated from one another, by Socrates and then similarly by all the Socratic schools, and the philosophers looked down on eloquence and the orators on wisdom, and never touched anything from the side of the other study except what this group borrowed from that one, or that one from this; whereas they would have drawn from the common supply indifferently if they had been willing to remain in the partnership of early days. (3.29.72)

Cicero's overall message in *De Oratore*, argued through the voice of Crassus, urges the reintegration of rhetoric with other topics, especially politics and ethics. A key ethical precept of Cicero's rhetoric is that the orator must have knowledge of his subject matter. Knowledge by itself does not make a good orator, but it is a sine qua non of the good orator. The critique of others in the dialogue, who represent the counter voice that Cicero argues with (but in so doing reveals his own doubts), is that he may be advancing an unattainable ideal: Can any speaker actually have sufficient knowledge of all subjects? Can speakers not speak until they have sufficient knowledge (a criterion that would seem to promote continual silence)?

Throughout *De Oratore*, Cicero describes the ethical duties of the orator. A theme running throughout the work is the importance of attention to detail and to "the facts of the case." In sounding this theme, Cicero reveals a point of disagreement with the philosophers who wallow in abstractions and delight in making "unnecessary divisions." Cicero's pragmatic ethical dictum requires focus on the particular and contextual aspects of any situation. This is a point that postmodern ethics, especially feminist ethics, emphasizes—and it is a point that will become especially important (in Chapters 4 and 5) in the formation of an ethics for internetworked writing. Such an ethics must take serious account of the *technological* context of rhetorical action.

Cicero lists other important rhetorical-ethical criteria, and his manner of describing these criteria illustrates the integrated view he takes toward the two arts. For instance, we will not be surprised to hear that the history writer is obligated to "tell the truth" (2.15.62). Another important criterion is empathy with audience. Certainly the speaker must "know" the audience, have "range over men's souls, and explore their feelings and thoughts" (1.51.222). In addition, the rhetor "ought to feel the pulses of every class, time of life, and degree, and to taste the thoughts and feelings of those before whom he is pleading or intending to plead any cause" (1.52.223). The rhetor ought to be emotionally and psychologically committed to the audience, not merely feign interest: "It is impossible for the listener to feel indignation, hatred or ill-will, to be terrified of anything, or reduced to tears of compassion, unless all those emotions, which the advocate would inspire in the arbitrator, are visibly stamped or rather branded on the advocate himself" (*De Oratore*, 2.44.189). Here Cicero expresses the value of care and commitment to audience and admits deep feeling as a necessary part of the art, a rhetorical–ethical position we see echoed in feminist ethics (e.g., Noddings, 1984). It is also a principle sometimes invoked in discussions of the ethics of "lurking": Are members of electronic communities *obligated* to respond to requests for help out of a communal spirit of sharing and commitment, or can they continue to "lurk," to simply read and not post to a group?

Of course, an important feature of Cicero's rhetorical ethics is that the speaker must always appear to be, and must indeed be, virtuous (*De Oratore*, 2.43.182-184). In fact, Cicero obliterates the distinction between *be* and *seem* (which has plagued rhetoric). Cicero says, in effect, that you cannot fake it. We see this insistence on character also emphasized by Quintilian as well as by Isocrates (1929) in *Antidosis*:

The man who wishes to persuade people will not be negligent as to the matter of character; no, on the contrary, he will apply himself above all to establish a most honorable name among his fellow citizens; for who does not know that words carry greater conviction when spoken by men of good repute. (278)

Cicero's discussion in *De Oratore* anticipates in some ways themes and issues we will see emerging in postmodern rhetorical ethics (discussed in Chapters 4 and 5).

THE NEUTRAL VIEW OF RHETORIC

Although some would admit that rhetoric and ethics have an important relationship, they would question whether rhetoric as *art* (as opposed to the *practice* of rhetoric) can have an ethical component. They would insist on viewing rhetoric—understood either as a discipline or as a set of principles and strategies—as itself neutral. Rowland and Womack (1985), for instance, recognize that rhetorical acts can be judged moral or immoral, but that rhetoric as an art—that is, as a "body of systematic principles for creating discourse" (p. 13)—is itself amoral because it can "be used to discover persuasive devices which deceive or otherwise harm an audience" (p. 14).

Their argument rests on a certain view of the relationship between dialectic and rhetoric. Rowland and Womack see dialectic as separate from, and prior to, the art of rhetoric: Dialectic "actually discovers the truth that rhetoric makes persuasive"; rhetoric is "not the method of discovering probable truth ... [it] is the faculty of discovering the means to make those probable truths [discovered through dialectic] as persuasive as possible to an average audience" (p. 14). Rowland and Womack go on to say that "once particular devices have been given life in discourse, rhetoric becomes either moral or immoral according to its use" (p. 15). In other words, rhetoric does not make moral judgments. Forbes Hill (1983) holds a similar position. He recognizes that "any complete rhetoric needs to consider premises from ethics and politics—that is, premises that involve a man [sic] in moral choices," but he distinguishes ethics and rhetoric by stressing the "distinction between essence and properties": "The consideration of premises specific to ethics and politics is an important property of the art of rhetoric, but it is not part of its essence" (p. 26).

We can approach this issue by raising the question of the role of invention, and of dialectic as a type of invention, within rhetoric. For rhetoricians like Rowland and Womack, rhetoric does include invention, not invention as the process of discovering probable truths, but rather as the process of discovering the available means of persuading others of probable truths. This notion of invention forces a distinction between what we might call "rhetorical invention" and "dialectical invention," and thereby distances rhetoric from knowledge formation. That is, the rhetorical invention imagined by Rowland and Womack deals only with determining methods for persuading an audience to accept a given position ("discovering the available means of persuasion"—a definition that, although that of Aristotle's, is not, I would argue, a position he consistently maintains). In their sense, "rhetorical invention" does not involve invention of the position in the first place: Knowledge or truth is established through dialectic, not rhetoric.

Postmodern critical theory poses a serious challenge to this presumption, challenging the division on two grounds. The first problem is that this view assumes the possibility of a pure dialectic methodology, a dialectic that can proceed unaffected by rhetorical constraints such as audience and situation, a dialectic based on truth and fact, not opinion. (Is this the same as Habermas's idealized notion of communicative action?) One contribution of postmodern criticism is to notice that method itself is rhetorical, and that methods themselves are rhetorically invented entities. Dialectic is not prior to or free of rhetoric: It is itself subject to rhetoric, a point Chaim Perelman (1982) discussed:

> All who believe that they can disengage truth from opinion independently of argumentation have a profound disdain for rhetoric, which relates to opinions; they grant, at best, only a rhetoric which serves to propagate the truths guaranteed to speakers through intuition or self-evidence, but not a rhetoric which seeks to establish these truths. But if we do not concede that philosophical theses can be founded on self-evident intuitions, we must resort to argumentative techniques to make them prevail. The new rhetoric becomes the indispensable instrument of philosophy. (p. 7)

In Chapter 1 of *The Realm of Rhetoric*, Perelman argues that the traditional configuration of logic, dialectic, philosophy, and rhetoric needs to be refigured along different lines. He sees the basis and justification for such a refiguring within Aristotle's work, although this argument requires reading against the traditional interpretations of Aristotle's canon.

Postmodern critical theory challenges the presumed division of dialectic from rhetoric on a second ground as well: It assumes a linear communication process in which thought precedes language. Rowland and Womack reveal their reliance on a linear view of communication that sees writing and speech as secondary representations of thought. Ethical positions are established first through dialectic; rhetoric then figures how to persuade audiences to accept those truths. Jasper Neel (1988) refers to this view of the discovery process as the "classical notion" of communication:

> In the classical notion, . . . first there is thinking, then speaking serves as an instrument to represent thinking, and finally writing serves as an instrument to represent speaking. This means not only that writing remains exterior to and dependent on speaking and that speaking remains exterior to and dependent on thinking, but also that all systems of signification remain exterior to and dependent on whatever they signify. Language, in other words, must come after, remain outside of, and depend absolutely on meaning. (p. 110)

Of course, deconstruction has posed a serious challenge to this linearity, pointing out that such a position assumes a binary privileging thought over language and speech over writing (Derrida, 1977). Rowland and Womack's position rests on this binary, in their assumption that dialectic/thought precedes and takes precedence over rhetoric/language. The problem with this position is that it imagines dialectic as a kind of "pure discourse of thought" (is this philosophy discourse?) free from the taint of *kairos*. Derrida's position, as well as that of Perelman, is to question that assumption, to expose it *as* an assumption, as an unprovable warrant rather than as a certain ground. Derrida's position is that the opposite view has at least an equal probability of being true: that all discourse is subject to rhetorical constraints (Derrida, 1977; see also Porter, 1992a). Philosophical discourse, including ethics discourse, is not a metadiscourse that explains or has priority over rhetorical discourse. It is not immune from rhetoric because it is itself a type of rhetorical discourse.

Partly the argument here might be one between competing notions of rhetoric. On the one hand, there are those who advocate a compartmentalized rhetoric—a view of rhetoric as maintaining strict boundaries between itself and other disciplines, arts, or practices. On the other hand, some advocate an intertwined rhetoric—a rhetoric that accepts as natural and as enabling points of overlap between itself and other disciplines, arts, and practices. We might consider as advocates of compartmentalized rhetoric people such as the Cicero who wrote *De Inventione*, Peter Ramus, and George Campbell. Those who take a more open view of rhetoric include the Cicero who wrote *De Oratore*, Gorgias, and Kenneth Burke. Aristotle seems to be somewhere in between because his work is so complex—some might say inconsistent—that he can be claimed by both sides.

This difference between types of rhetorics recalls Lanham's (1993) distinction between "verbal rhetoric" and "architectonic rhetoric" (which he borrows from Richard McKeon). According to Lanham, verbal rhetoric focuses on formal features of discourse, whereas the architectonic sort views rhetoric "as the overarching *paideia* Cicero and Quintilian sought to describe" (p. 166). Lanham goes on to develop what he calls a "strong defense" of rhetoric, one that takes an architectonic view of the art as encompassing and intermingling with lots of issues that conventionally get grouped under different disciplinary headings (philosophy, communication, ethics, etc.).

THE NEW RHETORIC AND OTHER MODERN/ RATIONALISTIC VIEWS

The classical rhetoric of Aristotle and the Cicero of *De Oratore* advocates a complicated and integrated view of rhetoric as imbricated with ethics—in part this view derives from the understanding of rhetoric as including the activity of invention. If we hold the position that rhetoric includes invention—that is, if we open the door to admit invention as a proper topic of rhetoric—then I believe that we then admit questions of truth, knowledge, and power, as well as ethics. We are, in Perelman's terms, breaching the old boundaries between philosophy and rhetoric. Notice that we are not saying that the areas are the same, only that we must recognize and value their points of overlap and intersection. Maybe our nice neat classification system disappears, and our ground becomes a little shakier, but we gain something in terms of flexibility and explanatory adequacy.

In the 20th century, it was the new rhetoricians of the 1950s and 1960s—called by Walter Beale (1990) the "first awakening"—who first recognized that rhetoric included topical invention or dialectic. Several of them—most notably Kenneth Burke, Richard Weaver, Karl Wallace, and Chaim Perelman—assigned ethics a necessary role in this "new rhetoric." The new rhetoricians saw the issue of ethics as actually a logical outcome of the revival of invention. That is, if we view invention as a legitimate, indeed necessary, focus of rhetoric—that is, if we move beyond a limited notion of rhetoric as a technical activity (see Crowley, 1989)—then we are obliged to consider how invention involves the constitution and distribution of knowledge. This, in turn, leads us to inquiries about the relationship between rhetoric and politics/power (i.e., how knowledge is used) and, eventually, to ethics (i.e., the aims of that use of knowledge).

What is the New Rhetoric? There have been several "new rhetorics," but the New Rhetoric of the 1950s and 1960s refers both to a theoretical shift within communication theory and to its subsequent effects on composition curricula (Porter, 1992a, p. 52). It started, post-World War II, as a rediscovery of classical rhetoric, but developed beyond that in the 1950s and 1960s to develop a truly new rhetoric calling on principles from contemporary philosophy, cognitive and developmental psychology, and literary theory. The chief significance of the New Rhetoric was in rejecting the limited view of rhetoric represented in formalism (with its emphasis on style and correctness as the true basis of the art) and in recovering a broad classical sense of the art of rhetoric as including issues of context, topical invention, and audience.

Kenneth Burke and Richard Weaver, who were among the earliest of these new rhetoricians, represent two divergent positions about the rhetoric-ethics relationship. Both see the rhetoric-ethics connection as important, but they configure it differently. For Burke, rhetoric is important because it helps us determine what is ethical: Rhetoric is inevitably involved in the process of determining what is ethical. In Burkean terms, a piece of writing is seen as agency, as the means or instrument by which agents (writers) act in order to achieve their purposes. Burke (1969) sees a close relation between rhetoric and ethics because truth arises out of the "synthesis" of rhetorical dialectic (p. 53). Any individual speech does not present truth so much as it engages in a process that encourages the truth to emerge.

Weaver's view is theoretically akin to that of Rowland and Womack: Rhetoric is important, but only because it is the necessary (evil?) means by which people are persuaded to be ethical. In Burke's view rhetoric and ethics are interdependent: They interrelate with and support one another at various points; neither has priority. Weaver's view sees ethics—in the form of traditional precepts expressed through language—as prior to and determining of rhetoric, although necessarily reliant on rhetoric. Weaver noticed the slippery, relativistic nature of language (especially the rhetoric of "ultimate terms") and looked for ethical stability in both tradition (by which he meant a reading of the classical tradition favoring

Plato and, to a lesser extent, Aristotle over the sophists) and "rationality": "An ethics of rhetoric requires that ultimate terms be ultimate in some rational sense. The only way to achieve that objective is through an ordering of our own minds and our own passions" (Weaver, 1970, p. 111).

For Weaver, there is a single Great Tradition, which is most readily accessible in classical philosophy, particularly Plato. Granted, this tradition is complex, and it recognizes the complexity of certain questions about the human condition, but nonetheless it is a unified tradition that stands against the great enemies of Truth—Relativism and its discursive counterpart Rhetoric.

Discussions of ethics in the field of rhetoric have traditionally gravitated around Weaver's view, probably because Weaver (1953) more prominently situates his program under the banner of ethics. (It is hard to invoke the term *rhetorical ethics* without invoking the ghost of Richard Weaver.) Burke's view, a more contextual view, is actually much closer to that of Aristotle. Although in Aristotle's corpus ethics and rhetoric are treated in two separate works (*Rhetoric* and *Nicomachean Ethics*), the two works have almost a hypertextual relationship, constantly referring to and overlapping one another. The concept connecting the two areas is *phronesis* (judgment or practical wisdom), which is the basis for both ethical and rhetorical activity.

Other new rhetoricians explored the relationship between ethics and rhetoric, most notably, Chaim Perelman (1982), Perelman and Olbrechts-Tyteca (1969), Stephen Toulmin, and Karl Wallace (1963), and later, in the same vein, Richard Johannesen (1990, 1991). Wallace and Perelman look for ethical stability within abstract rhetorical structures; for Perelman the basis for ethical judgment is the universal audience, for Wallace it is "good reasons." Karl Wallace (1963) constructs an argument that rhetorical invention must include ethical invention as part of its system:

> First, rhetorical theory must deal with the substance of discourse as well as with the structure and style. Second, the basic materials of discourse are (1) ethical and moral values and (2) information relevant to these. Third, ethics deals with the theory of goods and values, and from ethics rhetoric can make adaptations that will result in a modern system of topics. (p. 240)

Wallace's argument is that the "substance of rhetoric" includes questions and issues regarding ethics. He proceeds to suggest a set of ethical *topoi* ("value categories"), that rhetors can apply.

In *The Realm of Rhetoric* (1982), Perelman destabilizes the ground of analytical philosophy by demonstrating that audience is a factor of every argumentative situation. Perelman challenges the distinction between dialectic and rhetoric, in effect making all practical discourse a type of "new rhetoric." All discourse—except some purely formal statements of a mathematical or self-fulfilling variety (arguments from definition, for instance, or tautologies, as in "lying is wrong")—is rhetorical.

As a philosopher Perelman is uncomfortable with a logic based mainly on audience "adherence." He believes that two people agreeing does not necessarily make a truth (recalling Plato's critique of belief as a basis for truth). The majority can be wrong; the community can be wrong. So by what standard can truth be judged?

Perelman builds his standard very carefully based on general premises that are not universal in any absolute sense (i.e., they are not true in all instances), but that are universal in a general sense (i.e., they apply as presumptions; we may assume them to be true unless something else is demonstrated). Presumptions are not universal truths because, Perelman admits, circumstances ("facts") can render them invalid. However, they are assumed to be true unless proven otherwise. Innocent until proven guilty is one common presumption of U.S. jurisprudence. Perelman cites some others: "The presumption that the quality of an act reveals the quality of the person responsible for it; the presumption of natural trustfulness by which our first reaction is to accept what someone tells us as being true" (p. 25). Presumptions serve as contingent ethical principles, representing what is *probably* true in any given case—with the caveat that the specific context may require an adjustment, or rejection, of the principle.

These new rhetoricians tend to look for stabilizing principles in rhetoric—whether the principles are the "universal audience" or "good reasons"—to provide a touchstone for ethical decision making. The communicative ethics program of Jürgen Habermas and his followers is to a great extent an effort to develop a universal rhetorical ethics in the same line of thought as that of the New Rhetoric (see Chapter 4 for discussion of Habermas's discourse ethic).

There are other important views of the ethics–rhetoric relationship, ones that are probably more commonly held views culturally, although perhaps less so in rhetoric theory. The instrumental view sees language as a pipeline; ethical language use is that use which places the fewest barriers between the audience and the facts (or the Truth). Plain style advocates advance their rhetoric on ethical grounds. (We can see the roots of this movement in the birth of the science paradigm, in Ramus's *Dialectic*, in the Puritan attack on metaphor, in the language philosophy of John Locke, and in the stylistic tracts of the Royal Society.) In "Politics and the English Language" (1956), George Orwell, the archetypal plain stylist, describes the ethical problems with the political prose of his time, deploring the rhetorical inflation of totalitarian regimes. For Orwell, "good prose is like a window pane." Although he admits that all language is political, he pines for a "clear, direct, and neutral" language that will permit the truest picture of reality. This kind of representational view of language—that an ethical style is a transparent style, putting the fewest obstacles between the word and the thing the word represents—becomes enshrined as a stylistic norm in the formalist handbook tradition. We see in Strunk and White's *The Elements of Style* (1979), for instance, the insistence on "clear language," based on the assumptions (a) that the writer knows the truth and so is morally responsible for presenting it as clearly as possible, and (b) that the morally best language is that which posits a one-to-one correspondence between the word and the thing.

Berel Lang (1991) represents another common view toward the ethics of rhetoric. He recognizes that all language use has moral implications. His answer to the problem of how to promote ethical writing—and it is the answer for many in composition—is the personal essay, a form he sees as offering the least opportunity for immorality. The expressivist tradition in general posits that the final arbiter of truth is the self, and that, therefore, the best writing is that which arises from self-experience, self-critique, and self-reflection. That writing which is least true is that which merely imitates the work of others, or which attempts gross flattery of an audience (or which attempts to persuade at all), or which affects scholarly or intellectual pretensions. Persuasion is in fact a suspect aim in this tradition (Porter, 1992a). Moral writing is defined by genre, with the personal essay being the most ethical form and all others being lesser to some extent or other.

All these constructions recognize the ethical implications of language use and posit some kind of foundation for settling the ethical dilemma: whether it be in the style used (Orwell), the form or genre employed (Lang), or in some more abstract construction like the universal audience (Perelman) or "good reasons" (Wallace). Perelman sees the need for some norm for judging the validity of arguments. His answer is the construct of the universal audience, which provides a rational basis for deciding disagreement; he attempts to manifest the values of the universal audience in the form of presumptions, which describe what is probably true. Richard Weaver looks to "tradition" as offering an ethical basis for rhetoric.

Postmodern rhetorical-ethical theory—discussed in Chapters 4 and 5—challenges all these foundational bases. Although all have some strengths, none provides by itself an adequate theory for explaining the range of discourse—or the range of ways discourse can be viewed as ethical or unethical. None sufficiently addresses questions of justice or oppression because these theories remain wedded to a view of rhetoric as text rather than act.

What is important to realize, and what I hope this overview has shown, is that not all calls to ethics are the same. Some emerge from an attenuated if not downright hostile view of rhetoric—and it is important to distinguish my call from those. My view sees rhetoric as a worthy art, sees invention as an integral part of rhetoric, and sees rhetoric and ethics operating as co-equal participants in the construction of subjectivities and standpoints. Establishing how this works in terms of the distinct rhetorical dynamic of internetworked writing is the focus of Chapters 5 and 6.

3

Recovering an Ethics for Rhetoric and Writing: Postmodern Views

---

Marx was rightly suspicious of the attempt to occupy a position above the fray.
—Feenberg, 1991, p. 143

Postmodern theory provides another perspective on rhetorical ethics (see Porter, 1993a). Postmodernism challenges the rationalist rhetorical ethics Weaver, Wallace, and others attempt to establish on two grounds: (a) seeing the search for a single ground—whether that ground is within or outside of rhetoric—as itself misguided and not logically necessary; and (b) viewing ethics not as a fixed set of precepts, or as "the basic materials of discourse" (Wallace, 1963, p. 240), but as an ongoing process. Postmodernism challenges the foundationalist assumptions that reside at the center of most ethical discussions.

Postmodernism is difficult to define, and, as Lester Faigley (1992) points out, it may be self-contradictory to do so (p. 3; see also Sullivan & Porter, 1997, Chap. 2). Still, we can characterize postmodern theory (as opposed to postmodern aesthetics, for instance) as characterized by its "radical critiques of knowledge and the sign" (Faigley, 1992, p. 8; Hassan, 1993; Lyotard, 1984) and by its challenging of the tenets of certain established intellectual orders (modernism, humanism, Enlightenment liberalism). We might add that it is a radical critique of ethics, too, at least as traditionally constructed. Faigley describes postmodernism's critique of traditional ethics as taking the position that:

There is nothing outside contingent discourses to which a discourse of values can be grounded—no eternal truths, no universal human experience, no universal human rights, no overriding narrative of human progress. This assumption carries many radical implications. The foundational concepts associated with artistic judgment such as "universal value" and "intrinsic merit," with science such as "truth" and "objectivity," and with ethics and law such as "rights" and "freedoms" suddenly have no meaning outside of particular discourses and are deeply involved in the qualities they are alleged to be describing objectively. . . . Postmodern theory offers a sustained critique of a unified discourse of humane values by revealing how such a discourse results from a dichotomy between what is held to be universal and what is particular and contingent. A unified discourse of human values follows from the ideal of impartial moral reason, where from a disinterested and detached standpoint the particularities of different social contexts can be abstracted into universals. (pp. 8, 46)

Postmodernism challenges the possibility of a "disinterested and detached standpoint" that has universal standing. However, it also recognizes two inevitabilities about standpoints: (a) Every discourse is a new act of power that takes a stance in an already established discursive system of power; whenever you write, you take a position and you establish a value vis-à-vis existing systems; and (b) different standpoints will inevitably conflict.

A postmodern approach to ethics differs from traditional ethics primarily in its contingent nature; it sees ethics as grounded in fluctuating criteria, in difference, or in community or local practices. It does not rely on, nor would it attempt to seek, a universal common ground for ethical action. In this sense it is highly compatible with pluralistic rhetorics. The critical challenge in developing such an ethics is building a model that accommodates the postmodern critique of traditional ethics while at the same time resisting the traditional ethicists' charge of "relativism."

The question I am asking is this: Is it possible to reconfigure ethics and rhetoric in light of postmodern precepts? Could there be such a thing as a postmodern ethics? Obviously there is (see Bauman, 1993; Brown, 1995; Caputo, 1993; Critchley, 1992; McCance, 1996, Wyschogrod, 1990). A number of leading postmodern theorists—among them Foucault, Lyotard, and Irigaray—have explored such a possibility. Foucault begins to develop this discussion in the second and third volumes of *The History of Sexuality* (1985, 1986a); Lyotard most explicitly in *Just Gaming* (Lyotard & Thébaud, 1985) and, to an extent, in *Peregrinations* (1988a); and Irigaray in *An Ethics of Sexual Difference* (1984/1993). Obviously the process of tracking the development of postmodern ethical thought is a vast one (and it is explored in greater depth in Chapters 4 and 7). In this overview I call attention to the possibility of it, with reference to Foucault's focus on the constitution of the self, to Lyotard's treatment of obligation and duty, and to Irigaray's focus on difference, as these discussions describe what I see as two primary components of postmodern ethics: construction of the ethical subject and the necessity of ethical action.

FOUCAULT AND THE ETHICAL SUBJECT

Foucault sees ethics as the necessary third axis of his historical analytic (Davidson, 1986; Foucault, 1983; 1984b, 1984c). Archaeology is the analytic by which he examines how knowledge is constructed; genealogy investigates the relations between power (or action) and knowledge. The third focus is on ethics, which investigates how "we constitute ourselves as moral agents" (Foucault, 1984c, p. 351). These axes appear chronologically in Foucault's work, but they are not discrete nor are they stages; rather, each axis implies the other. As Foucault began his project of identifying systems of knowledge, he realized that these systems were implicated with systems of power (*Discipline and Punish*, 1979, is the book that marks the intersection of the two concerns). Later he realized that systems of power/knowledge were also implicated with the ethical issue of the constitution of the subject.

Near the end of his life, Foucault became more concerned in his lectures and interviews with the moral, political, and historical problematics of truth telling (see Bernauer, 1987, p. 72). Although he was never able to engage this project fully, the consideration of power and the political clearly led him to ethical questions. His ethical project never got very far, and it centered mainly on the "ethic of the care of the self"—which, to most ethicists, is only a small part of the whole subject. Yet he did address this question: How does one define ethical behavior in a world where discursive practice is necessarily an exercise of power?

Foucault's study of ethics begins in *The History of Sexuality* with his examination of the ancient Greeks' notion of ethics. The question for the Greeks, as Foucault perceives it, is the issue of what kind of life to lead—How should we live?—a question at the core of Aristotle's *Politics*. (Foucault focuses in particular on sexual and dietary mores.) The question of the "aesthetics of life" presupposes a "should"—a norm or ideal existence, sometimes established through written codes, but often only implicit in the actions of a people, which are sometimes at odds with and resistant to extant codes. Foucault's interest is in examining how various cultures (ancient Greek, 19th-Century Victorian) developed ethical standards, and how individuals within those cultures constituted themselves as moral beings in relation to cultural mores.

Foucault does not provide very much discussion of the third axis of his project, the ethical axis. We have relatively few references in his later work, mostly interviews, but enough to see that it was emerging as an important concern tied to his interest in the relation of knowledge to power and the constitution of the subject. The significance of Foucault calling attention to this set of questions is to notice that ethics is, has to be, a crucial component of social activity (which is to say, also rhetoric). Foucault's discussion also insists that the power-knowledge investigation will necessarily be incomplete without a consideration of the moral/ethical component that always presupposes a "should," serving as a driving and motivating force for action within the power-knowledge matrix. The self is defined, ethically, in terms of its relationship to these codes and mores. Ethics always involves a positioning, even if that positioning is only temporary. The self—which could be a singular "I" or a plural "we"—is constituted through a process of positioning among various sites or various communities. Self in this sense, is of course, not to be understood as transcendental, a priori, or un-self-determined. Self is rather postures evident in discourses, positions taken or adopted. Ethics then comes closer to the classical notion of *ethos* (character). Ethics is the process by which this individual character is constructed, through alignment with and within various communities. (Of course, Kantian ethics focuses more on the constitution of the single and consistent moral *self*, whereas postmodern ethics focuses more on the various *selves* that writers construct, say, in various electronic communities.)

Foucault's contribution is to see ethics as a set of situated, constituted relations rather than a static set of ahistorical or metaphysical standards. (We see a similar point made in feminist ethics. For instance, see Mullett, 1987, who describes feminist ethics as an ethics of relationality versus the rationality of traditional ethics; see Chapter 4 for further discussion.) That is not to eliminate the possibility that there can be transhistorical standards—traditions of various sorts do, after all, leverage quite a bit of influence; the past does exercise a power and may indeed constitute a certain authority. However, Past and Tradition are to be recognized for what they are—not ahistorical or metaphysical, but very much arising out of historical contexts and very much constructed by previous communities. (Foucault's entire project is after all an historical one: Understanding the genealogy of concepts, of institutions, of discursive practices is vital to a critical understanding of the self.) Thus, the kind of ethics this leads toward is not a "here and now" situationalism denying the validity of other communities or previous communities, but one that examines them critically.

There is one point of particular methodological importance in Foucault's project: Studying the actual formalized ethical codes of a culture or community never provides a complete picture of the ethics of that group. We have to examine a whole set of interrelated practices that constitute the behavior of individuals and read the codes not as authoritative, explanatory, or ultimately descriptive, but as another set of practices themselves that influence and interact with, but by no means, determine individual activities. Bernauer (1987) recognizes the importance of this methodological point: "The ethical substance of his [Foucault's] treatise puts forward a domain for analysis which overcomes the theory-practice dualism. It is composed, not of institutions, theories or ideologies but of practices" (p. 74). The focus on *practices* is an important one to the postmodern ethical project, and one I return to later in this chapter.

LYOTARD AND THE ISSUE OF OBLIGATION

Lyotard's treatment of ethics resembles Foucault's in its wrestling with the problem of the ethics of rhetorical standpoint. In *Peregrinations* (1988a), Lyotard sees ethics as the determination of a "should" for a "we." Reviving Aristotle's central question in *The Politics*, he asks: How should we in various communities act? What should we believe? How should we think? And how do we justify those actions, those beliefs, those thoughts? The notion of the good is tied to a "we," and every action, including every discursive action, invokes the good of the we. In *Peregrinations*, Lyotard examines various critical postures that he himself held, including indifference and irony. Rejecting both indifference and irony as viable critical postures, he arrives at duty and at obligation—not a duty or obligation to a particular position, but rather a duty "to be obliged" (that is, to something), an attachment, a commitment, a belief. Lyotard goes on to describe the "pure obligation," the "duty of being obliged," which, for him, drives political action:

> Every political deliberation or decision [or, could we add, rhetorical act?] either explicitly or implicitly involves a reference to and, as much as possible, an answer to the issue of what "we" ought to be or become in the present circumstances. The "we" at stake here thus designates a community whose existence belongs to the determination of what we ought to be or become and indeed to the determination of how to do it . . . .Whatever the question, an obligation is implied. (p. 35)

Lyotard's realization—one carefully and painstakingly arrived at, after rejecting the postures of irony and indifference—is that there is no escaping obligation and judgment. Rhetorical acts presume both an obligation and a judgment, which are part of, not prior to, the rhetorical act. This duty, this drive to obligation and action, derives from community, but not community in the sense of universal common grounds, not a universal audience, and not an unruly mob. Rather this duty derives from a "local we," a "we" that is bound and localized in various ways, perhaps by culture, by disciplinary affiliation, by theological predisposition, and certainly by some combination of these (and other) influences. We might consider this "we" as a local rather than a universal audience. A Lyotardian ethics, then, has to do with the commitment of self to some community: How is this commitment formed? What understandings does the commitment imply? In this system, ethical principles exist, but there are numerous and competing ethical sites, with equal validity (see Chap. 4, Figure 4.1).

Disagreeing with ethicists like Levinas, Buber, and Noddings, who see the personal I–thou relationship as the ideal, Lyotard (1988b) views the I–you relationship with considerable suspicion: "By turning the I into its you, the other makes him or herself master, and turns the I into his or her hostage" (p. 111). Dialogue requires the objectifying of participants into fixed roles, with the *I* defining the *you* as different and at the same time monopolizing it, which Lyotard sees as a form of terrorism. To reach out to another Lyotard sees as a form of strangulation rather than embrace. In any case, the *I* and the *you* are both flimsy referents for constructing a discourse ethic.

So what is one left to do? Obligation and commitment are inevitable, but upon what are they to be constructed? As Lyotard (1988b) points out, Kant develops the concept of "universal humanity" (the *sensus communis*)—the "community of practical, reasonable beings" (p. 125), a precursor of Perelman's universal audience. Lyotard agrees it is possible to conceptualize such a community, but unnecessary and perhaps unethical. Lyotard describes how Kant's move is self-refuting: Kant produces a discourse that claims to be prior to all discursive acts—including itself, hence the contradiction—and that serves as the guiding principle underlying them. In short, the move of rationalist philosophy that Lyotard challenges (it is also Habermas's move) is the move of producing discourse that claims it is a special metadiscourse outside the realm of normal discourse, but that nevertheless provides the criteria for judging normal discourse. (For a discussion of Lyotard's ethics, particularly its relation to Kantian ethics, see Beardsworth, 1992.)

It is this last move that postmodernism challenges: One cannot get outside language. Yet, unlike many postmodernists, Lyotard does not shrink from the critical question: Given this state of affairs, how do we justify ourselves? Lyotard recognizes the need for justification. Any act of writing—or, for that matter, any act of *not* writing but silence—requires a commitment. We cannot escape from a positioning of ourselves in any rhetorical undertaking.

Lyotard looks to the genres of discourse as defined by communities as providing a locale for answering this question. There are discourse rules, or game rules, in the sense of *nomoi*, but they are different at the practical or local level, and there is no generic or universal set of rules (or Rule) regulating them. That is, difference is fundamental, just difference or conflict between discursive positions. In *The Differend* (1988b), Lyotard calls frequently on the litigation model: Whenever there are communities conflict is inevitable, and yet some decision must always be made, without the assistance of a universal tribunal.

So how are differences settled? The suggestion in *The Differend* is that communities have to talk—litigate or argue, if you like—and in so doing create a new game that enables them to create a new third community. Rhetoric, then, becomes a means by which new communities are established, and that is the process by which old communities' conflicts are settled. The game rules of this third community should not be assigned universal status, just "new" status as arising from a community conflict.

If this view of discourse ethics leads to any kind of explicit directive, it is this: Talk, and through talk create a new community. On a practical level, we see such a solution frequently applied to the creation of new electronic communities on the networks. When a discussion thread in an electronic community is deemed tangential to the main interests of the group, what happens is often, first, an argument about what is appropriate subject matter for the list, but then, second, a dissolution of the original group. The dissatisfied sect breaks off, schismatically, and forms a new LISTSERV community. In a sense the technology encourages such dissolution because it is relatively easy, technologically, to form a new community—and it is relatively difficult, via electronic postings, to reconcile deep rifts.

However, Lyotard is also suspicious of the "we," of the consensus that can also be a form of terrorism—and if there is a form of relative freedom it is made possible by the principle of multiplicity. Talk should not attempt to elide difference, but celebrate it. It is this commitment to pluralism we see most clearly expressed in *Just Gaming*.

In *Just Gaming* (Lyotard & Thébaud, 1985), Lyotard considers the problem of judgment in postmodern thought. Denying the possibility of a *sensus communis*, Lyotard picks up the issue of how judgment can be justified without universals or general metalanguage. Lyotard begins by acknowledging two points: one, that prescriptions are inevitable, "fundamental even" (p. 59); and two, that "one cannot derive prescriptions from descriptions" (p. 59).

The strategy that Lyotard develops is casuistic: One works "case by case," a strategy that "can only be implemented in the light of practice" (p. 28), in a negotiation (in *The Differend*, 1988b, Lyotard uses the word "litigation") between sides. This negotiation is a kind of "game," but not "game" in the casual or recreational sense. In fact, the French title, *Au Juste*, focuses on justice, the end of discourse, rather than on "gaming," which for Lyotard is the means toward the end. There are discourse conventions, game rules, and the discursive subject plays within and with the conventions in order to secure an advantage.

Lyotard's discourse model—which he considers both a "pagan" model and a sophistic one—might be faulted for its agonism, for seeing conflict, not cooperation, as the basis for discourse. In this model, morality emerges from the contest of antagonistic *opinions*, there being no other stuff out of which to construct morality. As communities build morality through this process of gaming, an Idea might emerge: not an a priori principle, but an Idea that serves as an imaginative goal (or "horizon") toward which communities strive. At the same time this Idea should not be treated as a totalizing a priori: It should not control the singularity of cases, and it should not become static.

In the final chapter of *Just Gaming*, Lyotard anticipates what will be the most serious criticism of his vision: that such a view inevitably leads toward a "horizon of unity and of totality" (p. 95), toward the reconstitution of a hegemonic "we," the dominating consensus of community, or the terror of the majority (which means "great fear"). So Lyotard asks whether politics could "regulate itself by the idea of minority and plurality" (p. 96). In this case Lyotard almost creates a general discourse principle, although he stops just short of that: Respect plurality, respect multiplicity. A political community can guarantee its own morality only by supporting its own critique and by allowing for dissenting opinions not only to be heard but even to risk the identity of the community. Lyotard recognizes the paradox of this move, finally:

The justice of multiplicity: it is assured, paradoxically enough, by a prescriptive of universal value. It prescribes the observance of the singular justice of each game such as it has just been situated: formalism of the rules and imagination in the moves. It authorizes the "violence" that accompanies the work of the imagination. It prohibits terror, that is, the blackmail of death toward one's partners, the blackmail that a prescriptive system does not fail to make use of in order to become the majority in most of the games and over most of their pragmatic positions. ... Justice here does not consist merely in the observance of the rules; as in all the games, it consists in working at the limits of what the rules permit, in order to invent new moves, perhaps new rules and therefore new games. (p. 100)

Discourse is a game with serious stakes. Justice—and we must have a means of deciding what justice is in any case—is determined through a process of "gaming," a kind of negotiation in which participants push at the margins of the rules in order to secure an advantage. Yet Lyotard (1984) insists that we recognize, and respect, the "heterogeneity of language games" (p. xxv). That is, do not try to do what Habermas attempts: Do not try to regulate the rules of language games into a single Rule, but recognize the differences between language games and, at the same time, the inevitability that communities will collide and conflict will occur. Judgments must be made, that is inevitable, but they must be made with the presumption in the direction of hetero- rather than homogeneity. That is the only thing that protects us from the dominance of consensus and the terror of the majority. (For a discussion of Lyotard's notion of justice in the context of political ethics, see Barron, 1992.)

IRIGARAY AND THE CELEBRATION OF BODILY DIFFERENCE

In *An Ethics of Sexual Difference* (1984/1993), Luce Irigaray identifies sexual difference as "one of the major philosophical issues, if not the issue, of our age" (p. 5). She notes that throughout history "man has been the subject of discourse, whether in theory, morality, or politics" (p. 6). Irigaray turns to developing an ethics that is connected to sexual difference and that recognizes the presence—and perhaps, the authority—of a feminine ethics that constitutes itself quite differently from the "masculine and paternal" (pp. 6–7) systems (e.g., natural law) that have dominated the discussions of ethics: "An ethical imperative would seem to require a practical and theoretical revision of the role historically allotted to woman" (p. 117). We must "ask science to reconsider the nonneutrality of the supposedly universal subject that constitutes its scientific theory and practice," because, in fact, "the self-proclaimed universal is the equivalent of an idiolect of men, a masculine imaginary, a sexed world" (p. 121). Furthermore, Irigaray urges us to recognize that "discourse has a *sex*" (p. 112, emphasis in original).

For Irigaray, ethics refers to the way we construct our identities and our relations with one another—and the source of our relations lies in the morphological differences between men and women and in the physical dynamic of heterosexual intercourse. For Irigaray, physical love (*eros*) is the principle that bridges opposites, desire is the driving force of love, and the caress, or touch, is love's "most elementary gesture" (p. 186). With this emphasis, Irigaray brings a set of terms into ethics that have not traditionally been foregrounded. Although Christian ethics, of course, emphasizes love, Christian love (*agape*) is more of a spiritual love-in-a-community kind than the sensible, sensual, and one-to-one physical love (*eros*) that Irigaray imagines as most basic. Irigaray's notion of love is also different from the emphasis on love (*philia*) in Aristotle's rhetorical and ethical system, which stresses the spirit of friendliness that should characterize social and rhetorical relations. Irigaray attempts to rescue the *physical* from the subordinated status it has been assigned in traditional ethical systems. The body matters, in other words. The passion of wonder is also important to Irigaray, a quality that can serve to link men and women—awe in regard to the Other who is a mystery—and this quality can manifest itself in the "sexual encounter [that] would be a festive celebration and not a disguised or polemical form of the master–slave relationship" (p. 17). All in all, Irigaray attempts to change the very terms of the discussion of Western ethics: from a masculine, abstract, and property-based ethic of justice to an affirmative ethic of celebration in the sharing of difference in a very physical and material way.

This focus on *difference* is the key feature of Irigaray's ethics—and indeed of postmodern ethics generally: that is, the argument that difference is just as fundamental as similarity (in Irigaray's system, more so), and that similarity (or commonality) should not be assumed to be the higher or determining factor of ethics, as the Great Western Tradition has all along assumed. As Irigaray points out, the focus on similarity—or the humanity common to us all—has often meant that the female is obscured, neglected, subordinated, or denied. The fundamental differences between male and female sexuality—for example, the male sex organ is external and so in a sense is apart from man; the female sex organ is internal and enveloping—are not to be glossed over, Irigaray suggests, as merely incidental differences between a more important and fundamental humanity. The challenge that faces any ethics of sexual difference is to allow for the embrace, the sharing, the union—the true touch or caress—that is not also at the same time an effacement or erasure of another. In terms of Irigaray's construction, she sees it as important that women begin with "love of self," with acknowledging and celebrating their own sexual identity, in a sense forming their own distinct community, "*a world for women*" (p. 109), or their "own ethical site" (p. 199). In this articulation, Irigaray recognizes the need for a female community that does not allow the masculine principle to continue to dominate the site of ethics under the banner of neutrality or humanity.

Foucault and Lyotard both develop ethical discussions focusing on the individual's relationship to various communities, and so their ethics have a social emphasis and a justice emphasis that is unlike Irigaray's. Their approaches also are decidedly rhetorical in the sense that they consider the problem of taking and justifying discursive standpoints. An especially important component of both their discussions is being sensitive to the ways in which any community can marginalize as well as provide identities for individuals. We must have communities—and yet communities can cause us difficulties whenever they obscure diverse identities. "Sameness" is "deadly" (Irigaray, 1984/1993, p. 191) because there is no reaching out to the other but simply an erasure of our otherness. In a sense, postmodern ethics supports a subversiveness that we do not find in traditional ethics, a point that Charles Scott (1990) sees as a sine qua non of postmodern ethics:

> Learning to name things anew, to become alert to exclusions and to forgotten aspects in a people's history, to overhear what is usually drowned out by the predominant values, to rethink what is ordinarily taken for granted, to find out how to hold itself in question: these are aspects of the thought of the question of ethics. There is a subversiveness in such processes vis-à-vis the normal and ordinary, a subversiveness not unlike that of poets and philosophers who are routinely excluded and silenced by totalitarian regimes. (pp. 7–8)

Scott puts his finger on another important feature of postmodern ethics: It works to revive and rediscover the marginalized, what has been lost and excluded "in a people's history." In this aspect, postmodern ethics not only listens to alternate voices, but it also works actively to uncover those voices. Recognition not of "The Other" but of Others (plural) is a critical principle that emerges from postmodern ethics. We must engage and embrace—and love, says Irigaray—difference in order to arrive at justice (in Lyotard's system) or to achieve the kind of transcendent celebratory meeting that is the *telos* of Irigaray's ethic. In postmodern ethics Love of Other replaces Rule.

A second principle emerging from this discussion, then, and one that I discuss in the next section of this chapter, is process. Postmodern ethics refers to an inquiry procedure, a process rather than a static set of a priori principles applied to historical situations. In postmodern ethics, Scott (1990) says,

> The emphasis falls on a continuing process of thinking that diagnoses, criticizes, clarifies by means of questions, destructures the components of meaning and power that silently shape our lives together, and also questions the values and concepts that have rule-governing and axiomatic power in our culture. The emphasis does not fall on the possible complete systematic accounts that prescribe definitive solutions to problems, "right" structures of value, originary or utopian visions of preferred types of personal identity. Thinking and writing, rather, take place in the questionableness and the problems that arise in the constellation of belief, know-

ledge, and evaluation that constitute us and set the parameters of what we may legitimately desire and the manners in which we normally relate to people and things. (p. 7)

Considering the relationship of rhetoric to ethics, Victoria Kahn (1985) also sees the importance of practical and social activity as its emphasis on procedure (know how) as opposed to subject matter:

> Its results are practical, not theoretical; rather than providing us with a set of theoretical principles it engages us in a reflexive activity of practical reasoning, and it is that *activity* rather than the subject matter under discussion that is of primary importance, for it refines the faculty of judgment that will enable us to reason appropriately in each particular case. Furthermore, both in origin and effect the *usus* or activity of disputation is a social one: it requires an interlocutor. (p. 57, emphasis in original)

THEORY AND PRACTICE, ETHICS AND WRITING

Conventional Enlightenment and deontological notions of ethics rely on a perspective that sees ethics—and, more generally, theory—as an explanatory and determining set of universal precepts, a metanarrative that justifies historical and situated action. Ethics within this framework is determining what the principles are through a theoretical, philosophical, and/or theological methodology (such as dialectic) and then determining how the general principles apply to particular situations. General theories, or a priori principles, discipline specific practices or historical contexts.

Of course the view that abstract concepts and precepts can function as rules participates in the theory–practice binary, privileging the role of theory in explaining and determining practice. A number of researchers in a variety of fields have challenged the privileging of theory over practice—in a number of its various manifestations—and are arguing for a balanced perspective that integrates theory and "situatedness." The basis for this critique also lies in researchers' acknowledgment of the historicized nature of all inquiry and thought (vs. the deontological, or a-historical, approach of other ethicists and methodologists). Their argument supports the need for a situated ethic, one that (a) takes into account the "particular and contingent" (Faigley, 1992, p. 46), for instance, the influence of technological structures on social relations (how the ethical rules of a newsgroup are different from those for a LISTSERV group); (b) grants ethical authority to the *nomoi* of local electronic communities (e.g., the norms for behavior to a great extent, but not entirely, are decided on a local basis, by distinct groups); and (c) supports a case approach to rhetorical-ethical decision making.

A number of researchers from a variety of fields, including professional writing (see Sullivan & Porter, 1993b) and research methodology (see Sullivan &

Porter, 1997), have noticed the dominant tendency in academic scholarship to privilege theory (often portrayed as "structure" or "method") over practice and have begun to challenge this presumed superiority, arguing for the significance of practice (see Lobkowicz, 1967). Pierre Bourdieu's (1977) analysis of the theory-practice dynamic represents his break from what he refers to as the "positionality of the objectivist stance" he associates with traditional social science research. Bourdieu points out that to understand a cultural activity, such as the gift-giving ritual of the Kabyle culture, one must understand the timing of that activity. The static structuralist paradigm does not account for the timing, the situatedness of the ritual, or what rhetoric terms *kairos* (see Kinneavy, 1986; Phelps, 1988, pp. 230–231). Theory (in this instance understood to be an all-encompassing structure or framework of understanding) does not account for the "positionality" of the ritual. *Kairos* is a critical element of rhetorical ethics, as well as casuistry. *Kairos* refers to appropriateness, to the timing of a rhetorical event, or to cultural conventions existing at any given moment that give the rhetorical utterance its shape and context. *Kairos* refers not only to the particular momentary situation, but also to "due measure, appropriateness, fitness" generally (Sheard, 1993, p. 292).

In her discussion of usability methodology, Lucy Suchman (1987) explores the relationship between plans (which function as theory or structure) and the situated actions of the users of a copying machine. She notes that "European navigators" (her analogy for the Western rationalist) tend to view plans as abstract and prior structures, as determining or at least guiding behavior. However, her observations of office workers learning to use new copying machines indicate that such users proceed more like "Trukese navigators": They know where they want to go, but they do not have any prior navigational plan for getting there. They proceed in ad hoc fashion, letting the unfolding events of the situation (rather than the preconceived plan) determine what they will do next. The problem, according to Suchman, is that researchers seldom distinguish between the plan (as intention) and the explanatory structure. Her point is that as researchers we must begin to understand structure as "an emergent product of situated action, rather than its foundation" (p. 67).

Michel de Certeau (1984) sees practice as necessarily resistant to and opposed to theory. Clifford Geertz (1983) notes how "knowledge" must be a local phenomenon. In their study of design of computer systems, Terry Winograd and Fernando Flores (1986) challenge the rationalistic paradigm (which applies systematic general rules, which are viewed as explanatory hypotheses, to solve problems), pointing out that "the meanings of items cannot be fixed without reference to the context in which they occur" (p. 19). All these researchers and theorists have noticed that "theory alone, by its very nature as abstraction, as generalization, cannot account completely for the situational, the specific instance of practice. That is not to dismiss theory, but simply to say that it ought not to be perceived as all-determining or all-explaining" (Sullivan & Porter, 1993b).

In rhetoric/composition, Carolyn Miller and Louise Wetherbee Phelps have both recognized the limitations of theory and have worked toward a dynamic view of composing theory that recognizes the necessary contribution of practice. For example, Miller (1989) identifies praxis as a middle ground between theory and practice, a higher form of practice. Praxis is more than a simple addition of or compromise between theory and practice; it represents a new kind of critical positioning. It is a practice, conscious of itself, that calls on "prudential reasoning" for the sake not only of production but for "right conduct" as well. It is informed action, as well as politically and ethically conscious action that in its functioning overlaps practical and productive knowledge (see Freire, 1970/1993, on the transforming purpose of praxis).

The judgment that enables praxis is "practical wisdom," that is, *phronesis*, sometimes translated as "prudence," after the Latin *prudentia* (see Book 6 of *Nicomachean Ethics*). According to Garver (1987), prudence inserts itself into that gap "between apprehending a rule (*episteme*) and applying it (*techne*)" (p. 16). Prudence "requires that the writer find some middle ground between too much universality—the superfluous … proclamation of moralizing principles—and too much particularity" (p. 39). Ethically, prudence is "halfway between an ethics of principles, in which those principles univocally dictate action … and an ethics of consequences, in which the successful result is all" (p. 12). Thus, praxis is in this sense sophistic and contingent in nature.

Praxis refers to "practical rhetoric," focused on local writing activities (practice), informed by as well as informing general principles (theory) and calling on "prudential reasoning." Praxis recognizes the "inseparable relation between reflection and action" (see Phelps, 1988, on Freire, p. 211; Schön, 1983, on professional action as reflection-in-action). The way Miller and Phelps have used praxis might be loosely translated as "reflective action," after Schön's discussion. "Reflective action" refers to a thoughtful procedure that is neither "theory" (in the sense of *theoria*, or epistemic/scientific knowledge) nor mere "practice" (in the sense of "habits"—what people regularly do). Praxis is more than merely high-level practice (i.e., doing rote, well-defined tasks). The way Schön describes it, certain kinds of professional areas are defined by the activity of praxis: a kind of thinking that does not start with theoretical knowledge or abstract models (which are then applied to situations), but that begins with immersion in local situations and then uses epistemic theory as heuristic rather than as explanatory or determining. Praxis aims for action (that is, situated response) rather than knowledge.

The major discussions of praxis in rhetoric/composition—by Miller, Phelps, and Garver—view praxis as a type of thought/action that questions the validity and usefulness of the theory–practice distinction, yet that must, ironically, rely on that binary for its explanation and justification. Praxis occupies the realm of the probable and is connected by Miller, Garver, and others to Aristotle's notions of practical *and* productive knowledge, types of knowledge that have not been well understood in the post-Enlightenment era, and types of knowledge that Descartes dismissed as no knowledge at all. The standard in the Enlightenment era is scientific knowledge. Those trying to revive praxis for composition are trying to carve out a space for a practical/productive knowledge within the framework of rhetorical invention.

Several researchers and theorists have been urging rhetoric/composition toward this perspective. Martin Jacobi (1990), for instance, argues that ethical practice requires a social dialectic, an interaction between rhetor and audience. (He sees the enthymeme as the formal vehicle enabling this interaction.) According to Michael Kelly (1989), a comprehensive ethical behavior requires three kinds of dialectic: (a) "the single agent's attempt to make a decision about how to act morally in a particular case ... [which involves] conflict within his consciousness between different norms" (p. 177); (b) "the mediation between ethical practice and the demands placed on it by other types of human practice" (p. 178); and (c) the task of rendering "explicit both the dialectics within the practical reason and practical philosophy and the relationships between these two dialectical moments" (p. 178). Kelly stresses the importance of "ethical critique," which requires maintaining a balance between the exercise of power and ethical reflection: "Power threatens and limits reflection, yet reflection constantly challenges power" (p. 185). Arthur Walzer (1989) looks to the speech-act theory of H. Paul Grice for rhetorical principles that will help writers and speakers make ethical decisions in situations involving possible "misleading inference." Walzer's approach to ethics is to show how an abstract set of principles (e.g., Grice's maxims) can usefully be applied to writing situations. The maxims do not generate a definitive answer because "applying" the maxims means using them as a guide in interpreting practice. James Raymond (1989) refers to this kind of process as a "rhetoric as bricolage," a version of rhetoric depending on "a collection of perspectives that yield useful insights in this situation or that, but always partial insights, never the whole truth" (p. 389). It is "the practice of simultaneously exploiting and resisting generalizations" (p. 397; see also Kahn, 1985; and Leff, 1978, on "epistemic rhetoric and the problem of values," p. 64ff.).

What these theorists and researchers are noticing is (a) that rhetorical action always involves a negotiation between competing positions and perspectives, or between abstract principles and theories and particular needs and circumstances; and (b) that rhetorical action always involves ethical judgment because the very act of composing establishes relations between writers and audiences, or relations depending on some notions of "rightness" and "wrongness." In their work on casuistic ethics Jonsen and Toulmin (1988) have tried to develop a heuristic strategy for making such rhetorical-ethical decisions.

Figure 3.1 illustrates the process these theorists are describing by identifying some of the elements constituting a postmodern rhetorical ethics. It attempts to show that writing itself as an activity requires negotiating principles, theories, and strategies from a number of domains; placing those principles, theories, and

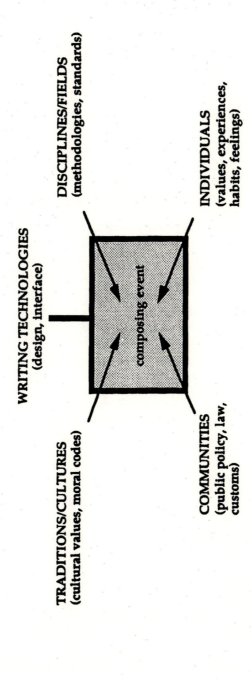

WRITING TECHNOLOGIES
(design, interface)

DISCIPLINES/FIELDS
(methodologies, standards)

INDIVIDUALS
(values, experiences,
habits, feelings)

composing event

TRADITIONS/CULTURES
(cultural values, moral codes)

COMMUNITIES
(public policy, law,
customs)

FIGURE 3.1.   The ethical writing situation.

strategies in dynamic tension; and making composing judgments or commitments based on those dynamics. In this scheme, abstract ethical precepts do not determine decisions; rather, decisions are negotiated among various sites of authority, in an antilogical, *dissoi logoi* system of checks and balances. The material site for this interaction—the technology supporting the internetworked writing activity—contributes to the negotiation of the rhetorical–ethical position.

Traditional ethicists look for their dominant and determining principles in the Tradition/Culture circle. According to their view, certain values found through certain kinds of analogic and analytic reasoning procedures (like dialectic) and manifested in certain kinds of texts (e.g., scripture, "philosophy talk") provide foundational principles. Within this theory-privileging paradigm, the problem for ethics is to interpret these principles for particular circumstances, or to judge between competing principles. Within this paradigm, unethical behavior is thought to derive from allowing circumstances or immediate needs to drive a decision. Unethical corporate behavior, for instance, is assumed to derive from a perspective that uses the value of corporate success as the dominant principle (Porter, 1993d). According to most deontological ethicists, this approach is not ethical because it does not derive from an ethical tradition outside of a particular institutional structure. Weaver (1953), for instance, sees "arguments from circumstance" as "the nearest of all arguments to purest expediency" (p. 57).

In a postmodern ethics, no particular site claims controlling status, but there are sites nevertheless. Ethical judgment in this scheme is the process of placing principles from various sites in dialectic. Authority derives not from any particular set of principles, but from their interaction and through a process of negotiation similar to what Lyotard describes in *Just Gaming* (Lyotard & Thébaud, 1985). The process of writing within this particular composing model is one of negotiation between various positions, and the claim this chapter makes is that this process of negotiation necessarily involves examining the ways that knowledge, power, and ethics intersect through language use. Such judgments are unavoidable (although it is certainly possible to fashion a rhetoric that avoids these judgments by saying that such judgments are outside of the art). Postmodernism urges us to see ethics not simply as something borrowed from these various loci; it is not to be thought of as a whole content that comes to the composing event. Rather, every writing act is itself an ethical process, not simply a presentation of an already preformed ethical position.

Postmodern ethics does not assume that there is "some bedrock of common human values" (Faigley, 1992, p. 162) underlying all rhetorical activities that we can invoke to solve our differences. It does however insist that all rhetorical values are also statements about human values. It begins by recognizing the fundamental principle of diversity—that is, the differences between our values must be acknowledged and respected—and yet goes on to accept the realization that at times we still need to cooperate in order to make decisions when our different values collide, as they will eventually. Rhetoric as an art has a prominent role to play in this process of negotiation and cooperation. It will not provide answers to specific ethical questions, nor is it neutral. Yet it does posit certain ethical values concerning the grounds of communication, and in that respect it will provide practical procedural advice.

RHETORIC AS NEUTRAL VERSUS RHETORIC AS ETHICALLY COMMITTED

This perspective that I am developing rests on a view of rhetoric as a mode of inquiry with its own distinct procedures and topics. That is, as Janice Lauer (1984) argues, rhetoric includes invention; it is not simply an art of developing "a thesis already at hand" (p. 136). I see Crassus's view of the rhetor being knowledgeable in all subjects as an unattainable ideal. The rhetorician does not need to know all subjects and indeed cannot. However, we might posit as a more reasonable goal that the rhetorician should know the processes by which he or she can become knowledgeable in that which he or she needs to talk about. In other words, we can shift the criterion to knowing procedures (know-how) rather than knowledge in the epistemic sense (know-that).

For the most part the notions of productive art and productive knowledge have been lost to Western thought, as Janet Atwill (1990) has pointed out, squeezed out in the binary between theory and practice, between theoretical or scientific knowledge (*episteme*) on the one hand and practice (or practical knowledge) on the other. I think it important to maintain the distinct focus on rhetoric as *techne*, as productive art—at the same time I disagree with those who would argue the ethical neutrality of *techne*.

Atwill and Lauer (1995) carve out a distinct disciplinary space for rhetoric as a productive art (*techne*), an exercise with which I am in agreement. However, they insist on arguing the *ethical neutrality* of productive arts: Rhetoric does not have an "end in itself," says Janet Atwill (1990). Atwill says that with Aristotle "productive knowledge has neither political nor epistemological ends" (p. 12); "productive knowledge can have no 'ends in itself'" (p. 171); and "a productive art can never be concerned with determinate knowledge or value" (p. 172). With this move Atwill seems to divide rhetoric from ethics, which with Aristotle is a practical art that does have definite ends. To the degree rhetoric has an end, it is persuasion of the listener or reader, but it has no specific social or cultural end. Productive knowledge has no end in itself: Its origin or first principle (*arche*) is in the artist and its *telos* is in the user (Aristotle, *Nicomachean Ethics* 1976, 140a5–15). This way, according to Atwill (1990), Aristotle

> attempted to ensure that rhetoric could neither authorize itself as knowledge for its own sake nor be the instrument of a specific social and political objective. Instead, rhetoric was situated in a space where values were in contest. ... It is precisely this

epistemological and ethical indeterminacy ... that the theory/practice binary suppresses. (p. 8)

Atwill might be making this line of argument to resist the philosophers setting the terms for rhetoric and reducing it to an inferior form of theoretical knowledge. If *techne* and morals become confused, we are back to Plato/Socrates' critique of rhetoric. We must detach and delineate rhetoric in order to save it. Atwill describes a view of rhetoric as neutral, in the sense of relativistic: It proceeds based on a kind of sophistic antilogic that can serve any and all sides of a debate. Yet far from being neutral or aethical, the rhetorical relativism that Atwill sketches is an ethical position. To call it nonethical is to buy into Plato's distinctions between true and false knowledge—and to end up on the wrong side. (There is another way around this binary—praxis.)

Atwill and Lauer make this move in order to prevent philosophy from setting the terms for rhetoric, an aim I am sympathetic with. I see frequent examples of philosophers and literary theorists who blur the distinction between rhetoric and ethics or philosophy and end up dismissing, neglecting, or subordinating rhetoric once again. (Kahn, 1985, and Nussbaum, 1986, are two notable examples.) Separating rhetoric from ethics is one way to counter the Western Tradition's subordination and eventual dismissal of rhetoric—and also a way, politically, to establish the importance of writing instruction as more than "mere" style or grammar. Their answer to this disciplinary battle is to separate the contestants and give to each their due territory—separate but equal—because the blurring of the arts has tended to lead, in the past, to neglect of rhetoric.

Postmodernism may have the theoretical power and pragmatic focus to change that tendency. The tactic postmodernism uses is to let rhetoric set the terms for philosophy. This is by no means a new idea, although it is a radical one. It is, after all, what Perelman suggested in his rhetoric. It is, after all, the central thesis of social constructionist rhetorics. Flip the terms of the binary, as Derrida says, in order to show that any privileging within the binary is an arbitrary act.

The question of rhetoric as productive art pertains to issues about the neutrality of technology. In what sense is a gun—or a computer—a neutral tool? Certainly I can use a gun for good or for ill. If I defend my children with it against a crazed attacker, in that sense it serves a positive purpose within its ethical context of use. U.S. soldiers can wave their guns in a manner that is intended to provide food for starving Somalians, and this might be perceived as a "good" use of the tool. The gun rights' advocates push this view of tool as neutral: The person, not the tool itself, uses it in a good or bad manner. The goodness or badness of the tool is in its *telos*, its end or use, not in the thing itself.

However, there is another sense in which a gun, any gun, is by no means a neutral tool. Its very structure presupposes a certain approach to solving problems, and it exists in a cultural and social system of use. It contrasts with other tools; instead of a gun I could wield my pen, my voice, wave my fist, or put out an open hand. In a cultural context of use, a gun is a violent choice. The gun exists in a culture of use, in a system of operation in which it already has a value. In the U.S. Constitution the right of the individual to bear arms is given legal sanction, whereas in some other countries where the good of the community is paramount, the gun is perceived as a threat to the health and welfare of citizens. In that sense, it is part of a system of value.

This distinction is one that Feenberg (1991) discusses in *Critical Theory of Technology*. Borrowing from Weber, Feenberg distinguishes between formal (or instrumental) and substantive views toward technology. If you isolate a system as a formal or abstracted entity, then it can indeed appear to be neutral, but that move to formalize is illusory: "[T]he decontextualized elements from which the biased system is built up *are* in fact neutral in their abstract form.... . [But] Critical Theory shatters the illusion by recovering the lost contexts ... " (p. 181). It is this insistence on *contextualizing* the principles of the art (or the features of a technology)—that is, examining the art or technology in terms of its practical contexts of use (social and political), its institutional settings, it disciplinary affiliations, and its historical positions—that characterizes the postmodern perspective toward art and technology.

Foucault (1979) recognizes this in his discussion of institutions such as the prison: Any technology or object or institution or architecture is already part of a system of use; that system presupposes an archaeology of knowledge, a genealogy of power relations, and an ethics of identity—a "should" or a set of norms for ideal conditions and also an ideal identity for subjects. To abstract the tool out of the system is to leave out too much. The gun, like the prison or the hospital or the computer—or like any rhetoric—is only neutral if you abstract it from its climate of use, which in practical application is never possible. As a human *design* (see Buchanan, 1989; Kinross, 1989) in a certain time and place (culture), a rhetoric is always already ethically and politically imbricated.

Rhetoric is a technology—and there is no neutral technology because all technologies are always already invested with a category bias; they are always socially and culturally situated (as Atwill indeed admits), constructed out of specific historical circumstances and reflecting the biases of that context. Some rhetorics value audience (e.g., the New Rhetoric) investing audience with importance in contributing to the construction of knowledge (Porter, 1992a). Other rhetorics neglect audience, or even show disdain for audience (expressivism for instance), and in adopting this position they establish an ethical value (expressivism says that what the audience thinks is not as important as what the writer thinks). In its design a particular rhetoric can be a strategy either for domination or for democratization. The rhetoric that constructs the audience as a passive receiver of the message determined by the author and that talks only to the rhetor about strategies for changing the audience over to his point of view is a rhetoric of domination. The rhetoric that constructs the audience as an interlocutor, as a source of knowledge, and as a necessary participant in the construction of discourse is a rhetoric of democratization.

A rhetoric may be used for good or for ill within its context of use, but its very structure also already suggests a use. For example, any heuristic, like the nine-cell tagmemic heuristic or the Burkean pentad, is a grid, and as Foucault tells us any grid creates a system of knowledge (or a system for producing knowledge) which both includes and excludes possibilities. A grid is a practice of power, and that practice always posits identities, or ideal roles, for speakers and writers. As Foucault came to realize in his later work on "the ethical axis" (Davidson, 1986), the exercise of power/knowledge has an ethical component. Grids suggest an action and criteria for the conditions of knowledge. In this sense, heuristics are ethically committed structures.

If rhetoric wishes to contribute in useful ways to the discussion and negotiation of major public issues, if it hopes to address the problem of competing social values, then it must reconstruct its historical and conceptual relationship to ethics—and both ethics and rhetoric must recognize their reliance on the practice of writing as tied to technology. This chapter begins such a process by suggesting that rhetoric must recognize its importance to, as well as its interconnections with, ethics (conceived generally as a process of inquiry into questions of value). Although often critical of traditional ethics, postmodern theory actually provides us with a model for a flexible ethics that is compatible with rhetoric/composition and that leads writing teachers toward a heuristic for exploring competing values, which are an unavoidable feature of any writing context. This approach provides a way to "teach ethics" without "teaching people what to think."

From the perspective of rhetoric-as-composing, writing is both product and action, an action with political and ethical consequences. Every act of writing is an attempt to change an audience, and the ethical question that must intersect that attempt pertains to the ultimate goal of the action, which—if it is not precisely "the social good"—will be someone's sense of "the good." We do not need Aristotle to remind us that all writing has an aim, that all writing is rhetorical, and therefore that all writing has an ethical component: It aims for the good of somebody or something.

It is important to understand the use of the term *ethics* emerging here. By *ethics* I do not mean a particular moral code (as in the articulation "Christian ethics"). I am referring, rather, to *rhetorical ethics*—a set of implicit understandings between writer and audience about their relationship. Ethics in this sense is not an answer but is more a critical inquiry into how the writer determines what is good and desirable. Such inquiry necessarily leads toward a standpoint about what is good or desirable for a given situation.

Ethics in the postmodern sense does not refer to a static body of foundational principles, laws, and procedures. It is not to be confused with particular moral codes or with particular sets of statements about what is appropriate or inappropriate behavior or practice. Ethics is not a set of answers, but rather a mode of questioning and a manner of positioning. That questioning certainly involves principles, but it always involves mediating between competing principles and judging those principles in light of particular circumstances. It is, in a word, *kairotic*. Ethics is decision making, but it is decision making that involves question and critique. It is informed, critical, and pluralistic decision making.

Louise Phelps (1988) has perhaps come the closest of any to recognizing the importance of this issue for rhetoric/composition:

> It is clear that in the activities with which composition is concerned—writing, reading, educational interactions—we cannot neatly separate out ethical acts that depend on ethical knowledge, artistic decisions that depend on *techne*, textual interpretations that represent hermeneutical knowledge, and so on. Instead, there is a whole situation in which *phronesis* is the form of reasoning by which teachers constantly adapt for new circumstances knowledge that is itself mixed and subject to change. (p. 218)

What I am referring to as a rhetorical ethics addresses the *should* of writing activities: What *should* the writer do? To answer this question, the writer must explore several lines of inquiry: What ethical constraints (i.e., understandings between reader and writer) are operating in any given writing situation? How does the writing help constitute or shape those conventions? By what inquiry procedure can the writer determine what those conventions might be? Should those conventions be changed, and how might they be changed? From the writer's point of view, ethics has to do with determining (and perhaps even changing) the principles or codes that establish, maintain, and guide relations between writer and audience and with considering the political and ethical consequences of our composing: What gives me the right to attempt to change this audience? By what authority do I claim this right? Am I changing the audience for the better? (Whatever "the better" might be.) Is it for my betterment, theirs, or both of ours? How can I be sure of that trust and responsibility? Such questions force us to think about the ethical implications of our writing actions. Given this broad view of ethics, every act of internetworked writing requires ethical questioning. Given this view, ethics is not just a matter of the occasional problematic episode; rather, ethics, like audience, is a factor of every rhetorical act.

The art of rhetoric does not provide specific answers to specific problems, such as the issue of whether or not LISTSERV owners have the ethical right to cancel subscribers who post unwanted or off-subject messages to a list. The art does provide, or should provide, guidance as to the kinds of ethical procedures one might exercise in making such a decision. In other words, it provides ethical guidance in the form of procedures (e.g., negotiating strategies) and heuristics for making ethical decisions. It suggests the process through which ethical conflicts can be adjudicated. It helps us generate options. It calls our attention to the discursive system itself, as system, and provides us with the means to critique the system (constituted by medium, forum, community, genre, etc.). Rhetoric is also sensitive to the mandates of specific practices, specific technologies, specific community interchanges, specific technologies, and specific bureaucracies of power. Because rhetoric is a situated art, it is ethically committed to the situated, the contingent, the historical (see Farrell, 1993). This commitment positions the art in an ethical continuum, as discussed in Chapter 4. Any claims by rhetoricians to the ethical neutrality of the art will not hold.

Ethical judgments are unavoidable if you plan to write or teach writing. To teach or to practice writing as a rhetorical activity requires that you advocate some notion about the nature of social relations. It requires taking a stand that something is "to the good," at least relative to some other thing that you are not doing. It establishes a value and assumes a vision of what is good and just and of how people should relate to one another. All writing is also fundamentally a praxis, an act of vision, of utopian vision, pushing us to be something better.

4

Complicating Rhetorical-Ethical Stances

The work of the Right is done very well, and spontaneously, by the Left on its own.
—Baudrillard, 1983, p. 30

I don't believe there can be a society without relations of power.
—Foucault, 1987, p. 18

Oremus. Lead us not into sticking labels all over one another lest we fall into the grave error of taxonomania.
—Swearingen, 1991, p. 161

How do we constitute and situate ourselves ethically as writers/publishers of electronic discourse, or as listowners, managers, or developers of network groups and archives, or as teachers in internetworked writing classrooms? What principles can we invoke or stances adopt for assistance in guiding our ethical choices or in doing ethical writing, especially when the traditional sources of ethics have been challenged by the postmodern critique of Western metaphysics and rationality? Lyotard and Thébaud (1985) say that "generally speaking, writing is irresponsible" (p. 8), although maybe they were speaking ironically. Is it possible to have *responsible* (at least relatively so) writing?

In this chapter I consider a variety of possible ethical stances and configure their implications for internetworked writing. The purpose of this chapter is to lay out ethical alternatives to the dominant ethical framework influencing discussions of internetworked writing: To the extent that there is one, it is liberal individualism.

LIBERAL-INDIVIDUALISM AND THE POLITICS OF
ELECTRONIC DISCOURSE

Howard Rheingold and Mitchell Kapor (co-founder and President of the Electronic Frontier Foundation, or EFF), and others associated with EFF, have taken a more or less absolute free-speech position toward discourse on the networks. Rheingold (1991) thinks that "Even the most obnoxious expressions deserve protection, on the grounds that restrictions on antisocial communications can easily be extended to communications that don't jibe with the political views or morals of those in power at the time" (p. 46).

Kapor (1991) advocates "freedom of speech on networks" except in "exceptional cases" (p. 162). Both of their positions are warranted by the view that network participants can for the most part police themselves. Even though they admit the likelihood that there will always be some nasty incidents (like the Jake Baker episode), social pressure brought to bear will solve the problems. Their response to electronic harassment is to just ignore harassers and they will go away.

The problem, as they see it, is government bureaucracy (especially law enforcement agencies) and Big Business who is trying to control what should be a free citizens' network. Rheingold (1991) identifies the villains as the Secret Service, the FBI, and the National Science Foundation. The "defenders" are the Electronic Frontier Foundation, the American Civil Liberties Union, and Computer Professionals for Social Responsibility (CPSR). Meeks (1994) sees the bad guys as the National Security Agency, the FBI, and "other assorted spook agencies." John Perry Barlow (1993) admonishes the Clinton Administration for not living up to the campaign expectation that it would stand up to the evil governmental bureaucracies (surprisingly, as he says, because "hell, a lot of them are Deadheads"). Barlow chides the Clinton Administration for instead giving in to the old paradigm "Guardian Class," those hanging on to a Cold War mentality that justifies violation of individual rights under the auspices of protecting U.S. citizens from terrorism. Kapor (1991) sees legal and governmental institutions as a threat to civil liberties. The stories he tells, like the government raid on Steve Jackson's files, remind us of the ignorance of law enforcement agencies and their attempts to curtail individual freedoms.

Rheingold (1993) is a grassroots optimist. According to Rheingold, if only government bureaucracies and Big Business would stay out of the way and leave us alone, everything would be fine. People are fine. The technology is fine. The problem is big organization and government. The Panopticon is what will happen if the government gets control. Without interference virtual communities will inevitably grow and prosper, like microorganisms in petri dishes (p. 6)—that is Rheingold's metaphor, the community as fungus. Another metaphor of his is the network as Great American Picnic. (p. 20). This is another version of the level-playing field, town-hall metaphor—a popular one for liberal individualists.

When you examine the particular features that constitute Rheingold's ideal electronic citizen, his vision seems less benign. Rheingold's community is white and upper-middle class, with the leisure time to surf the Net. It is mostly male, mostly baby boomers and their offspring, mainly centered in the cultural space between San Francisco and Silicon Valley. They are technologically sophisticated yuppies, but yuppies with a 1960s social conscience. They are liberals, but not radicals. They are, in Rheingold's own words, the "granola-eating utopians" (p. 48). They are (this is not in Rheingold's own words) the people who are most like Rheingold.

The irony of Rheingold's position is that although he is a liberal-individualist, the nominal emphasis in his book is as the title suggests: virtual communities. Rheingold, though, is by no means a communitarian. In his view communities are simply collections of individuals: "Virtual communities are social aggregations that emerge from the Net when enough people carry on those public discussions long enough, with sufficient human feeling, to form webs of personal relationships in cyberspace" (p. 5). This construction of community is a Rawlsian contractarian one: The community is constituted by individuals (i.e., it does not preexist individuals) and gains its authority only through the rights granted it by the individuals in it. (Such a position is not at all the same as communitarianism, discussed later in this chapter.)

I am in the main supportive of Rheingold's, Kapor's, and others' attempts to protect civil liberties on the network and to act as advocates for electronic citizens. Abuses and violations of individual rights have occurred. Free speech is a good thing (we can all agree on that), and government invasion of privacy and censorship of discourse should be resisted.

Many of their concerns are valid; for instance, Meeks (1994) points out how the government seems to be moving toward approval of the FBI's request for "putting a trapdoor into digital switches, allowing agents easy access to phone conversations," and other forms of electronic communication. There is continued fear (in 1996) that the Clinton Administration in collusion with the Republican-controlled Congress will propose legislation that will favor copyright owners rather than users of information by putting restrictions on the fair use of electronic text (Jacobson, 1995). Such legislation would work in favor of publishers' and property owners' interests to the detriment of teachers and students. Similarly, there is a strong desire in the U.S. Congress to punish those who use the Internet to distribute "obscene" or "pornographic" material. The so-called Gorton-Exon Communications Decency Act, which was included as part of a comprehensive telecommunications bill approved by both the U.S. Senate and House of Representatives and signed into law by President Clinton in early 1996 (see Wilson, 1995), was intended to make Internet service providers liable for pornographic material stored on their electronic databases (whether or not the service provider had put that material there or even had knowledge of it). (However, in June 1996, a federal court overturned the decency act on the grounds that it stifled free speech—a decision that free network advocates vigorously applauded—see Quittner, 1996; Simons, 1996). The argument for rhetorical ethics in this book should not be read as support for the Exon Bill, or for any comparable government intrusion on writers' activities. I argue for the opposite actually: Ultimately, my call for greater awareness and appreciation for ethics is offered as an *alternative* to this sort of heavy-handed, top-down legal or legislative response.

I have no quarrel with EFF's effort to lobby government action in the direction of protecting the individual's rights to free speech and privacy. However, I see their efforts as most appropriately aimed at law and public policy. The principles they advocate may be sound legal ones, but they are questionable ethical ones, and they do not provide guidelines for writing or for teaching writing. Rheingold is one, in particular, who steps over the line into ethical questions involving electronic communities. Kapor's brand of electronic freedom—which advocates "freedom of speech on electronic networks," except in "exceptional cases" (p. 162)—is a position that will lead, ironically, to the increased commercialization of the nets. The free speech philosophy coupled with an open-market economics will lead to commercial control—and that will mean that the only denizens of the Net will be those who can afford it—that is, the granola-eating utopians in Silicon Valley and Redmond, but not the students in inner-city schools in Gary, IN or in rural schools in South Carolina.

The extreme position that these advocates take will, I am afraid, lead to other kinds of abuses. First, the position of *absolute* anti-State intervention is a hard one to defend, if one examines the problematic cases. Should the State not intervene when a husband beats his wife? Or when a member of the Faith Assembly Church refuses to allow her child to receive necessary medical attention? Are these "private" matters only?

Granted, the nature of the harm is different in these cases. The issue in internetworked writing hinges on the possible harm of "only words" (MacKinnon, 1993). When do words alone constitute harm or physical threat to an individual? The Jake Baker case (see Chapter 6) points to an instance in which the courts initially determined that in this particular context the student's fictional story was more than simply fiction. In using a real classmate's name and in fantasizing about rape/torture in personal e-mail, Jake Baker blurred the fiction/nonfiction line just enough to get himself jailed. Given their context of use, his words alone constituted a threat to a person's physical well-being.

Those who advocate an absolute free speech position—based on what Catharine MacKinnon (1993) refers to as "the stupid theory of equality" (p. 98)—do not sufficiently acknowledge the intimidating power of violent speech, the capacity of speech to silence especially those who have been historically silenced and marginalized. Nor can such a view address an ethical issue like "spamming" (also known as "mondo posting")—that is, the question of how (or whether) to control blanket postings of political or commercial messages to numerous newsgroups or, increasingly, LISTSERV discussion groups. Neither

Rheingold or Kapor take any heed of the relatively low participation of women in network activity. America Online reports that 84% of its subscribers are male. CompuServe reports that 88% of its users are male ("It's a man's, man's, man's world on-line," 1995, p. B1). Exact numbers for the Internet at large are harder to come by, but estimates suggest that 65% to 95% of Internet users are male. Nor do they consider the numerous critiques that suggest that the internetworked environment may be a hostile place for women (Hawisher & Sullivan, in press; Selfe, 1996; Takayoshi, 1994).

The liberal-individualist image of networks—what they are, as well as what they could or should be—fails to recognize the role of power in any discursive arrangement and fails to acknowledge differences among participants, not just race, gender, and age differences, but differences in values as well, that is, different ethics, different attitudes about the way things ought to be, fundamental differences in how we orient ourselves to the world, and how we make it. Those differences get obliterated by the kind of homogenizing metaphors that Rheingold invokes, but they also get obliterated in the political philosophy that informs his vision. As Rawls (1971) articulates this position in *A Theory of Justice*, it is a philosophy that supposes that "each person possesses an inviolability founded on justice that even the welfare of society as a whole cannot override" (p. 3).

A number of postmodern theorists have raised challenges to this sort of discursive model. Many are questioning whether a bill of rights for electronic use based on a liberal Enlightenment ethic—with its constructs of *man*, free speech, and *individual* human rights—is adequate for dealing with the postmodern phenomenon of electronic discourse via networks. Martha Cooper (1991) points out how both Classical and Enlightenment traditions are based on "a vision of face-to-face communication" between equal and opposite (and male) advocates, each of whom has "the possibility of obtaining accurate information and choosing among policy alternatives." (p. 26) She calls this "an image of autonomous individuals"—what we have come to know as "the level playing field" assumption about discourse rights. (p. 26)

Michel Foucault (1987) points out that there is no ideal speech situation free from institutional hierarchies, traditional alignments, and power relations. All discourse occurs already in a situated practice of power relations. Although the liberal Enlightenment view assumes an assembly of people speaking their minds freely—as Rawls (1971) says: "It seems reasonable to suppose that the parties in the original position are equal" (p. 19)—no such assembly does or can exist:

> The thought that there could be a state of communication which would be such that the games of truth could circulate freely, without obstacles, without constraint and without coercive effects, seems to me to be Utopia. It is being blind to the fact that relations of power are not something bad in themselves, from which one must free one's self. I don't believe there can be a society without relations of power, if you

understand them as means by which individuals try to conduct, to determine the behaviors of others. The problem is not of trying to dissolve them in the utopia of a perfectly transparent communication, but to give one's self the rules of law, the techniques of management, and also the ethics, the *ethos*, the practice of self, which would allow these games of power to be played with a minimum of domination. (Foucault, 1987, p. 18)

Foucault's entire research project of studying institutions like the prison and the hospital argues that the *principles* of justice and freedom espoused by Enlightenment philosophers were seldom realized in *practice* (that is, in the institutions and bureaucracies that their advocates constructed). In a way, he suggests, the utopian ideal makes things worse (and this is the basis of his quarrel with Habermas) because it can have the effect of obscuring the exercise of power and thus making it more invincible in its invisibility.

Benhabib's (1992) chapter on "Models of Public Space," from *Situating the Self*, also considers the limitations of "the liberal model of public space." Her critique is based on the elision of "legal" and "ethical" within such a model:

An additional limitation of the liberal model of public space is that it conceives of political relations all too often narrowly along the model of juridical ones. ... The liberal principle of dialogic neutrality, while it expresses one of the main principles of the modern legal system, is too restrictive and frozen in application to the dynamics of power struggles in actual political processes. (pp. 99–100)

Foucault and Benhabib serve as examples of how the liberal-individualist political metaphor is being challenged by postmodernist ethicists: that is, on the basis of its failure to recognize that human relations always already occur in a system of power; on its inadequacy to handle "tough ethical cases" that will inevitably emerge (as discussed in Chapter 5), and on its legalistic view of ethical problems (an impractical view for day-to-day ethical writing issues, as well as a potentially expensive one). The liberal-individualist view does not address the material conditions of the networked writing situation or the fundamental inequalities and differences that exist there. Foucault reminds us that all discourse occurs already in a situated practice of power relations, institutional hierarchies, and alignments.

Rheingold thinks that under the skin everybody is the same, and that given non-interference by Evil Powers we will eventually work out our differences and form one big comfortable Virtual Community. This strikes me as seemingly benign, but actually an insidious utopian goal—a dystopia. The image is of the world as a New England townhall meeting, with all citizens participating in an equal forum, except we know that the forum was never equal, and that not everyone got to speak (Phillips, 1993).

This metaphor, which is also a model of discursive relations, is incapable of dealing with the tough ethical cases that are occurring in networked communities. It does not deal well with the collision of differences; it simply hopes that differences can be worked out. This kind of ethical approach cannot begin to understand or deal with ethnic slaughter in Rwanda. It cannot begin to deal with the problem of gang violence and drive-by shootings in Cleveland and Los Angeles. Nor can it understand how women might be intimidated into silence in an electronic community because of angry and hostile postings by men.

In Rheingold's virtual community, women are just supposed to ignore harassment. At this point, Rheingold is just not sufficiently aware of historical factors in the exercise of power. At other points he is not aware of the economics of power that inevitably inhabit electronic spaces. The technology in his vision is supposed to simply "be there" to support our social activity. It is not clear to me how it is supposed to get there and stay there without some kind of business, government, or organizational "interference." *Organization* is a bad word in Rheingold's vocabulary. He just does not see the fact that he belongs to organizations (like Well and EFF), too, that in large part help him construct the view of community he espouses—and that it is largely through organization of some kind that large-scale action is made possible. (Rheingold sees Well and EFF as "communities" rather than "organizations" such as IBM, Microsoft, and the FBI. Communities are benign, organizations and institutions are malicious.)

Is the First Amendment a desirable first principle for discursive practice on electronic networks? Richard Bernstein (1994) identifies a troubling emergent sentiment that views the First Amendment as the last line of defense for white heterosexual men. The First Amendment, according to Bernstein, is being invoked to protect men's rights to use sexually harassing and racist speech as a way to counter what many of them perceive to be an unfair affirmative action in favor of blacks and women. By keeping the playing field level through broad interpretation of the First Amendment, those in power can be assured of staying in power. Bernstein's point is not to dismiss the First Amendment, but simply to suggest that, although it may be a widely held *legal* principle, the First Amendment does not have and should not be granted universal status as an *ethical* principle, as many are wont to do. Similarly, Catharine MacKinnon thinks that the First and the Fourteenth Amendment (which mandates equal protection for all citizens) should counterbalance each other; without the Fourteenth Amendment the First Amendment can become a tool of dominance. Likewise, I argue for viewing the First Amendment not as the final determining authority for all discursive relations, but rather as one of several important and competing principles that a writer must apply heuristically to render a judgment about the ethics of any electronic discursive activity.

The appeal to free speech is one that Stanley Fish (1994) sees as both a conservative and a liberal strategy; he sees both conservatives and liberals as committed to defending foundational views of community (although, of course, their views of the ideal community differ). Fish distrusts the abstract appeal to principle because such abstractions often obscure differences in how people construct the terms and differences in the way they are applied:

> When words and phrases [such as *free speech* and *neutrality* and *Reason*] are invoked, it is almost always as part of an effort to deprive moral and legal problems of their histories so that merely formal calculations can then be performed on phenomena that have been flattened out and no longer have their real-world shape. (p. viii)

Fish (1994) notes that there is really no such thing as free speech—and he thinks it is a good thing. He calls the First Amendment "the First Refuge of Scoundrels" (p. 102). He notes that in cases involving hate speech, the neutrality or fairness argument is often used to advocate continuing a policy (or practice) of hate, oppression, and harassment.

The absolute free speech position, as advocated by the Electronic Frontier Foundation, assumes an ideal speech situation as its core model of discourse—a speech situation in which everybody is more or less reasonable and more or less equal—or even, if not, has an equal and inviolable right to speak. This view participates in the American myth of the classless society, which insists "Of course we are all equal!" Of course, this is not true, especially as pertaining to access to literacy (Stuckey, 1991).

This view does not address fundamental inequalities in the material nature of the writing situation. Some people have access to computers and modems; others do not. Some know how to manipulate newsgroup technology; others don't. Large and muscular white males with shaved heads and swastikas on their arms can intimidate smaller women into silence—and they do. In 1992, a student at Carnegie Mellon posted lewd and "offensive" messages on the electronic bulletin board maintained by and for the campus Women's Center. His postings had the effect of shutting down the newsgroup and intimidating some members into silence. Invoking the First Amendment, the liberal-individualist position defends his right to do that—and it is at that precise point that the ethics of the liberal-individualist position fails.

MAPPING POSITIONS

Rheingold and Kapor think that their position is the only reasonable alternative to a system of strict, top-down governmental control, but there are numerous alternatives that should be considered in any discussion of network ethics. Figure 4.1 is my representation of various rhetorical-ethical positions we might see as relevant to the discussion of the ethics of internetworked writing. Patricia Sullivan and I refer to this sort of mapping as a kind of basketball shot chart (Porter & Sullivan, 1996; Sullivan & Porter, 1997), a way of identifying places where various

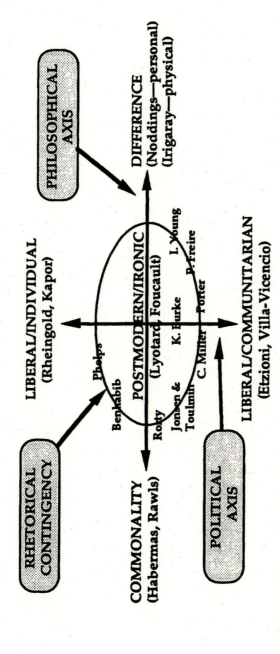

FIGURE 4.1. Rhetorical-ethical positions.

advocates stand when they take their shots, that is, when they make their ethical pronouncements. The chart is designed to show the diversity of, as well as tensions between, various kinds of ethical systems.

This kind of chart is a postmodern mapping. Similar mapping procedures can be found in Pierre Bourdieu's *Homo Academicus* (1988), in which he charts the faculty at the University of Paris, and in Edward Soja's *Postmodern Geographies* (1989), in which he draws various maps of the city of Los Angeles to show diverse perspectives on the city. Patricia Sullivan and I have used this mapping procedure to distinguish research epistemologies in professional writing (Sullivan & Porter, 1993b); to configure different curricular views toward professional writing within departments of English (Sullivan & Porter, 1993a); and to configure methodological positions in rhetoric/composition, professional writing, and computers and composition (Porter & Sullivan, 1996; Sullivan & Porter, 1997; see also Barton & Barton, 1993). Although she does not use actual visual diagrams, Seyla Benhabib uses a comparable mapping strategy in her alignment of ethical positions in *Situating the Self* (1992). She distinguishes between the universalist (a-historical) position of Habermas and what she sees as various forms of neo-Aristotelian or Hegelian historicized positions.

The purpose of this mapping is not to describe things "the way they are." Rather, Figure 4.1 attempts to complicate the binary universe (good/bad) of Rheingold and Kapor by showing a range of ethical systems providing alternatives to the liberal/individual position. What it reveals is, first, that there *are* different positions. Second, it attempts to align these positions along two main axes: (a) the horizontal axis is the *philosophical* axis of commonality/difference, which indicates to what degree an ethical system emphasizes similarities or commonalities (e.g., to what extent does it essentialize "self") or to what degree it emphasizes differences or dualities; and (b) the vertical axis is the *political* axis of one/many, which indicates to what degree a system stresses the individual or the communal. The positions at the outer extremes of the chart represent the positions of greatest certainty (and hence are the positions where the highest degree of ethical construction is possible); those positions in the center of the chart represent the positions of greatest irony and uncertainty (and hence are the positions where the highest degree of ethical criticism is possible).

The place on the border of the circle is the position of rhetorical contingency. It is the nomadic position that focuses on the practice, on the situation, on the circumstances, on *kairos*, on the particular participants, on the particular technologies, on the distinct history of the community, and on its development. Its bias is in the direction of the particular, the historical, the contingent, not in the direction of insisting on any single, transhistorical standpoint. This is the position of rhetorical ethics.

Other mappings of these ethical frameworks are, of course, possible, and I should point out some of the oddities of this map. (I am grateful to the faculty and graduate students at Miami University of Ohio, particularly Jim Sosnoski and

Susan Jarratt, for helping me think through some of the implications of the map.) Figure 4.1 puts Noddings and Irigaray in the same location (stress on difference), but a map distinguishing types of feminism would surely highlight their important differences (Ebert, 1991). Stanley Fish (1994) might be inclined to put the liberal/individuals and the liberal/communitarians together in the same location, as he sees both supporting traditional values (and both equally wrong). Seyla Benhabib's (1992) nonvisual "map" begins by distinguishing between historicized and ahistoricized ethical systems, her main category distinction. Of course, Figure 4.1 does not show differences in terms of how technology is treated (or not) in any given ethical framework.

Figure 4.1 does not provide a *single* clear place for either Marxist or feminist positions, and that is because I see these theorists as occupying different positions, depending on their brand of feminism or Marxism. For the most part, though, Marxist and neo-Marxist positions occupy the bottom half of this grid because such positions tend to favor group and social points of view over individual ones. Feminists generally (although by no means exclusively) occupy the right half of the grid, which emphasizes the quality of difference.

The postmodern geographer who uses such maps should make several things clear. It is important to tell readers (a) what particular types of relations form the main focus of the map; (b) that the map presents not an objective description of a territory, but a political judgment about a territory; (c) that any map, as a grid, always obscures and marginalizes some entities; and (d) that other depictions are certainly possible (and so I have done. ; -).

COMMUNITARIAN APPROACHES

Rheingold occupies a position that privileges individual identity and rights extending from that identity as the originating source for ethics and law. In general, approaches to dealing with rhetorical/ethical problems on the networks have been very individual-oriented. Even self-proclaimed postmodern positions (such as are often expressed in computers and composition forums like MBU-L) often end up circling back and becoming a kind of "liberal postmodernism," which still places its ethical focus on the individual writer, the student self.

It is especially hard for those reading from mainstream U.S. culture to see beyond the god-term "individual rights," but if you read African communitarian theory or liberation theology you can see how the principles "we" believe to be inviolable can in fact be problematic. You begin to see how the concepts "individual rights" and "human rights" are actually very different constructs.

On the other end of the axis from the liberal-individual position is the social-communitarian position, which posits that rights and responsibilities originate in communities, and that "what is good for the community" should ultimately take precedence over individual rights in matters of tough ethical decision making (see Baynes, 1990; Bellah, Madsen, Sullivan, Swidler, & Tipton, 1985; D'Entrèves, 1992; Devine, 1992; Miller, 1993).

Amitai Etzioni (1993) sees communitarianism as providing a necessary middle ground in U.S. politics between the absolutist Authoritarians (groups like the Moral Majority) and Radical Individualists (groups like the ACLU). (Kapor and Rheingold would fall into the category of Radical Individualists, although Etzioni does not consider issues involving internetworked writing.) Etzioni's interest is in "balancing individual rights with social needs" (p. 182), and his argument is warranted by a belief in one's innate responsibilities to communities (social, familial, academic, electronic, disciplinary, professional, institutional, political, etc.) and by a principle of reciprocity (although not in a strict *quid pro quo* economic sense).

One example Etzioni uses to identify his position is the question of the ethics of airport electronic security gates. Although the ACLU originally opposed the use of such gates as violating the rights of the individual (who must be presumed innocent), Etzioni sees those gates as a good communitarian solution, treating everyone equally (and so not innately unjust) and also protecting all from terrorism. The analogy would extend well to security and privacy issues for internetworked writing, suggesting that in the communitarian view some "invasion" of privacy—for example, trespass into someone's email account—might be allowable in order to protect users from electronic terrorism in the form of viruses, as long as any such policy is applied equally and fairly to all users, and is used to *protect*, not to *monitor*. The irony here is that certain intrusions that restrict individual behaviors may be necessary (desirable) for the common good.

In *A Theology of Reconstruction* (1992), Charles Villa-Vicencio advances his case for the communitarian agenda, beginning by noting that the liberal Enlightenment view of individuality is tied to a troubling economic agenda: free-market capitalism. As a South African, Villa-Vicencio writes from a context in which the liberal Enlightenment codes—indeed the verbatim principles of the U.S. Constitution—were used in conjunction with a strict rule-of-law philosophy to uphold a system of apartheid:

> The dominant western, libertarian, individualistic understanding of humanity (seen in the American *Bill of Rights*, the *Rights of Man* included in the French constitution and, to a lesser extent, in sections of the *Universal Declaration of Human Rights* read in isolation from the entire text) stands in contradiction to this emphasis [i.e., African communal ethics]. In these declarations the rights of individuals all too often in reality means the rights of *some* individuals at the cost of other individuals. (p. 166)

Villa Vicencio contends that the Rawlsian theory of justice, which starts with individual liberties, assumes a more or less free society to begin with: Such a theory of justice "fits a society within which there is more or less equal distribution of wealth better than it does situations which show vast discrepancies between the rich and the poor, which is a dominant feature of South African society and an increasing number of contemporary capitalist countries" (p. 236). Villa-Vicencio challenges the assumption of the sanctity of private ownership.

Villa-Vicencio sees the liberal Enlightenment view as presupposing a society of more or less equal participants, who have more or less the same access to wealth, and who already have equal rights under the constitution. In a society or community with inherently inequal participants, or with a long history of inequality, the appeal to the liberal enlightenment view may have the effect of maintaining the status quo (see Fish, 1994, p. 76). In a culture where access to computer writing technology is unequal—like U.S. culture (see Piller, 1992)— the liberal-individualist view can have the effect of maintaining inequality by further distancing the haves from the have nots.

Villa-Vicencio (1992) offers an "alternative to western individualism" (p. 172), which merges Christian ecumenical ethics and African communal ethics and builds from the principles of reciprocity and Christian charity (see also West, 1991):

> The African world view emerges as a striking alternative to western individualism. It is at the same time an alternative to ideologies that reduce people to by-products of social and economic forces. ... Individual development and aspirations ... are tempered in traditional African society by the needs of the community. (p. 172)

Villa-Vicencio sees such an ethics as grounded in theology, but also as having a secular and political manifestation that he sees as evident in the United Nations' *Universal Declaration of Human Rights*:

> Theology grounds the human rights debate within a personal-communal sense of existence which transcends the divide between western individualism and collectivist notions of human rights, characteristic of much within the secular debate on human rights. (p. 155)

Villa-Vicencio thinks that theology provides a missing perspective to secular ethics, and he invokes theological principles he feels can command broad consent, even by those opposed to any form of theological intrusion into political affairs. Theology provides a point of critique outside the borders of national boundaries. Villa-Vicencio starts with the principle of "love your neighbor," which, as he says, is "for the Christian, a familiar *doctrinal* notion, but one that is not often given practical expression within the context of Western individualism" (p. 174 emphasis in original). On the contrary, liberal-individualism can often take the form of an isolationism (p. 169) and a neglect of others, which Villa-Vicencio sees as inherently unethical.

An important feature of Villa-Vicencio's communal ethics is that its sense of community arises from, *but is not tied to*, particular sociological or geographical groups. He is talking about using a tribal and family-based communal model in order to construct a transcommunal ethic; the community he imagines is a global one. In addition, the communal ethic that Villa-Vicencio (1992) advocates has a strong presumption in "favor[ing] the poor and marginalized members of society in defining and prioritizing human rights" (p. 160). Presumption in favor of the weak and marginalized is an ethic that rhetoric/composition has not often advocated, but it can easily be forged into a principle for treatment of others in electronic communities.

The point here is that there are alternate ethics that Kapor, Rheingold, and others do not address, but that raise a serious challenge to their assumptions about what is, or should be, "right":

> The ethic being appealed for requires an outlook on life significantly different to that contained within the creeds of liberal individualism. At the same time it affirms the democratic right and the ability of all people to share in the shaping of society; something often denied ordinary citizens within centrally controlled collectivist societies, ruled by a political elite. It is an ethic which is grounded in a vision of humanity within which each will no longer be responsible solely for him or herself. (Villa-Vicencio, 1992, p. 162)

We see a communitarian, reciprocity-based ethic articulated in the Connolly, Gilbert, and Lyman "Bill of Rights for Electronic Citizens" (1991a, 1991b). Connolly et al. realize that most who have tried to write an electronic bill of rights have begun with a commitment to the liberal ideal, which is inadequate for dealing with the postmodern phenomenon of electronic discourse via networks. Because Connolly et al. are more interested in developing principles that pertain to and support "the electronic community of researchers" (1991b, p. 54), they develop an ethic based on a gift-exchange system of property as an alternative to the conventional property rights system of Western capitalism and Enlightenment liberalism. In this respect, their bill of rights for electronic citizens is compatible with Villa-Vicencio's communitarian ethic and poses a clear alternative to policies based on liberal individualism.

We should be clear about what Villa-Vicencio (1992) is proposing in his communitarian ethic: *not* that we should abandon the individual in favor of the state or government, which is the binary that EFF assumes offer us our only two choices. Villa-Vicencio's position is that the "community" is something different, offering a mediating ground between the "individual" and the "state." In traditional African society, "the extended family unit and village membership ... function as an intermediary between the individual and the state" (p. 172). He argues for including the community as an important (and currently missing) feature of human rights legislation—and I would agree that the notions of "community" and "forum" (Porter, 1992a) are important constructs currently missing from most discussions of public policy on electronic networks.

I am not offering Villa-Vicencio's ethic as an alternative we should necessarily adopt. What I am saying is that we need to question the individualist ethic that supports many of the statements about ethics and legality on electronic networks. The liberal-individualist position receives solid support within computers and composition and from rhetoric/composition because it dovetails neatly with the field's individualist focus on activities of the solitary writer. Despite the considerable emphasis on collaboration and social construction, the field's principle orientation is still the individual student writer (and also, "the text"), and the field still favors an individualist ethic (albeit largely an implicit one) over communitarian and other sorts of ethical positions.

Some have accused the communitarian position in general of being soft on power—that is, for not recognizing the institutional inequalities that might exist in a given community (and that function to enable relations within that community); for not allowing space for the critique of community; and for not addressing the tough issue of incommensurability between communities. Communitarianism in some of its Anglo-American, conservative forms can promote intolerance of the Other or the individual in the name of the public good. Elizabeth Frazer and Nicola Lacey (1993) critique communitarian theory from a feminist perspective, pointing out that "the communitarian emphasis on traditional discourses and practices inevitably reproduces the dichotomized thinking characteristic of western culture" (p. 168). Among other things, this thinking leads to "the invisibility of gender in political theory" (p. 213). They wonder whether communitarians have really escaped the "implicitly male individualism of liberal theories" (p. 146).

Frazer and Lacey's critique aims at the communitarian philosophy articulated by Anglo-American theorists like Habermas, MacIntyre, Taylor, and Rorty. Similarly, Derek Phillips (1993) critiques the American communitarian theories of Bellah and MacIntyre for their utopian readings of American history. The golden past that such communitarians urge us toward, says Phillips, was in fact "a hierarchic political order resting on the natural right of the wise to rule the less wise" (p. 62). Frazer and Lacey's and Phillips' critiques remind us to distinguish between various types of communitarian theory.

The Anglo-American theory of Etzioni, Bellah, and MacIntyre is a type of communitarianism that suffers from many of the same faults as liberal individualism. It essentializes "community" in the same way that the liberal position could be said to essentialize the individual. But this is not the only form of communitarianism. Neither Frazer and Lacey nor Phillips consider postcolonial forms of communitarianism nor Marxist and neo-Marxist forms (such as liberation theology), which might be seen to practice in very different ways—although these, too, might be challenged on the grounds of obscuring gender difference.

The limitation of the Anglo-American communitarian position is, I believe, the potential threat it poses to the marginalized groups, the minorities, that constitute any social community. One corrective to this problem can be found in the

Marxist version of communitarianism that is found in liberation theology. Liberation theology attempts to situate theology in the material conditions of a people (as opposed to its more traditional location in metaphysics). Liberation theology attempts to move theology from the realm of "theory" to that of praxis. Theology in this system is seen not only as a descriptive tool or as a means of spiritual action, but as a lever of critique for enacting social change. As a theory of economics, liberation theology opposes three things: "Profit as the key motive for economic progress, competition as the supreme law of economics, and private ownership of the means of production as an absolute right that has no limits and carries no corresponding social obligation" (Smith, 1991, p. 125; see also Berryman, 1987; Boff & Boff, 1986; Gutièrrez, 1973).

According to Enrique Dussel (1988), the basic (and absolute) principle of liberation ethics is this: Liberate the poor (p. 73). He sees the basis for this ethic in both New Testament scripture and in the theory of Karl Marx (who, he says, has been misinterpreted as "collectivist" rather than what he really is—"communal"). The community that Dussel imagines as operative here is an ideal ethical community that works against the existing social order (which primarily dominates and oppresses, at the very least by turning its back on the poor). This version of communitarianism is very different from those in the Anglo-American tradition. Its critical difference is that such a communitarianism has in it a preferential option for the poor. What prevents its becoming a kind of oppressive majority rule is the chief operating principle that the operation of the community must presume in favor of the poor—by which Dussel means the economically disadvantaged, but which could be extended to cover all marginalized and oppressed groups in a community (see Sullivan & Porter, 1997).

THE COMMON RULES FOR DISCOURSE—HABERMASIAN DISCOURSE ETHICS

Although not explicitly allied with the figures of the New Rhetoric and not aware of their contributions (even though he does invoke Toulmin), Jürgen Habermas represents a more recent attempt to build a communication ethics based on an ideal of rationality. Universalist positions such as Habermas's argue the necessity of universal and ahistorical principles that govern historical and situated events. There must be a standpoint of critique beyond the individual and outside of any historical community, and rationality provides the means of constructing such a standpoint (Benhabib & Dallmayr, 1990; Kelly, 1990).

In *Moral Consciousness and Communicative Action* (1990), Habermas outlines the basis of his discourse ethics, which rests on two key principles: Principle U establishes that for a norm to be valid (a) all must accept it, and (b) it has to satisfy the interests of all affected by it (p. 65). Principle D shifts the site of this determination to "practical discourse": A norm is valid only if it meets "with the approval of all affected in their capacity as participants in a practical discourse" (p. 66). Habermas admits that these are "improbable conditions" (p. 88), but his point is to establish these conditions as a norm, not as a description of real discourse events. His purpose is to refute both ethical relativism and ethical skepticism by explaining "how moral judgments can be justified" (p. 120). He challenges postmodernist positions on the grounds of their being "performative contradictions." That is, he challenges how anyone could state categorically that "pluralism should be our ethical position," or that "there are no universal rules for discourse." Both statements contradict themselves, according to Habermas, because their very existence relies on an adherence to universal rules of argumentation.

Habermas's contribution to Kantian ethics is to complicate the categorical imperative. It is not sufficient to allow the individual to make the determination about ethical law, but rather Habermas shifts the grounds of the decision from the individual to an "intersubjective process," a "cooperative process of argumentation" (p. 67). In short, Habermas's communicative ethic requires rhetoric— although he avoids stressing the term *rhetoric* (he does, however, mention it).

Habermas's move also involves shifting the role of philosophy. In a complex pluralistic world, philosophy can perhaps no longer tell us directly what we should do, that is, it cannot provide answers to *constative* questions (questions about moral content or substance). Philosophical ethicists like Rawls lose their philosophical authority whenever they "stray into substantive issues" (p. 122). The role Habermas envisions for philosophy is to address *regulative* questions, that is, questions about procedure or discursive norms. Philosophy can provide formal guidance regarding the rules and processes of argumentation, especially with regards to the rules for participation in discourse. It is this distinction that is crucial for understanding Habermasian discourse ethics—and it is this distinction that proves most useful in developing a rhetorical ethics for electronic discourse.

Seyla Benhabib (1992) identifies the two main tenets of Habermasian discourse ethics as the *principle of universal moral respect* and the *principle of egalitarian reciprocity*. The principle of universal moral respect recognizes "the right of all beings capable of speech and action to be participants in the moral conversation." (p. 29) The principle of egalitarian reciprocity specifies that "within such conversations each has the same symmetrical rights to various speech acts, to initiate new topics, to ask for reflection about the presuppositions of the conversation, etc." (p. 29). Again, Benhabib reminds us, the point is not that such principles reflect actual discursive practices, but that they do serve as criteria for moral justification of past action. These principles do not tell us whether a given action is right or wrong, but they can provide guidance for our behavior as writers.

It is important to note that Habermas does not deny the necessity of situated judgment or the operation of *phronesis*, or "hermeneutic prudence." In fact, such judgments are an unavoidable part of the social condition. That Habermas's discursive regulations are impractical has been pointed out—by Habermas himself. The subrules that his discourse ethic generates—such as Rule 3.2.b, "everyone is allowed to introduce any assertion whatever into the discourse" (p. 89)—seem ludicrously impractical. What if one of the assertions introduced into the discourse has a "chilling effect,"—that is, it discourages others from contributing, as has often happened in electronic discourse?

The question is whether such idealized rules have any practical value whatsoever in addressing the difficult problems of human ethics. Habermas is not interested, however, in addressing cases. His interest lies in building from the philosophical-ethical tradition a case for a universal set of discourse norms. Ultimately this is not a great deal of help to the practical rhetorician: Even if we are willing to accept his norms as valid, we are still left with the huge task of dealing with the messiness of real human communication and ethical dilemmas. The norms do not take us very far, although some who need philosophical assurance of the existence of such norms might perhaps gain some comfort and solace.

A further question can be raised about the norms themselves—and has been, for instance, by Lyotard and Foucault. If humans cannot arrive at a consensus regarding constative questions, why should it be easier to come to agreement regarding regulative questions? Why should we suppose that there are *universal* regulative rules for discourse? Certainly there are rules for discourse (even Lyotard admits), but why must they be regarded as universal? In taking the position he does, Habermas fails to acknowledge his own critical bias: his belief in the universality of Western thinking, particularly in Western philosophical thought, that posits "formal abstractions" as having normative if not determining jurisdiction over human action. Analysis is superior to feeling. Rationality should control human behavior. Both rationality and analysis are "neutral" in their operation, and universal norms (even if derived from Western modes of thinking) have "a validity that extends beyond the perspective of a particular culture" (Habermas, 1990, p. 116).

These assumptions are precisely the ones, of course, that are most aggressively challenged by feminists, neo-Marxists, and postmodern ironists—groups whose arguments Habermas only marginally addresses. It is the messiness of discursive *practice*, the "practice of everyday life" (p. 108), the variance of cultures, the range of communication technologies, and the significant difference of gender that Habermas's theory neglects, avoids, and underestimates, although at times he does pay lip service to "lifeworld experiences," and at one point in *Moral Consciousness* (pp. 108–109) even argues for the dependence of universal morality on practice. Habermas's effort to establish ethical norms using a philosophy discourse that claims a preferential position outside the realm of rhetoric is a move that rhetoric ought to challenge, and indeed *has*, most prominently by Perelman in *The Realm of Rhetoric* (1982).

Habermas does establish an important principle of rhetorical ethics—that argument has to be public to achieve validity. The contribution of Habermas's discourse ethic is (a) that he is questioning Kant's assumption that the determination of ethical behavior can be an individual reflection, and (b) that he is situating that ethical decision making within a rhetorical context. However, it is important to understand that Habermas is not at all suggesting, as Rorty does, that consensus determines validity. Habermas is saying that public dialogue is a necessary component of validity, but *not* that public consensus determines what is probably true.

Habermas's discourse ethics does not attempt to control the substance of discourse, but rather its procedure:

> Discourse ethics does not set up substantive orientations. Instead, it establishes a *procedure* based on presuppositions and designed to guarantee the impartiality of the process of judging. Practical discourse is a procedure for testing the validity of hypothetical norms, not for producing justified norms. ... The principle of discourse ethics prohibits singling out with philosophical authority any specific normative contents (as, for example, certain principles of distribute justice) as the definitive content of moral theory. Once a normative theory like Rawls's theory of justice strays into substantive issues, it becomes just one contribution to practical discourse among many, even though it may be an especially competent one. It no longer helps to ground the moral point of view that characterizes practical discourses *as such*. (p. 122, emphasis in original)

Habermas's argument (as developed primarily in *Moral Consciousness and Communicative Action*, 1990) points the way to a nonfoundational rationality. Habermas agrees with Rorty's critique of foundationalism, but not with his rationality stance. Thus, Habermas provides us with an example of a prorationality position that addresses the postmodern critique of rationality (especially as offered by Rorty):

> The question of the context-specific application of universal norms should not be confused with the question of their justification. Since moral norms do not contain their own rules of application, acting on the basis of moral insight requires the additional competence of hermeneutic prudence, or in Kantian terminology, reflective judgment. But this in no ways puts into question the prior decision in favor of a universalistic position. (pp. 179–180)

Habermas suggests that discourse situations presume a rationality (p. 30). He cannot imagine a discourse ethic without one. To my way of thinking, he assumes the superiority of rationality rather than argues for it: He never actually addresses the challenge that Rorty (and Derrida) pose to the whole idea of rationality.

Habermas buys into the stage model of ethical development (Kohlberg in particular), which places in the highest and most developed position ethics based on principles (rather than groups or individuals)(p. 167). He is conscious of the critiques that have been leveled against such a privileging, and in some ways he distances himself from the linearity of Kohlberg's model (p. 173). However, in the final analysis, Habermas accepts the presumed superiority of the model that puts deontological ethical decision making into the position of moral and developmental superiority. He is conscious of the critique of this system on the basis of its being Western and male and logocentric. He provides an explicit response to Carol Gilligan's critique of Kohlberg (p. 179), and, more generally, he dismisses the presumptions of feminist ethics. He sees universalist ethics as possible and as preferable to the "contextual relativism" represented by Gilligan. Habermas imagines an ideal world of argument, in which principled *men* can discuss their differences on an equal playing field, not without regard for particularities (Habermas does say that the dictates of practical situations must be considered), but with proper regard for their status as secondary. Emotion has a suspect status, as does personal commitment to oneself, to other individuals, or even to specific social settings.

One important contribution of discourse ethics is to acknowledge the importance of the rhetorical audience to ethical determinations. Both of the principles that Benhabib articulates—universal moral respect and egalitarian reciprocity—could be seen to guide relations between writers and audiences. In fact, Benhabib is one of the few to recognize this connection. In her description of Habermasian discourse ethics (as seen through the lens of Hannah Arendt's thought), Benhabib reformulates the universal validity principle to say that your actions should take into account "the perspective of everyone else in such a way that you would be in a position to 'woo their consent.' … The moral principle of enlarged thought enjoins us to view each person as one to whom I owe the moral respect to consider their standpoint" (p. 136). Benhabib does not invoke the term *audience* (of course), nor does Habermas, but the principle here says not only that one must "respect others," but it goes further to suggest concrete criteria for determining what form that "respect" should take. You should treat them as an *audience*, that is, someone whom you are trying to persuade.

In advancing this position Benhabib does not examine some of the more troubling implications of the persuasive model. Persuasion can, of course, be manipulative. There is also decidedly double edge to the "wooing" metaphor she invokes. Neither she nor Habermas know enough about rhetoric, especially about its long and ongoing discussion about the ethics of persuasion. However, the point here is that Benhabib's articulation, couched within her justification of discourse ethics, argues the need to deal with the concept of audience as a fundamental component of its basic universality tenet. It is at this juncture where discourse ethics recognizes its reliance on, and its critical point of overlap with, rhetoric.

Like many philosophers of rationalist discourse, Habermas's approach does not assign sufficient credit to the social and political contexts for discourse, or to the legitimate role of *pathos* in the play of discursive relations, or to the material conditions that support discourse, or to the differences and diversities (and power

relations) that support discursive activity (criticisms that Benhabib has also articulated). Discourse situations occur because there are institutions and technologies in place that permit those discourses and that guide their dynamic. Those
institutions and technologies are not incidental to the discourse: They shape and
influence and restrict it in fundamental ways. Those institutions and technologies
provide a forum for discourse, and that forum includes historical factors, community conventions, and specialized rules for discourse that are not incidental to the
discourse itself. These institutions and technologies help constitute—we might
say, simply, constitute—discursive relations in the first place. It is at this precise
point where we can see the difference between Habermas's vision of communication and that of Foucault. Although Foucault views the institutions and technologies of discourse as significant, Habermas views them as secondary; in fact, in
Moral Consciousness and Communicative Action (1990) he never treats them.

We can also see chaos theory as providing an indirect critique of Habermas's
assumptions about the conditions of discourse. Chaos theory tells us that initial,
particular conditions in the development of an emergent phenomenon (say, for
instance, the birth of an electronic community)—even seemingly insignificant
events—are key to guiding the outcome of natural phenomena (such as the
weather). Similarly, initial, particular material conditions of a discourse setting
are key to understanding its subsequent dynamic. One of the failures of the New
Rhetoric is, in its insistence on establishing universal or at least generalizable
rules for discourse, that it does not sufficiently credit the particular conditions for
discursive practices.

Habermas appreciates the need to have a rhetorical ethics, but his answer to
the problem is to return to the metadiscourse of philosophy as providing the metanarrative for rhetoric. Here is where a distinction is necessary. Rhetoric is not
philosophy; rhetoric is not subject to philosophy; rhetoric is not the handmaiden
of philosophy. The initial rhetorical move of philosophy (Plato's move) was to
assume the existence of a metalanguage outside of "normal" language that would
be a superior form of language. As Foucault (1972) points out, the claim to truth
is the essential rhetorical move authorizing philosophy: Philosophy creates the
distinction between "true" and "false" language. Validity in this model comes
from an appeal, by the philosopher, to a higher level of abstraction: Appeal to
specific events and circumstances and individuals is suspect. Habermas, although
he is sensitive to the critique of universality, concedes the "weak" nature of universal ethical claims, and is cautious about limiting the ability of philosophy to
address human problems, still proceeds, methodologically, with the assumption
that philosophy represents a higher and privileged form of language use. He still
grants philosophy master discipline status.

Rhetoric's view is to see philosophy language as not ontologically different,
but rather just different, a kind of language still subject to rhetoric with its own
conventions and rules, historically constituted and situated, and with its own disciplinary (and hence, institutional) parameters. Although philosophy distrusts

nomos, rhetoric invests *nomos*, local language, with power. Why should rhetoric have any more right than philosophy to make this move? No *more* right—the point is that rhetoric recognizes it as a rhetorical move, its own move included.

Habermas sketches an ideal for communicative action, insisting that we need to construct a place outside of rhetorical activity in order to judge rhetorical activity. Foucault and others challenge this move, reminding us that all such moves to find a place "beyond rhetoric" are an especially arrogant form of rhetoric: I speak the truth, you do not. At best, such a move expresses an ideal that can never be achieved.

The ethical approach I advocate in this study is like Habermas's in its emphasis on the procedural. However, it is very unlike Habermas's in most other respects, but most especially in its rhetorical emphasis. Habermas's (1990) disdain for rhetoric is palpable: He makes clear his preference for the formalized and the abstracted (vs. the situated and concrete), and he views philosophy as the one true "guardian of rationality" (p. 20). He does acknowledge the importance of Toulmin's focus on moral argumentation, but he does not acknowledge Toulmin's reliance on a rhetorical frame (e.g., Toulmin's warrant is an audience belief), nor does he seem conscious of the relevance of Perelman's work, which connects the realm of argumentation explicitly to rhetoric.

Finally, I believe there are pieces of Habermas's discourse ethic that are valuable and importable—but, like Benhabib, I believe they require significant supplementation, most particularly in the direction of acknowledging the situated and rhetorical nature of human ethical relations.

FUNDAMENTAL DIFFERENCES—NODDINGS AND THE ETHIC OF CARING

In Chapter 3, I examined Luce Irigaray's (1984/1993) "ethic of sexual difference" and showed how it provides a substantial critique of Western ethics' move toward an homogenous and liberal ethic of neutrality. Irigaray's basic position—that it is difference (sexual difference), not sameness, that is essential in nature—opens up the way to an ethic stressing difference, which offers a significant alternative to most masculine ethics.

Nel Noddings' (1984) argument for "caring" provides another important component in our development of a rhetorical ethics sensitive to difference. Although Noddings is by no means a feminist in the same sense as Irigaray, Noddings calls her book *Caring* a "practical ethics from the feminine view" (p. 3). She sums up her position this way:

> Women, in particular, seem to approach moral problems by placing themselves as nearly as possible in concrete situations and assuming personal responsibility for the choices to be made. They define themselves in terms of *caring* and work their

way through moral problems from the position of one-caring. ... Our motivation in caring is directed toward the welfare, protection, or enhancement of the cared-for. (pp. 8, 23)

Nel Noddings's particular brand of feminist ethics looks for moral justification within the human spirit and explicitly rejects as a basis for ethics any divine deity or metaphysical logic or generalization of the individual or ethic of principle. The universal ethic of principle is fatally flawed because it "abstract[s] away from concrete situations" the very qualities that "gave rise to the moral question in the situation" (p. 85). In other words, the move to abstract ethical problems focuses on what is common among ethical situations, but in that abstracting move the particular circumstances that are key to the ethical situation are obliterated.

The ethic of caring is a development within the general movement of feminism and women's studies that arises most directly out of the work of Noddings and Carol Gilligan (*In a Different Voice*, 1993), whose book on the moral development of women challenges Kohlberg's model of ethical development. Gilligan questions, first, why the moral responses of men should be assumed to be the norm for moral development; and, second, why a situated, concrete, and personal response to ethical problems should be assumed to be at a lower level of ethical development than abstracted and formal kinds of deontological ethics. Noddings, Gilligan, and their followers (e.g., Larrabee, 1993) develop through the articulation of this ethic of caring a dramatic alternative to deontological and utilitarian ethical frameworks.

Noddings, for instance, distinguishes her ethic of caring from the deontological and masculine ethic of principle as well as from the liberal-individualist rights ethic. Noddings's ethical model is a dialogic one, which pairs the "cared-for" and the "one-caring" in a mutually supportive relationship. The focus of her ethic is on the caring relationship between these two parties. Unlike Irigaray, who constructs her ethic from the physicality of the male–female difference (and the sexuality of the male–female union), Noddings's ethic constructs itself from a different basic relationship—the mother–child relationship.

The strength of Noddings's approach is that it raises the ethical standard for human behavior: "Respect for" others is minimal in her estimation. You have to move beyond "respect," which can seem to permit a benign neglect, to a position of "caring," where one actively works for the welfare of others. Like many forms of Christian ethics, this ethic promotes positive action, although Noddings expresses serious doubts about the ability of Christian ethics and religious ethics generally to promote a genuine spirit of caring.

Noddings makes ethics personal as well. Her position is that the masculine ethic of principle relies on abstractions that remain unsituated, impractical, and impersonal. White traditional masculine ethicists have stressed the importance of impersonality (termed *objectivity*) in moral reasoning, but Noddings directly challenges the assumption that abstract and impersonal reasoning is superior (e.g., she criticizes the warrants of Kohlberg's framework). She takes issue with the traditional view that sees women's personal approach to caring as a less developed form of ethical reasoning. She sees the personal approach as the highest form: For her, moral criteria arise ultimately out of personal feelings of caring for others, and the mother–child relationship may provide the ideal model for ethical relations generally. Invoking Buber, she sees the basis of ethics as residing in personal one-to-one commitment.

It is in her focus on dialogic, one-to-one ethics where Noddings's ethic may prove incompatible with rhetoric. What about community, the relationship between Self and others (plural)? Like Rheingold, Noddings takes a negative view of organizations—and by implication communities. For her, more often than not communities are likely to impede the development of an "ethical ideal" (p. 117). She doubts seriously, for instance, whether organized religion really bolsters ethical behavior.

The irony of Noddings approach is that she is willing to grant the possibility of an ethical ideal to the individual, but not to communities. Her trust and faith in the individual is a matter of faith, no more or less capable of actual demonstration than another's distrust of the individual and faith and trust in the community. The one or the many? Noddings's approach is an ethic of mutual cooperation, but it is not a social or community ethic—and it is an ethic that depends ultimately on the Enlightenment assumption of individuality. The difference is that Noddings's ideal ethical individual is a "caring woman" rather than an objective, reasoning man. In fact, she says, "the duty to enhance the ethical ideal, the commitment to caring, invokes a duty to promote skepticism and noninstitutional affiliation" (p. 103). Noddings's hostility toward institutions is extreme.

However, Noddings's approach does contribute an important set of questions to our emerging rhetorical-ethical heuristic: What does it mean to be a "caring writer"? Or a "caring writing teacher"? Or a "caring LISTSERV manager"? Writing in this ethic is to be viewed personally: It has an effect on individual persons. In this respect Noddings's ethic of caring provides a necessary counterbalance to communitarian ethics. I as writer must be careful in my actions to be caring toward my potential readers. We cannot see ourselves as obligated only to the larger community. Our concern for community must also be personal concern for individuals in the community. This position stands counter to views that "the ends always justify the means," or that "the good of the group outweighs the good of the individual." Louise Wetherbee Phelps (1992) has argued that Noddings ethic of caring should be a kind of first ethical principle in the composition classroom, that writing teachers have to make personal concern for students as individuals the primary ethic of teaching. (Interestingly, Susan Mallon Ross, 1994a, argues for a technical communication ethic that balances the Habermasian "ethic of justice" with the feminist "ethic of care." Invoking Benhabib, Ross considers how such an ethic might work in the "domain of environmental policy-making" [p. 338].)

POSTMODERN IRONY

At the center of Figure 4.1, we have what I call the position of "postmodern irony." These are the people who look at all the other positions and critique them, seeing their limitations and inadequacies, noticing all their contradictions and arbitrary essentializing gestures.

Teresa Ebert (1991) develops a similar category in her discussion of *ludic postmodernism*, a term that she opposes to *resistance postmodernism*. (I discuss an alternative to resistance postmodernism in Chapter 7.) According to Ebert, ludic postmodernists focus on the play of "disembodied signifiers" and of differ-ence: "Through textualizing strategies such as parody and pastiche, they seek to drive a wedge between signifier (word) and signified (meaning) and thus vacate the established relations between language and the world" (p. 887). The problem with ludic postmodernism is that although it develops a sharp critical edge, it lacks the capacity for strong commitment or for social and political transforma-tion. By disconnecting themselves from social and material conditions, ludic postmodernists render themselves politically impotent.

Stanley Fish may be the most thoroughly ironic of the postmodern ironists. His critical stance in *There's No Such Thing as Copyright* (1994) is to demon-strate that everything is political and to stand opposed to nearly everything—except for his own posture of radical skepticism. (In practice, Fish does seem to want to make some positive assertions. He wants to insist that the Holocaust hap-pened, and that there are "facts" somewhere, but he does not make it clear in *There's No Such Thing as Copyright* where such positive knowledge is located or how we are to construct it.)

Fish shoots down everyone else's efforts to establish a program for positive action and assertion, and thus leaves some doubts as to whether any program of positive action and assertion could be valid according to the criteria of his critical methodology. He believes that the best position is the radical opposition to any attempt to assert an ideal form of rhetoric, ethics, or politics. Antilogic, exercised through the deployment of Theory, is his preferred critical stance. We should not believe in any gods, he insists, and in so asserting that belief it becomes the god he offers us.

Not many postmodern ironists have been willing to take up the problem of deciding what we should do when we write and how we should justify the posi-tions we take. Many follow the line of Fish, remaining satisfied with simply resisting others' attempt to build systems, but some have—for example, Foucault, Kristeva, and Lyotard (as discussed in Chapter 3). It is perfectly possible for there to be a constructed or committed postmodern ethics. Despite Ebert's placement of Lyotard and Irigaray in the postmodern ludic category, I do not think that their position is as devoid of ethical and political potency as Ebert suggests.

Lyotard in *Just Gaming* (Lyotard & Thébaud, 1985) playfully adopts the position of ultrairony, but unlike Fish is at least willing to acknowledge that you have to make ethical decisions even if, in his mind, you can't ultimately justify them. Power is awesome, but we cannot let that freeze us into inaction. Writing may be irresponsible, as Lyotard says (unless he is being ironic), but *not* writing may be more irresponsible.

Lyotard advocates an ethics of pluralism generally—at the same time he realizes the limits of pluralism (see Kekes, 1993). At some point differences will collide, and there have to be some criteria by which a judgment can be made. In *Just Gaming* (1985), Lyotard and Thébaud articulate the problem of the postmodern ironist: "One is without criteria, yet one must decide" (p. 17). They accept that even in the face of a radical critique of metaphysics, of rationalist and deontological ethics, we must have the ability to judge that some things are just and others unjust. We must be able to see the Holocaust as a great evil and to be willing to oppose terrorism. Such ethical distinctions are necessary, even if there is no non-arbitrary ethical system, and even though he distrusts the chief ethical systems that provide support for this response. The ethical system he advocates he calls paganism, but is actually Aristotelian in its reliance on a situated practical judgment exercises in specific cases. What is most dangerous to Lyotard is the "politics of opinion" (what he sees as the tyranny of the majority) and the failure to act when necessary.

Emilia Steuerman (1992) asks the question whether Lyotard is a ludic postmodernist (committed only to the endless celebration of play and to laughter), or whether there is a point of commitment in Lyotard's ethic. Steuerman sees two sides to Lyotard. Certainly there is an ironic side to Lyotard that stresses "impotency" (if laughter is impotency)—that is, that leads us to the conclusion that because there are no criteria we cannot decide. However, Steuerman sees another model in Lyotard, one emphasizing "potency." In this mode we engage in language games agonistically by challenging efforts to totalize (when we recognize them) and by inventing new rules (p. 114). According to Steuerman, Lyotard "stresses the need for the invention and creation of new rules" (p. 113). In this respect Steuerman sees the agendas of modernity and postmodernity as operating in a dialectic dance. Postmodernism is not a rejection and replacement of modernism, but a fulfillment of it. As Beardsworth (1992) suggests, the "post" in postmodernity should "not imply a temporal succession" (p. 52). Steuerman sees the discourse ethics of Lyotard and Habermas as serving as necessary complements to one another.

Lyotard and others recognize that "pluralism" will not work, ultimately, as a final ethical position. It is not up to the challenge raised by "tough cases." ("Tough cases" refer to any incidents or ethical stories that challenge the basis of your own ethical system—see Toner, 1996.) Why will pluralism not work? First,

Lyotard and Benhabib both recognize the problem of essentializing pluralism—once you make that gesture you are engaging in a totalizing act that deconstructive and postmodern critiques have fulminated against. Second, pluralism in most instantiations assumes a level playing field metaphor, which leaves us incapable of dealing with tough cases (i.e., the problems that inevitably result when differences collide—which they always do). Without a moral position of some sort, you are left with "let the differences work it out"—the true postmodern ironist cannot justify taking any stand—which is likely to leave the more powerful position intact. This is why postmodern irony could end up being as politically impotent as liberal individualism, especially in situations of material, social, or economic inequality. (This is one reason why Zavarzadeh and Morton, 1994, critique postmodern ethics.)

Often, postmodern theorists in composition, even relatively radical ones adopting cultural studies' pedagogies, follow a line of critique that circles back to the focus on the individual writer. This individual is now a less stable, deconstructed subject, a tentative subject (not autonomous, not cognitively a priori)—but the dominance of individualism gets reinscribed, and, in fact, an old New Critical role gets reinvented: the Critic. The art of rhetoric is coopted into an art for the individual, and an art of critique rather than cooperation, and the role of the composition teacher is to "arm" individuals and let them have at it. This is a convenient way for composition teachers to mouth the precepts of postmodernism or liberalism or conservatism (they can take their choice) while remaining aloof from its political and ethical implications (i.e., choice). Teachers can be avant garde and intellectually interesting and, at the same time, keep their hands clean and themselves out of the fray.

However, the postmodern world is not going to let us—especially not if we are teaching writing on computer networks, where such choices are hard thrust upon us. Our theories are going to be—are already being—carried kicking and screaming into a world of racism, sexual abuse and harassment, increasing violence, and into a society where the emergent and desperate answer seems to be build more jails or revoke computer accounts.

Lester Faigley (1992) and Iris Marion Young (1990) argue for a politics and an ethics of difference rather than one based on an homogeneous or unified community. Both call on an urban model of difference. As Faigley says, paraphrasing Young, "in cities people are more open to the possibilities of interacting with strangers and often find stimulation in such interactions" (p. 232). Postmodern ethics must support "openness to heterogeneity," and yet at the same time practically recognize that heterogeneity can lead to conflict—the bad kind. I am not talking about rhetorical conflict between equal participants on the level playing field of discourse. I am talking about racial and sexual harassment, the silencing of the less powerful, the jailing of those we cannot deal with, the effacement of the rural and urban poor. "Openness to heterogeneity" cannot mean in our classrooms that we teach an uncommitted pluralism. This is the key ethical challenge facing postmodern irony.

LOCATING RHETORICAL CONTINGENCY

The theorists who occupy the outer extremes of the diagram tend to be those who present the most "certain" positions (the "construct" position, the position of strength for constructing solid ethical answers). Those in the middle of the diagram take the position of most uncertainty and greatest skepticism (the "critique" position, the position of strength for critiquing others' certainties). People who occupy all the extremes—the extreme outer or the extreme middle—tend to be in, or to be doing, philosophy, and they tend to be Big T Theory sorts of people. I have also noticed that those at the extremes are mostly, although not exclusively, men. Those occupying the intermediate border region—what we might call the region of rhetorical flexibility and choice—are mostly, although by no means exclusively, women. The space on the borders of the circle is where the rhetoricians are—the place of rhetorical ethics.

Where do we map feminist ethics on the chart? Well, we can chart it numerous places because different feminist ethicists occupy different positions. Feminist approaches to ethics, with their focus on concrete situations and distinct personal relations, are highly compatible with the dualistic position (Noddings, for example). We have also seen at least one example of an ethicist—Seyla Benhabib—who tries to develop a universalist feminist discourse ethic. Lisa Sowle Cahill (1990) develops a feminist theological ethic with ties to Marxist liberation theology. Cahill's core principle is that "all human beings exist in spatial and material relationships which not only are constitutive of individual identity but are also the conditions of possibility of human communities and institutions" (p. 55). With this articulation, Cahill challenges traditional theology's nearly exclusive focus on the spiritual and nonmaterial side of human nature and works to create a space for the acknowledgment of the worth of women within a disciplinary framework (theology) that has not traditionally recognized women's issues as distinct from that of men.

Feminist positions share, according to Cole and Coultrap-McQuin (1992), a commitment to "two basic assumptions relevant to moral life: (1) women and their values are of profound moral significance in and of themselves; (2) social institutions and practices have encouraged discrimination against women and the suppression of their moral views" (p. 1). Feminist ethics often defines itself in opposition to deontological ethical systems (like Kant's) based on notions of justice and abstract impartiality. Feminist ethicists point out that these so-called impartial or abstract systems actually "derive predominantly from men's experience" and are "largely male-directed enterprises" (p. 2), which have the result of dismissing or obscuring an entire set of moral values that have, or should have, potency in public life. These moral values are those, especially, affiliated with the personal, the affective, and the familial. They are values that give greater credit to the specific details of situated human experience, to the "concrete, everyday world" (Donovan, 1985, p. 173; see also Benhabib, 1992), and to the commitment of human relations, rather than to principles whose claims to validity rest on their abstract and impartial qualities. Feminist ethics, in its emphasis on "attachment, particularity, emotion, and intersubjectivity" (Cole & Coultrap-McQuin, 1992, p. 5), challenges and overturns the assumptions of most traditional deontological ethical systems. As Cahill (1990) says, "Feminists emphasize not only the historicity of moral agency but also its communal or social character" (p. 52).

Another important emphasis of feminist ethics to rhetorical ethics is its reconceptualizing of the notion of the moral situation. Ethics from the feminist point of view is not limited only to issues involving ethical dilemmas and crises, but also has a more day-to-day application—it has to do more broadly with *relations*.

There are different strands of feminist ethics, of course, but generally feminist positions, whether held by women or by men, tend to occupy the place of rhetorical ethics, emphasizing the necessity for situated choice. This positioning confirms Jarratt's (1991) view that sophistic rhetoric is a feminist rhetoric with ethical implications. We see a more community-based social version of feminist ethics in Susan Jarratt's *Rereading the Sophists*. Jarratt views sophistic rhetoric as a feminist rhetoric and one with significant ethical implications. The sophists believed that law and truth derived from *nomoi*, local habits or customs that could change from city to city, region to region. The philosophers in the Platonic tradition, of course, challenged this sort of relativism, insisting on the ideal of Truth (*logos*, universal laws that would be acommunal).

The sophists' vision of truth is cast in history as the jaded, cynical view: "Truth is what you can get people to believe in." That sentence casts the rhetorician in the role of manipulator, changing the truth whimsically to suit whatever motives he or she happens to represent at the moment. However, another version of the sophistic position is less cynical: "Truth is what people believe the truth to be." This statement—seemingly tautological but actually not—acknowledges the role of human participation in the construction of truth and suggests that the role of the rhetor is to take that truth seriously. Truth is socially and culturally constituted, but that does not mean that it cannot be taken seriously. In fact, "what people believe" is the basis for rhetoric.

In this chapter, I have tried to show a variety of ethical frameworks that can serve as alternatives to the liberal-individual framework that often dominates public and network discussions of the ethics of electronic discourse. There *are* alternative ethics—and in fact several that offer direct challenges to the popular forms of liberal individualism. In Chapters 6 and 7, I deploy these alternative frames in the service of a rhetorical ethic, a procedural ethic that will provide some guidelines (though few specific answers) for approaching ethical problems in internetworked writing. I try to clarify what I think it means to occupy the "nomadic position" on the border of the circle in Figure 4.1. The chief focus of this rhetorical ethic is *situated relations*—and in that sense the ethic I develop owes much to postmodern feminist and Marxist conceptions of ethics, although with a stronger rhetorical emphasis.

5

Legal and Ethical Issues in Cyberspace

> The protections which we will develop will rely far more on ethics and technology than on law.
> —Barlow, 1994

This chapter examines some of the key legal problems arising on electronic networks, and considers how writing activities and events on the Internet and World Wide Web pose problems for, or otherwise challenge, existing law. The purpose of this chapter is to point to cases and practices that argue for the necessity of moving beyond law to a more well-articulated cyberspace ethic that understands these issues and problems from a rhetorical frame (Porter, 1994d).

The discussion here is organized around several issues conventionally identified as critical to the discussion of computer ethics (e.g., access, privacy, intellectual property, harassment, netiquette), but configures these topics differently than computer ethicists typically do. I focus mainly on issues of *property* and *civility*. My purpose in making this adjustment is to focus more clearly on the problems and questions likely to be important to writers and writing teachers.

From the legal point of view, few of the questions explored in this chapter have definite answers. In fact, I intend to demonstrate that the legal point of view alone is insufficient to answer many of the questions that technical cyberwriters need to address. Why? For several reasons: (a) because the law is still predominantly print oriented and is likely to remain that way; (b) because the law is notoriously slow in keeping up with the problems raised by new technologies; (c) because even at best the law does not cover every particular contingency anyway; and (d) because "the law" is a complex, abstract, and often elusive concept, as Anne Wells Branscomb (1991) points out:

> Lawmaking is a complicated process that takes place in a larger universe than the confines of legislatures and courts. Many laws are never written. Many statutory laws are never enforced. Legal systems develop from community standards and consensual observance as well as from litigation and legislative determination. So, too, will the common law of cyberspace evolve as users express their concerns and seek consensual solutions to common problems. (p. 158)

What will become apparent through this treatment is the need to supplement the gaps in law by developing a *critical rhetorical ethic* that is sensitive to the particular rhetorical context(s) of electronic discourse; in other words, writers need a situated sense of "the common law of cyberspace" in addition to an understanding of the implications of statutory and case law. Cyberwriters need to consider "ethical hyperrealities" (Porter, 1997)—the ways in which electronic text itself, because it operates in a rhetorical environment so different from print media, may be considered exempt from legal considerations that are born out of and apply primarily to the world of print.

ISSUES OF PROPERTY

Access

Access to computer resources may well be the number one ethical issue for internetworked writing. Most discussions of computer ethics focus on justice issues among the *haves*—for example, when does an electronic posting threaten the rights of other electronic citizens? what constitutes electronic harassment? in what circumstances is spamming unethical?—without considering the status of the *have-nots*. Such questions do not foreground an essential justice issue that another set of questions would: How are computer resources shared and distributed in the public realm? Who decides who gets what type of computer resources? Who has access to computers?

From the standpoint of, for instance, Marxist liberation theology (e.g., Dussel, 1988) or communitarian theory (Villa Vicencio, 1992), the first principle of internetworked ethics might well be something like this: Work to insure that the poor and marginalized have access to internetworked resources, and make sure that such resources are fairly shared and distributed (such a sentiment is found frequently in discussions of access in computers and composition literature; see, for example, Hawisher, Selfe, Moran, & LeBlanc, 1996, pp. 257–262). Though there is no legal or constitutional imperative to "liberate the poor," most computer ethicists agree that this is a critical concern of computer ethics: how to allot, distribute, and pay for computer resources; and how to insure that computer resources are fairly shared and distributed in a society where full participation in the political life of the community may soon *require* computers.

There are three ways to think about access: in an infrastructural sense as technical *resources* (i.e., the machinery itself), in an educational sense as technical *literacy* (i.e., the skills and expertise necessary to use the resources), and in a social sense as *community acceptance*.

Most discussions of access refer only to the economic and technological sense of access. That is, users (students, faculty, the public) need access to the *technical machinery* for internetworked writing: a computer, a modem, communication software, a computer account. If they do not own the machinery themselves, they need convenient access to it. Such machinery must be in an accessible place (e.g., accessible to the physically challenged); there must be available terminals. We might consider such factors as the necessary material conditions of access.

How are such decisions made in a community or at a university? Are system design decisions driven by the "high-end users" (like engineering and computer science faculty)? Or are student and instructional needs given priority? Are allocations of resources and systemic decisions driven by a research or teaching emphasis? Does a state allocate its educational resources in a way that ensures that poor school systems, whether rural or urban, are not cut off from the technologies that can potentially enable students' access to economic and political power? Does state and federal legislation encourage the telecommunications industry to keep consumer costs at a level that will promote widespread use?

Equity of and access to computer resources pertain especially to school and computer system administrators: Are computer resources fairly and equitably allocated within school systems? Do all students have equal access to computers—or are computers made available only to honors students? The most significant political and financial issue for high school writing teachers in the next century may well be access to computers for writing. Writing in the 21st century will be electronic writing. Schools that have adequate technology will be able to prepare their students for writing in the world in which they will live. Schools that do not have the technology, or who don't know how to use it effectively, will not. How much computers actually help (or hinder) writing depends in large part on what technologies are available and how teachers use them. Using computers to teach writing requires a level of institutional support that is usually not afforded the traditional writing classroom. Even if schools have computers, if what they have are outdated computers with limited memory, hard-to-read screens, weak word-processing capabilities, no network access, no CD-ROM, and low-quality dot matrix printers, then writing teachers and student writers are not likely to find electronic writing beneficial, easy, or pleasurable. In one sense they may have computers and in another sense not have them: Counting computer terminals in classrooms is not per se an adequate measure of institutional support for computing.

The infrastructural support system for computers must include more than merely the capital for machinery. According to Charles Piller (1992), a mistake school corporations frequently make is allocating resources to purchase equipment but not providing sufficient follow-up support for teacher learning and training and for continuing maintenance of the equipment: "Nearly every school in America owns personal computers. But without expertise to use and maintain them, thousands of machines lie fallow. ... When computers are grafted onto dismal, underfunded schools that lack appropriate staff support, students and teachers rarely use them effectively" (pp. 221, 223). Of course, for many underfunded school systems, many in urban and rural areas, the problem may be more basic: access to *any* computers.

In another sense access refers to cognition and literacy, that is, users must *know how to use the machinery.* The technological apparatuses must be designed in a way that does not pose significant obstacles to users. My experience with computer systems and computer centers suggests that the computer industry has been slow to recognize access in this second sense—although there are some signs of an awakening.

Andrew Feenberg's (1991) "critical theory of technology" addresses access in this second sense—that is, focusing on the ethical and political relations between system design and use. His theory aims to counter the modernist notion of technology, which ends up installing in computer system design "the values and interests of ruling classes and elites" (p. 14). Feenberg thinks that the first generation philosophy of computer design—what he calls the "first cybernetics" (p. 106)—advances a mechanistic and instrumental view of human action, based on "rationalistic assumptions [that] are embodied in the technical code of the computer profession, [which are] the rules and procedures on the basis of which standard design decisions are made. It is this technical code which embodies the dominant image of the computer as a system of control, an automaton" (p. 99). Others who have critiqued the dominant, rationalistic view of technology include Winograd and Flores (1986) and Suchman (1987), who have offered an alternative to system design that focuses on the situated needs of users.

For a period of time, the campus computing center at my university would frequently make adjustments to the campus central server based on an instrumental view of users. They would make design decisions based on what was easiest or most efficient for their maintenance of the system, or what was most secure for data, with only secondary regard for the effect on users in general or on the needs of particular classes (especially writing classes). There was an assumption present that system design comes first, user training second—and there was also an attitude of impatience with users who could not learn to use the system. The assumption was that computer design was based on "rationality," and that users who could not use systems were not sufficiently capable of adopting this rationality. The onus for learning and adjustment was placed on the users (students and instructors); the dominant view was that users should adapt to system design, rather than design extending from users' needs. Clearly, the priority driving design decisions was not instructional needs.

Feenberg (1991) reverses the equation as he sees the emergence of a "second cybernetics," based on a Heidegerrian theory of action that "looks at the world from the standpoint of the involved subject rather than from that of the external observer" (p. 106). In the paradigm of this second cybernetic, engineers "come to terms with the complexity of the social system in which their tools will be employed" (p. 96). In this second cybernetic, user needs and social circumstances come first, driving design decisions.

So one aspect of the "ethics of access" is working to ensure that computer writing spaces are designed to suit writers' needs. Do the network writing tools that the computer center makes available help writers, or do they pose obstacles to their efforts as writers? Although most writing teachers will probably not see computer design as their strong suit, nor even any of their business, it is important for writing teachers in computer classrooms to participate in the design of those classrooms: both the physical design of the classroom as well as the design of network space (a point that has had strong support in computers and composition literature; see Selfe & Selfe, 1994).

The design of computer space—both classroom and network space—is not incidental to use or access. Rather, the design of such spaces influences access in fundamental ways, encouraging certain uses of technology, discouraging others, allowing freedom of expression, or promoting surveillance and control of others' writing (see Lopez, 1995). As Provenzo (1992) and Janangelo (1991) have pointed out, rationalistic system design can be a form of tyranny that inhibits ethical relations; some forms of computer design can even put the writing teacher in an ethically suspect position.

A third notion of access, one that hardly ever gets discussed in the literature on computer ethics, focuses on social acceptance. Are network participants made to feel welcome in network space (e.g., on newsgroups, LISTSERV discussion groups, bulletin boards)? Are *Auslanders* welcome in disciplinary discussion groups? Are women made to feel welcome in newsgroups focusing on the topic of technology? Does the dominant conversation in a group exclude participants on the basis of race, color, gender, or sexual preference?

An example springs to mind of a professional writing class at Purdue where the instructor set up a newsgroup for class discussions. During the first week of the newsgroup, a male computer science student posted a list of sexually explicit jokes about "dumb blondes." Women in the class found the remarks tasteless, intimidating, and offensive. Before any of them had a chance to post, they were already typecast on the newsgroup as occupying a subject position as ignorant sexual toys (see Chapter 6 for further discussion of this case). Such an incident points to an important aspect of access: that sometimes people use technology as a way to exclude others.

Intellectual Property

Ownership of text, citation of text, and the rights to distribute text comprise another key set of ethical issues in internetworked writing. In this area both legislation and conventions in print enter the discussion. (In interesting ways our ethical dilemmas on electronic networks illustrate some of the theoretical challenges to authorship voiced in postmodern theory; see Barthes, 1977; Foucault, 1984d; Lunsford & Ede, 1990; Smith, 1988.)

The basis for U.S. copyright law is the U.S. Constitution, which grants "Authors and Inventors the exclusive Right to their respective Writings and Discoveries," and the Copyright Act of 1976 (17 U.S.C. 101), which provides guidelines on, for instance, the copying of software programs. (The 1988 Berne Convention Implementation Act spells out guidelines for international copyright.) The basic tension in copyright ethics, reflected in the tensions in copyright law, is between the social right of access to information (based on the benefit a society accrues from being able to exchange and distribute information freely) and the right of the owner or author to fair recompense for the efforts of labor (Patterson & Lindberg, 1991). This issue takes the form of a debate on, for example, how electronic networks should be administered: Some advocate free access to and distribution of information on a government-supported Internet, whereas others believe that the commercialization of network resources is the best way to promote the development of creative and useful information. At the core of this discussion lie competing views of the role of the network in serving the social good. Will the social good be best served by making information freely available, or will the development of new information be best encouraged through a competitive and commercialized approach to information distribution? Should information be a shared resource, or a purchased one?

Fundamentally, according to the Copyright Act of 1976, electronic text is copyrightable because it is writing and thus exists in a tangible medium of expression. That does not mean, however, that such text cannot be reproduced. The Fair Use clause of U.S. copyright law exists to allow limited reproduction of texts without the approval of the copyright holder, *in some contexts*, in the interests of the benefit of society.

Cyberwriters and educators should pay special attention to section 107 of the Copyright Act of 1976, the Fair Use doctrine, which governs the reproduction of copyrighted materials for nonprofit educational purposes (as well as other purposes):

Sec. 107. ... the fair use of a copyrighted work ... for purposes such as criticism, comment, news reporting, teaching (including multiple copies for classroom use), scholarship, or research, is not an infringement of copyright. In determining whether the use made of a work in any particular case is a fair use the factors to be considered shall include

(1) the purpose and character of the use, including whether such use is of a commercial nature or is for nonprofit educational purposes;
(2) the nature of the copyrighted work;
(3) the amount and substantiality of the portion used in relation to the copyrighted work as a whole; and
(4) the effect of the use upon the potential market for or value of the copyrighted work.

The Fair Use doctrine is one of the most troubling aspects of copyright law for many because it expresses general factors influencing fair use decisions, but does not provide specific criteria. (The U.S. Congress deliberately declined to write in specific guidelines when drafting the law.) To the extent that specific criteria emerge at all, they emerge through case law—through the specific interpretations that courts develop for particular situations. As of yet, there is no established body of case law providing guidance for Fair Use of electronic text (Gilbert, 1990; Gilbert & Lyman, 1989).

Can electronic text be freely redistributed?

The fair use clause establishes that writers may reproduce others' words or images for appropriate purposes (e.g., instructional purposes; for purposes of criticism, rebuttal, and political satire), but there are restrictions. For instance, writers must credit their sources (e.g., following standard citation conventions) when they quote others' writings; failure to so acknowledge intellectual ownership is plagiarism. Writers and other borrowers are also limited as to how much of an original work they may reproduce (number of words is one but by no means the only factor determining what is allowable). Questions get even murkier, however, when it comes to considering how the fair use doctrine applies to electronic writing or, even murkier, how it might apply to electronic text developed for commercial purposes (e.g., on a corporate web site). In general, to the degree one uses others' electronic text for direct commercial gain, the fair use condition becomes less operable or may not apply at all.

Writers and writing teachers need to be aware, further, of the distinction between legal property rights (held by the person(s) who owns the document or work, often a publisher) and intellectual property rights (held by the entity assigned creative credit for the document or work—i.e., the author, who is usually a person or persons, but which can also be a conglomerate, a corporation, an organization, even a government). The legal owner is paid for the work; the intellectual owner is credited for its creation. The two are often not the same. Researchers and teachers in rhetoric/composition have seldom been interested in questions regarding *ownership* of text, preferring instead to focus on issues related to *authorship*. The reasons for this focus are sound enough: Ownership refers to legal property rights (and is the appropriate concern of the lawyer); authorship refers to rhetorical or literary credit, a different kind of capital. We can no longer accept the simple correspondence of the writer with the author. Nor should we accept that the author is always, or even usually, the owner.

The fluidity of electronic text makes copyright violations technically easier. Cut-and-paste options make it easy for writers to transport text without retyping and thus make boilerplating (and also plagiarism) easier. When writers are connected to network bulletin boards and to archived electronic files, they have access to a wealth of free-floating text, which they can easily download and import to word-processing files.

The fluidity of electronic writing and the hypertextual, rhizomatic nature of the Internet erode the romantic notions of source, origin, and authorship (Bolter, 1991; Faigley, 1992; Moulthrop, 1991; Poster, 1990). Although all text, whether electronic or print, is certainly "intertextual" in some sense (Porter, 1986), the conventions of print text do a better job of disguising its intertextual nature, partly because of its ability to support the pretense of permanence and fixity (and thus, origin and authorship). Baudrillard (1983) anticipates the problem of intellectual property in the electronic age: The problem of endless reproduction shatters the illusion of origin even more completely than does the printing press (pp. 100–101, 112). There is no original and no source: There are only copies, endlessly reproducible, redistributable, and malleable. For Baudrillard, "information" has no source, no origin: It merely is, available from various sites. So what does "authorship" signify in such a scene?

In the realm of the electronic network, the pretense of origin and fixity is more difficult to maintain (Bennett, 1993), although commercial publishers are working hard to lobby the U.S. Congress to pass legislation aimed at bringing electronic discourse under the control of print conventions (Weis, 1992). A bill under review in Congress in spring 1996, the National Information Infrastructure Copyright Protection Act of 1995 (H.R. 2441), commonly known as the Electronic Copyright Act, would extend print copyright laws to cover electronic information and make common cyberspace writing activities like browsing the web acts of copyright infringement in some circumstances (Working Group, 1995). (As of July 1996, discussion of this bill in committee had been suspended, but it is certain to be revised in a subsequent legislative session.)

If there is a common law emerging regarding the use of electronic writing on the networks, it is, according to network theorists and net lawyers, that:

> The medium is developing its own conventions for appropriate use ... conventions leaning toward free distribution of electronic text, at least on a network, with appropriate credit to source(s). ... A "common law" of bulletin boards is evolving in which re-posting messages is perfectly acceptable.

However, who says so? Where does this passage come from? The previous passage originally appeared without permission in an email conversation between Ann Okerson of SUNY-Albany and Bob Oakley, head of the Georgetown Law

Library. Okerson sent a report of this conversation to Stevan Harnad of Princeton, who sent it to Willard McCarty, editor of the Association of Electronic Scholarly Journals, who posted it on the Arachnet electronic list, where Tharon Howard picked it up and reposted it to Jim Porter, who put it in this chapter. All this occurred in the matter of a few days. The post has some authority based on who distributed and redistributed it and on the basis of its affirmation by noted intellectual property scholars (like Okerson)—but its origin is uncertain. Who is the original "author" of the quotation? In the form in which this quotation came to me it is impossible to tell—and how appropriate.

Electronic mail by its very discourse nature raises new issues (Hawisher & Moran, 1993; Kinkead, 1987; Ross, 1994b). On the one hand, electronic mail has some features of face-to-face spoken discourse (e.g., a telephone call). On the other hand, it also possesses some characteristics of writing (e.g., it lasts, it can be copied, archived, etc.). Anyone who has used it for any length of time realizes how easy it is to write a *flame* (an offensive, insulting, or sarcastic response to an electronic interlocutor). We sometimes write email as if we were talking to ourselves, as if it were a private journal entry, an immediate reaction—and then it goes out on the network, where it lives on in recorded format, gets redistributed, and maybe ends up in somebody's book. Email by its very discourse nature lives at the borders between speech and writing, between public and private discourse. It invites and encourages spontaneity, which means that our best thoughts, and our worst, can go flying through cyberspace, and outside it, to appear in contexts that we did not imagine when we first wrote them.

What understandings and expectations do people have when they write, read, or distribute electronic text, either on or off a network? Is electronic text a reusable resource (like a library's print materials)? Or is it hallway conversation—which might be seen, ethically at least, to be protected, private conversation? When might an electronic document constitute the "official business" of an organization, for which a company could be legally liable? (Can an electronic document have a contractual status? No, not yet, according to Victor Cosentino, 1994.) Does a writer need permission to quote a passage from electronic text in a print publication, to quote a passage from electronic text in another electronic publication, or to repost an electronic message to another site?

With snail mail and paper text we have more clearcut conventions, at least in theory if not practice. When I write as an official representative of Purdue University, I use official Purdue stationery, which signifies to the receiver that I am writing as an agent of that University. (Note: This use of Purdue stationery does not entitle the University to read my mail, even though the University pays for the stationery.) Purdue and, I imagine, other institutions have policies regarding the appropriate and inappropriate uses of stationery. For instance, I may not use Purdue stationery to write my state congressional representative, even if I am writing him or her about an academic issue.

However, what "stationery" authority does electronic text have? Here is one respect in which paper text has a distinct advantage: Stationery identifies an official documentary authority, usually by virtue of the distinctiveness of the stationery (which is partly a function of type face, font, and, usually, an official logo). Email does not yet recognize such distinctive features and distributes generic ASCII text, which will then be formatted in different ways at different sites, according to the software and hardware running at those sites. There is no way yet to sign email—and the signing act is what personalizes the letter and assigns it a clear authorship. (Although, of course, the author is not necessarily the same as the writer.)

How does one distinguish, then, an "official" statement from an individual opinion? Some email participants resort to posting disclaimers at the bottom of their messages—a statement that says, in effect, that the remarks are the writer's own and that his or her organization is in no way responsible for it. For instance, Carl Lydick of California Tech University issued this disclaimer to his postings to the comp-academic-freedom-talk list: "Unless what I'm saying is directly related to VAX/VMS, don't hold me or my organization responsible for it. If it IS related to VAX/VMS, you can try to hold me responsible for it, but my organization had nothing to do with it." Another convention of such disclaimers is the sometimes ironic aside, illustrated in Lydick's, that not even the writer is responsible for the content of the post.

How might the fair use doctrine apply to the redistribution of electronic text? Imagine this scenario: A student takes a portion of a message from a LISTSERV discussion and quotes it in a course paper, without securing permission of the original writer (and the group has no stated policy about reposting). The student then revises the paper for publication and sends it to the journal *Computers and Composition*. From the legal side, the Fair Use doctrine would seem to allow such a use, but this use could nonetheless constitute a significant betrayal of trust within an electronic community, and perhaps be unethical. To address writing issues like this one requires an exploration of the binary between public and private discourse.

Joseph Harris (1995), editor of *College Composition and Communication*, suggests a useful distinction—between "published work" and "semi-private writings" (p. 440)—that can provide some guidance to making such ethical determinations. Although Harris is referring to print materials, his distinction is partly applicable to electronic texts as well. He believes that "teaching materials, comments on student work, anecdotes from classrooms, informal talks, letters, memos, editorial reviews for journals ... should usually be considered private and quoted only with the consent of the people involved" (p. 440).

When applied in the electronic realm, such a principle suggests that a private email note should certainly not be redistributed or quoted in either an electronic or print publication without the consent of the writer. Yet that is an easy call. What about postings to electronic discussion groups? Although such postings are "public" in one sense, should they have a protected status within an electronic community, or can I quote any messages from the ACW-L discussion list (Alliance for Computers and Writing) in my publications without asking for writer or list approval? How do we go about answering that question? One operative principle (to be discussed in Chapters 6 and 7) says that the writer must make that decision considering the particular character of the list, the specific technological settings for the list (e.g., are posts archived? are they digested?), and the understandings, expectations, and policies that have been articulated within that community. From the point of view of the LISTSERV manager, it is important that understandings about use of community material be clearly articulated in the message welcoming new members to the list.

The strength of Harris's distinction is in giving us general criteria for making determinations about the status of online text. The fact that the binary between "public" and "private" is a questionable one, or that his distinction does not solve all our copyright problems in the huge gray area left by the binary (or any binary), should not prevent us from using such distinctions as heuristic guides.

One of the most helpful discussions involving the copyright of electronic information as it pertains to professional writing is Tharon Howard's chapter "Who 'Owns' Electronic Texts?" (1996a; see also Howard, 1996b; Jacobson, 1995; Okerson, 1996; Samuelson, 1994, 1995, 1996). Howard describes five particular scenarios that professional writers might face and considers how the professional writer might think through each scenario in terms of legal factors.

One of Howard's scenarios concerns the use of an email message posted to an electronic discussion group: Can I quote a portion of a message posted to an electronic discussion group (say, in a print publication)? As Howard says, current law seems to allow for such use of text under the Fair Use provision, but he also goes on to say that the form of the technology and the nature of the electronic group are factors that impact the *ethics* of that action. If the electronic group has defined itself as having a formal status as an electronic publication—for instance, by registering an ISSN number, by archiving or digesting postings to the group, or by applying some kind of editorial screening of messages—then those factors would seem to weigh in favor of allowing a writer to quote from portions of posted messages because the list is operating in some respects according to the conventions of a print journal.

If, however, the group has defined itself more informally, stressing "discussion" rather than "publication," and encouraging open and perhaps spontaneous postings, then another ethic of fair use ought to apply. Howard suggests that "the safest and most ethical course is to attempt to secure the permission of the email message's author before quoting from the message" (p. 193). I agree that this is generally true as a principle—it would constitute a serious betrayal of the trust of an electronic community to quote from a message that was posted in the heat of an exchange or in a process of inquiry and exploration. However, there are other circumstances (discussed later) that one has to weigh in making such a determination.

What about quoting from documents stored in World Wide Web archives? An emerging common law ethic suggests this rule of thumb: The presence of a document on a World Wide Web site is a de facto approval (an "implied license") to copy, republish, and quote from the document—given several necessary provisions: (a) the original author or site receives appropriate acknowledgment, (b) there are no other stipulations at the site that restrict such use (e.g., an editor's note prohibiting redistribution), and (c) the redistributed text remains within the realm of public domain—that is, the ethic says that I may not use freely distributed electronic text for direct commercial gain (e.g., selling copies of such a text).

The implied license principle as yet has no force whatsoever as a legal principle. However, it may function quite adequately as a common law of cyberspace, as an "ethical hyperreality"—that is, an ad hoc operating tenet guiding writing in cyberspace. This implied license principle is a "copyleft"-free text principle that commercial interests abhor and are fighting against because it blocks electronic publishers' efforts to develop web sites for significant commercial gain. The Electronic Copyright Act of 1995, at least in its July 1996 form, would help electronic publishers establish stricter fair use limitations on cyberspace than the emerging common law ethic cyberspace now recognizes. Even if there are other stipulations on the use of electronic text—for instance, a warning "do not quote from this passage without the expressed consent of the author"—we can legitimately question their legal force.

Here is another scenario: A Howard Rheingold editorial from the *San Francisco Examiner* is posted on a newsgroup, a public forum such as alt.comp.acad.freedom.news. One of your students takes it and reposts it on a LISTSERV discussion list. Another student transfers the document and reposts it on the class file server, where other students run off print copies on the lab printer. The teacher takes a print copy and distributes it in the next edition of the course packet. Then, a year later, the teacher publishes the editorial as a sample in her composition textbook. How many legal and ethical offenses are there in this sequence of events? Who is liable for what offenses? Are you as teacher liable for what your students illegally run off lab printers? (What if students store pornographic material on the class server? That might make your class more interesting, but could the police come in and haul you away?)

The cyberspace ethic now emerging seems to favor a presumption toward the free distribution of electronic text posted to newsgroups and archived LISTSERV lists (as long as the redistribution remains electronic). Thus the student's reposting of the Rheingold editorial to a LISTSERV discussion list would seem to be ethically allowable, as long as the editorial itself did not list any restrictions regarding its redistribution. Putting the editorial on the class file server and running off individual copies also falls under the heading of fair use. Where problems *might* arise is in the teacher's move to publish the editorial in a coursepack, at which point permissions might, from a strict legal point of view, be required if the editorial contains a clause prohibiting commercial use. At this juncture the teacher might make a reasoned practical judgment about whether the spirit of free distribution is maintained or harmed through the inclusion of the editorial in a coursepack. Should students be made to pay for an editorial that was intended to be freely distributed on the network, or is the payment simply a means of conveniently distributing work for the students' benefit? (Why can the teacher not distribute the editorial electronically?) Use of the editorial without permission in a textbook is clearly a copyright violation and also probably a violation of the cyberspace ethic promoting free distribution of electronic text (because it has moved the editorial out of its electronic context).

The variety of ways electronic documents can be produced, archived, distributed, and reproduced raises a serious challenge to conventional copyright law and to traditional notions of intellectual property. The right to redistribute others' messages is a key issue. Following conventional (i.e., print) fair use guidelines does not necessarily guarantee ethical use of electronic text. Different online groups develop their own policies regarding copyright and distribution of postings, to which members may be ethically (if not legally) obliged to adhere. Some groups' policies expressly forbid the redistribution of group messages without author consent. On other lists that do not have such explicit policy or that encourage conversational and spontaneous postings, participants might expect a principle of collegial privacy to apply and assume that their postings will not be redistributed without permission. Even if a conference technically permits reposting, conference members can feel that their rights of privacy are violated if their postings are quoted elsewhere without their permission. Here is where the practical ethical judgment of the writer comes into play. Noncontroversial or informative messages (e.g., conference announcements or bibliographical data) may not require permission; messages that carry sensitive information, controversial opinions, or innovative ideas are more likely to require permission. There is also an important distinction between reposting a message to another electronic bulletin board and quoting a message in a print forum.

Lists will often articulate an understanding, if not an actual copyright notice, governing the use of electronic messages. For example, on the moderated list Interpersonal Computing and Technology (IPCT-L), the editors judge whether submitted postings fall within the mission of the list; those that do not are returned to the sender. The policy statement for the list establishes that, unless otherwise specified by the author, the copyright for an individual posting is retained by the original author; and that archival, reproduction, or distribution of posted messages is not allowed except by written permission of the original author:

Copyrights of individual postings to, and archived files of, IPCT-L are retained by the original author unless specifically transferred. Copying, modification, publication or distribution of postings, or archives, of Interpersonal Computing and Technology Discussion List (IPCT-L) are not permitted except by the written permission of the original author(s) or the party to whom he/she has transferred copyright. (November 1, 1992)

This policy is a relatively restrictive one, one that is hard to enforce on the internetworked environment, and probably it is not meant to be enforced but to exist as a formal statement absolving IPCT-L of any responsibility for postings on the list. (Although, because the list is editorially screened, IPCT-L might be seen in this respect to be like a conventional publisher and so might be liable anyway.)

Compare the IPTC copyright policy to a second from the Rhetorical History and Terminology archive (RHAT):

All material entered into PTcs is copyrighted by AEE and PRE/TEXT. (See welcome message to PTcs.) However, subscribers to the list are given permission to copy any of the material on the list and to use it at their discretion on the condition that its authors be cited.

In addition, any contributor to Hist Rhet or RhetGlos retains a personal copyright to the materials he or she submitted and many publish them elsewhere without permission of the editors of AEE or PRE/TEXT. This permission does not extend to materials not authored by an individual. (March 5, 1995)

This policy permits free use of the material in the electronic archive, as long as authors are cited in the reuse of the material. This policy seems to suit an emergent cyberspace ethic that puts a high value on keeping the network free and allowing text to float at user's discretion. I am an advocate of that position myself, but the wording of the previous copyright statement does not guarantee that texts from this electronic archive will remain "free." The statement allows me to use this material at my discretion, but such a discretion would include my using this "free" text for my own commercial gain—say, if I put together a reference handbook of rhetorical terms constructed out of RhetGlos definitions. Is that a kind of use that the editors want to promote? Whether it is or it is not, this policy allows such a use.

To insure that electronic writing remains "free," editors, LISTSERV managers, and teachers should consider including "copyleft" statements: statements that indicate that although the material may be redistributed, it cannot be redistributed for commercial gain.

Who is responsible for electronic text?

The question of ownership of electronic text is not a matter of commercial or proprietary interest only. The other side of ownership is responsibility; intellectual property intersects with questions of authority and liability. Who is responsible for pornographic or libelous electronic text that may be in transit through various network sites or that may be deposited at a site without prior approval or knowledge? Although the law is not yet settled on this issue, teachers and administrators may be ethically responsible and legally liable for offensive materials stored on their computer systems or posted on their online conferences (see Elkin-Koren, 1995).

In May 1992, somebody reported to the police in Monroe Falls, OH, that minors were accessing adult materials over the Akron Anomaly Bulletin Board System. The systems operator did not "distribute" the materials directly, but they were in the electronic archive he maintained (he did not put them there), and a minor (who was set up by the police) was able to log in and retrieve the materials. The police seized the computer system and later arrested the systems operator, charging him with a misdemeanor (disseminating matter harmful to juveniles). Because a computer was involved, the police added felony charges (possession of criminal tools). In short, they treated the systems operator as a child pornographer. His lawyers argued that he should be treated as a librarian, but his electronic archive does not legally have the same status as a library. Essentially, its status is legally unclear (Cangialosi, 1989, describes a similar case).

The passage by the U.S. Congress of the Telecommunications Bill (signed into law in February 1996) establishes clear support for such extreme legal action. The Communications Decency provision of that bill makes service providers liable for pornographic material stored on electronic databases, even if the service providers did not put the material there and were not aware of its existence. In other words, the law establishes that service providers should be treated more as *publishers*, who must take responsibility for the distributed material, rather than as *common carriers*, who are simply providing the technological means of distribution (see Cangialosi, 1989, p. 278). Such a law, of course, will have the chilling effect of discouraging service providers from maintaining interactive web sites and will encourage increased surveillance of computer accounts by corporations and universities, who will need to institute such safeguards in order to protect themselves from obscenity charges.

In June 1996, this law was overturned by a panel of three federal judges in Philadelphia, who denounced the government's attempt "to regulate online content more closely than print or online content" (Quittner, 1996, p. 56). Although citizens' action groups like the American Civil Liberties Union and the American Library Association applauded this decision in favor of a free Internet, it is clear that the legal issues of liability and responsibility are far from settled. The decision is likely to be appealed to the Supreme Court, and even if it is upheld at that level, the U.S. Congress seems disposed to attempt another version of the Decency Act. Until such time as the legal issues become more settled, cyberwriters will need to acknowledge the responsibility and potential liability involved in maintaining electronic databases, especially interactive ones (for a more detailed discussion of liability issues for electronic databases, see Cangialosi, 1989; Elkin-Koren, 1995).

Is electronic text "private"?

Can teachers and systems administrators ethically monitor email and other electronic files? The clash between government control, educational control, and the individual writer's right to privacy highlights another key issue in the rhetorical ethics of internetworked writing (Parent, 1985; Piller, 1993a, 1993b; Thompson, DeTienne, & Smart, 1995).

The Fourth Amendment says that "the right of the people to be secure in their persons, houses, papers, and effects, against unreasonable searches and seizures, shall not be violated." The Fourth Amendment addresses privacy and personal security generally, but privacy on public information services is specifically addressed by the Electronic Communications Privacy Act of 1986 (18 U.S.C. 2510), which protects electronic mail from unwarranted search and seizure by government agencies and law enforcement officials. However, this act does not explicitly extend to private systems, such as in-house corporate email or to university computer systems, a gap that has resulted in some ethical and legal disagreements.

Shoars v. Epson America (1990) is a significant case in the process of deciding email privacy issues. In 1990, Alana Shoars filed a wrongful termination suit when she was fired (for insubordination) for criticizing her manager, who had been reading and making print-out copies of her email (Branscum, 1991). What was determined by the lower courts was that "neither state privacy statutes nor federal statutes address confidentiality of email in the workplace" (Branscomb, 1994, p. 93). The case was dismissed, thereby confirming the precedent that authorized managers may enter personal files in corporately owned messaging systems.

The Electronic Privacy Act of 1986 grants the same protection to public electronic discourse as is granted to telephone messages (Branscomb, 1994), but the law does not apply within corporately maintained electronic messaging systems; it only protects them from *outside* interference. As Oz (1994) says, "it does not cover communication in an organization's local area network" (p. 191). However, as Branscomb points out, distinguishing "inside" from "outside" can be murky because "many of the corporate messaging systems do have electronic gateways to public messaging systems" (p. 94). The distinction between "corporate" and "public" breaks down at some points, particularly on the web.

However, employees, teachers, and students should be aware of this fact: Companies (and universities) frequently monitor email, and thus far the law affirms their right to do so. In one study, 21.6% of the 301 surveyed companies "admitted searching employee files" (Branscomb, 1994, p. 93). According to the Communications Workers of America, 15 million U.S. workers are "subject to monitoring daily" (p. 95).

Many feel that practical ethical judgment should indicate that the privacy protections afforded U.S. first-class paper mail should extend to corporate and university electronic mail as well. Others point out that email is more like in-house mail, which may not have the same legal privacy protections (although ethical ones may obtain). Partly, the question hinges on which media analogy is most appropriate for electronic mail: Is email more like a letter or telephone conversation? More like a broadcast or a company file? The answers to such questions will help determine the legal status of employees' electronic text. A bill introduced in the U.S. Congress in 1991, The Privacy for Consumers and Workers Act (S. 516), aimed to address this matter by extending the right of privacy to employees' email. (The bill failed.)

Maintenance of email systems does require that system administrators occasionally monitor email, but how often and under what circumstances this is allowable is still under debate. It is one thing to enter computer accounts—in some circumstances, to open files—in order to solve some technical problems, but it is quite another to "open" electronic mail. Some administrators who have monitored email for purposes of determining acceptable content have been criticized for overstepping their authority.

Email at work or on campus does not have a legally protected status, but it is private. Until such time as the legal issue is settled, corporations and universities still have an ethical and relational obligation to provide, at the very least, advance warning to their employees and students that their email and electronic files might be examined. To not warn system users of this possibility is to deceive them and to violate the presumption of human trust, whether or not the act itself is finally determined to be legal or illegal. Until these matters become more firmly established by law, institutions should be sure (a) to communicate clearly their policies regarding the privacy of email (and the use of computer accounts generally), (b) to apply those policies fairly and consistently, and (c) to install some form of due process for judging alleged violations. With this approach, at least, users are less likely to be deceived about their privacy rights at work and on campus.

Are hypertext links allowable?

Nowhere are questions of law and ethics more murky than on the World Wide Web. The exponential growth of the Web, in conjunction with the use of graphic browsers like Mosaic and Netscape, has raised a number of new issues pertaining to the creation and distribution of online documents. (For instance, Netscape has a built-in function that makes it very easy to download graphic images from any web site.)

With the use of HTML text editors (e.g., Supertext and Web Weaver) and with the development of even more advanced web authoring tools (e.g., Adobe SiteMill), writers at web sites are easily able to create documents with internal links to other, remote sites. For instance, I have developed a statement on "ethics for professional writing"—a short statement of values aimed at professional writing students—that I placed on a web server at Purdue. I can identify one of the phrases in that statement—say, "business law"—as a hot spot. The hot spot is a link to another document or site that provides further information on that particular topic. When the reader clicks on that hot spot, he or she will call up another document, perhaps written by someone else and located at some other site.

Or is it at that other site? Where exactly is the document located, and does that matter in terms of the fair use and distribution of documents? Are such links actually duplications of that other document? Or are they more like bibliographic references? Do I as writer need permission to make a link to another site?

These and other such issues were extensively discussed on the CNI-COPYRIGHT electronic discussion list (CNI-COPYRIGHT@cni.org) during January/February 1995. The CNI-COPYRIGHT list is comprised of lawyers and law school professors (many of them intellectual property specialists), computer system administrators, librarians, and digital publishers. No clear consensus emerged from that discussion, except the universal agreement that these issues were complicated, and that there were as yet no clear legal answers and probably would not be until test cases arose to provide more concrete guidance.

However, one key binary emerged in the debate. A few on the list applied a strict interpretation of copyright law to conclude that any web link to another site, without the permission of the "linkee," was probably a copyright infringement, strictly speaking, because making a link (or activating it as a browser) constitutes reproducing an electronic text (because a copy is stored on the local computer's RAM). The argument proceeded along these lines: Because there are no clearly established legal precedents specifically for cyberwriting, the old print precedents apply, however inappropriate they may be to the web context. Until such time as multimedia law develops to address such circumstances, we are stuck with whatever law we now have.

Yet here is where a critical rhetorical ethic might provide some help to a developing cyberspace ethic. If we view hypertext as "rhizomatic" (Moulthrop, 1991)—that is, as not autonomous but as both conceptually and technologically connected intertextually—then we destabilize the notion of authorship to an extent that would seem to allow linkages of whatever sort (see Eldred & Fortune, 1992). The emergent consensus seems to be that the web itself, as a technological medium, implies an approval to "link freely." The critical view says that the electronic context provides a mitigating factor: If you as a writer connect your works to the World Wide Web, then that constitutes a public placement and *implies a license* (a key phrase in the discussion), allowing others to copy and view them without having to seek permission.

However, allowing "free" linkages does not solve two thorny problems. First, how should credit be assigned to intellectual work on the web? Linkages are never really "free" because they always involve the labor and effort of web writers. How should that work be credited? Second, how do we coordinate the idea of "free" linkages with the kinds of commercial services that are now appearing on the web? Can a commercial service charging its customers to access its web site then connect to noncommercial services—and thus, in effect, make money from others' freely shared web work?

One ethicist on the CNI-COPYRIGHT list felt that browsers should always heed author's labels, in ultimate respect to writers' right to control their own work. Most feel, however, that such a position runs counter to the spirit of the web, as well as the spirit of copyright, which urges a balance between protecting the author's work and promoting learning and progress.

Some restrictions impede learning and in fact have no legal force. I could put a phrase in this book saying, "No one may quote from this book, in any context, without written permission of the author." Yet such a restriction would put unfair restrictions on readers' rights. I cannot create my own counterlaw to the Fair Use doctrine. You would be perfectly within your legal and ethical rights to ignore my statement and to make use of my text within the guidelines of Fair Use. You *do* have the right, under the Fair Use clause, to quote from this book in your own work, subject to certain constraints (e.g., for the purpose of teaching, commentary, or critique). Society does have a right to use information for the benefit of all, although it does not have an absolute right to the particular form of expression of that information.

Here is an important exception to Howard's advice to "ask the author." What if my purpose in quoting from an electronic message is to critique the content of that message or to develop a politically counterposition? In other words, say that I am not simply reusing posted information in another context, but am perhaps rebutting it, correcting its errors, or disagreeing with its politics? In such an instance, the presumption may slide in favor of using the text *without* asking the author's permission, especially in cases when the author is unlikely to grant that information.

The ethic of *caring*, as developed by Nel Noddings, Carol Gilligan, and other feminist ethicists provides an operative principle here. Such an ethic takes the usual dictum "respect others" a step further to say that your ethical obligation is to *care* for the welfare of others as individuals, that is, to relate to them and work on their behalf as active care-givers. "Caring," for the writer in this context, would work to generate two lines of questioning: one pertaining to the author whose work might be used, and the other pertaining to the audience who might benefit from the author's work. As a writer invoking this ethic, I have to show care for both the author and my audience.

The Association for Computing Machinery (ACM, 1995) has developed a comprehensive set of policies guiding copyright for electronic publishing of ACM documents. One of the important principles of their copyright statement is its viewing an electronic link as a "form of citation" (p. 104). The policy recognizes that although, technically speaking, a link does involve "fetch[ing] a copy" (p. 105), from a rhetorical point of view a link on the web serves the same purpose as a citation in a print book or journal. The critical move made in such a policy is to let the rhetorical act take precedence over the technical, that is, to create a policy that takes into account the *rhetorical* rather than merely the *technical* nature of cyberwriting.

As intellectual property understandings have developed in 1996, it seems clear that there is a consensus that links are generally allowable on the World Wide Web, except under certain conditions. (See Oppedahl & Larson, 1996, discussion of "May I freely link to the web sites of others?" at <http://www.patents.com/weblaw.sht>.)

Are interface elements copyrightable?

Multimedia publishing technology generates its own distinct ethical issues. With the use of scanners and image-enhancement software writers can manipulate or combine copyrighted photos, art work, even digitized type fonts. Fair use allows for some copying and use of copyrighted images, but guidelines for use of visual images can be especially ambiguous. Can a student or teacher reproduce a copyrighted cartoon for use in a classroom assignment or for use in the school newspaper? Can visual icons be owned? Can templates be owned? What if a student takes a template presented during a class and uses it to create a brochure for a profit organization, without sharing the proceeds with the teacher of the class or asking the teacher's permission? Is that template copyrighted? (No, a template cannot be copyrighted, but the writer might be under an ethical obligation to credit the template's creator.) Is it permissible for a writer to scan a photo, then use a drawing program to trace part of that photo, then use the traced image as a silhouette for a company logo? There is no clear rule as to how much photo manipulation is allowable, except that the issue pertains to how much of the original photo was borrowed and how much of that original photo is recognizable in the newly created reproduction. Where law is not clear, careful practical ethical judgment will have to suffice.

How much manipulation of an electronic image is legally permissible? How much is ethically permissible? According to Ann Branscomb (1994), "It is too early to predict how the law will deal with electronic images" (p. 90), but a fair representation principle ought to proscribe, at least ethically, deceiving readers through the use of electronic imaging techniques. The principle is, of course, easy to articulate as a generality. What is harder is determining what *deception* means in any given case. Is it deception if no harm is done? (And what might constitute *harm*?) Is it okay if I manipulate an image for entertainment sake only? Or for advertising purposes (where people are likely to be more naturally alert to exaggerations and manipulations)? Provenzo (1992) warns of the dangers implicit in computer simulations and virtual reality, as used by business (pp. 176–180). Computer imaging makes graphic touchup all the easier and actually reduces the technological barriers to manipulation. The ease with which the technology can change pictures does not per se encourage their manipulation, but the technical constraints to manipulation are certainly lessened.

An interesting legal battle developed when the University of Illinois, copyright holder of the popular web browser Mosaic, charged Netscape Communications Corporation (NCC) with copyright infringement, claiming that the NCC web browser Netscape used features inappropriately "borrowed" from Mosaic (Blumenstyk, 1995). (The charge carried added weight because the person who developed Netscape for NCC also happened to work on the development of Mosaic when he was an undergraduate at Illinois.) NCC and the University of Illinois settled out of court, signing a private agreement that allowed both parties to continue to market and distribute their web browsers. Yet the issue remains alive: Can a cyberwriter imitate the interface features of other programs? At what points does "imitation" of features entail a copyright infringement?

Is the interface copyrightable? Samuelson, Davis, Kapor, and Reichman (1994) distinguish five types of "software entities" that may be protected in various ways: program code, program compilation as a whole, subcompilations, algorithms, and features. The first four of these entities refer more exclusively to the *operation of a computer program* and fall outside of the scope of copyright, which is concerned exclusively with *the reuse of written text* rather than the cloning of programs. However, the fifth element ("features") represents the gray area between computer programs as behaviors (or operations) and computer programs as text.

"Features of programs" are visual elements and designs that represent functions; they are a visual text that performs an accompanying behavior. They can be large or small, including everything from the macro feature of Lotus 1-2-3 to smaller elements like the zooming animation for Macintosh files, the tool bar (in numerous programs), the print preview (in numerous programs), color choices, button designs, and the like (Samuelson et al., 1995).

Are such features borrowable? Samuelson et al. think that "complex features should be regarded as subcompilations and protected" (p. 2385). However, they also note that "there has been relatively little objection to feature copying or migration among software developers, at least as long as the second adopter independently implemented the feature (i.e., wrote its own code)" (p. 2386). Their position thus argues that copying a design or feature *in a general sense* is allowable, as long as actual construction of the feature is done independently. In other words, if I like the "look and feel" of a particular dialogue box in a particular program, then I can imitate the design of that window myself, as long as I construct it independently. The design is not copyrightable as a text would be (see Pamela Samuelson's [1992, 1993] discussions of the "look-and-feel" cases).

Such a conclusion helps us answer a question regarding the design of web pages and sites. Is it allowable to copy the HTML source code for a document for use in one's own web site? The HTML source code for a document is not itself a *program* source code, so it is not protectable in the same sense as program code would be. The source code is also not per se text in the conventional sense, as it is a set of design markers—in other words, a style template. If I borrow Robin's source code simply to imitate the design of Robin's web site, but insert my own links and information (i.e., my own content), then I am not plagiarizing Robin's site, but am rather borrowing the look and feel of her design. Because the design does not perform any particularly unique function, there is no theft of code; there is no infringement of copyright.

On the other hand, ethical considerations might give me pause. To what degree am I learning from another's design and building on another's ideas, applying a transformative value as it were? Or to what degree am I simply copying a template? If a cyberwriter develops web sites in a parasitical fashion—simply taking others' designs and layouts and incorporating them as one's own—there may be an ethical loss of credibility, even if there is, strictly speaking, no legal infringement. Such an activity might also bespeak a lack of respect for others' web work. By the same token, those who build web sites should know that their codes are reusable. Does their location on the web presume an implied license to copy? Up to a point perhaps. Again, browsers like Netscape allow you to view and copy the HTML source code; but they do not advise you on the legal and ethical considerations involved in such technical activities.

A related question has to do with the copying of graphic images from a web site. Is it allowable to copy a diagram or photograph from one web site and import it to one's own? This issue has clearer answers. Images, like texts, are copyrightable; they are tangible forms of expression. Following the ACM linkage policy (which takes into consideration the rhetorical rather than merely technical nature of a web link), I could create a link to a text or image without a copyright violation (because, according to ACM policy, a link is like a citation). Yet I cannot move that text or image to my own site without clearly establishing the copyright status of that text or image. Copyright law and fair use provisions obtain in this case. Is it an image in the public domain? Has the web designer granted clear authorization to use an image? To what use am I planning to put the image (e.g., commercial vs. educational)? And how much of it am I planning to borrow? The emergent common law of web writing allows for a liberal interpretation of the distributability of web text and images, but there are nonetheless limits that must be observed (Bunnin, 1990; Van Bergen, 1992).

ISSUES OF CIVILITY: FREE SPEECH VERSUS REGULATION OF DISCOURSE

What constitutes civil behavior on the Internet? Such a question invites consideration of the free speech and censorship debate, which is exceedingly complex from a rhetorical ethical standpoint (Barringer, 1990; DeLoughry, 1996; Elmer-Dewitt, 1994, 1995; Lotus, 1993).

Advocates of an absolute free speech position begin their arguments and often end them as well, by citing the First Amendment to the U.S. Constitution, which articulates the basic principle of free speech: "Congress shall make no law ... abridging the freedom of speech." This principle raises questions about what kind of speech (or writing) can be prohibited, if any, and as to what degree the principle applies to writing produced by computer. The decision in the case of *Doe v. University of Michigan* (1989), which declared the University of Michigan's antiharassment policy unconstitutional because its overly broad definition of harassment threatened students' First Amendment rights, has led computer conference listowners and systems administrators to wonder whether forbidding or restricting so-called "hate speech" is constitutional. Can a campus system administrator legally or ethically revoke a student's email account for posting "offensive" messages (see Shade, 1996)?

One complexity of the free speech issue is in recognizing that there is such a thing, legally, as harassment, that is, speech, with its particular degree of abuse, constitutes an action (MacKinnon, 1993). Another complexity is noting that intellectual property and liability issues intersect with harassment issues. Assigning ownership is important to the question of liability (or fault): Who is *responsible* for internetworked writing that may be a form of harassment?

The increased use of electronic networking in writing classrooms raises questions about the ethics of that use. How do the principles and conventions that apply to conventional classroom discussion change in the electronic classroom? What happens when the students' right to free expression in the classroom (which can include the network) conflicts with the instructor's right, even responsibility, to maintain control in the classroom? What does the teacher do if a student posts an email message making sexual advances to another student in the class? Or if a student gets a sexually provocative message from a student in another class (which happened to one of my students, as reported in Takayoshi, 1994)? What if one of your students posts a racist or sexist comment on a public bulletin board? When is it the teacher's role to respond, and when is it the responsibility of the campus computing center to intervene by defining "inappropriate" uses of the network? It is not that this sort of problem cannot happen in traditional classroom settings, but my guess is it happens more frequently in the electronic network because of the intimacy and spontaneity of the medium and also because the medium is bringing together people with widely divergent views that are not used to sharing space with one another. The rules and conventions of practice are less well established on the Internet. What constitutes harassment and/or violation of privacy on the network? What if a student in your class uses his account to send repeated unwanted love messages to a student in another class? What if one student lures another into a MUD, then rapes her electronically, a situation described by Howard Rheingold (1993) and Julian Dibble (1993)? What about electronic stalking, in which a poster sends repeated unwanted messages to someone? Or in which a poster uses the network to lure minors into nonvirtual liaisons?

Does it matter if someone does these things during your class versus at home in the evening? What authority do you have over this situation? What responsibility? The answers might well lie between jurisdictions: It might involve you and your campus computing center, depending on how students' accounts are assigned through your university. Does your university's sexual harassment policy include a section on electronic harassment?

Numerous universities proscribe use of computer facilities for harassment, a policy that has, in some cases (e.g., the Jake Baker incident), proved difficult to implement. In November 1992, John Michael Polzer was arrested while seated at a computer terminal on the University of Minnesota campus. Although not a student, Polzer was arrested for using Internet Relay Chat (IRC) to send obscene and threatening messages to a female student at the University. However, this sort of direct and clear case of harassment does not pose much of an ethical problem, other grayer cases do.

In 1991, the Texas Educational Network (TENET) shut down USENET access shortly after turning it on because it was discovered that high school students were accessing the sexually explicit alt.sex* newsgroups. However, one view takes an absolute approach to free speech: No use of the network, other than obvious piracy, should be censored. There should be no bans related to hate speech or to use of the network for distributing sexually graphic materials, whether textual or visual (see Shade, 1996).

In 1992, a male student at Carnegie Mellon University was charged with violating the university's antiharassment policy for posting "offensive" messages on the electronic bulletin board maintained by the campus Women's Center. The student's repeated and lengthy postings described in graphic detail instances of sexual violence against women and insisted that it was the job of men everywhere to reestablish their physical mastery over women. The student's postings had the effect of shutting down discussion on the bulletin board, intimidating some members into silence and provoking angry response from others.

Should the student be reprimanded? Should his account be revoked? The issue centered on whether the student's postings constituted harassment or whether they were a protected form of free speech, especially because they were directly related to the topical identity of the newsgroup. Such issues hinge on a number of complex situational factors: for example, the incident happened at a private rather than public institution; the student's messages were aimed at feminists generally not at specific women (which, from one point of view, made the remarks "political" rather than "personal"); the messages were posted to a public bulletin board not to individuals; the university's student code explicitly allowed for free public expression of ideas, even controversial or potentially offensive ones.

One relevant principle (taken from the Netnews Bill of Rights, drafted by lawyers, systems administrators, and librarians as a guide to network usage; see Kadie, 1991) is that "materials should not be proscribed or removed [from public bulletin boards] because of partisan or doctrinal disapproval." The Electronic

Frontier Foundation (EFF)—an advocate of free speech on the networks—took the viewpoint that, because the student posted to a *public* bulletin board he had an absolute right to post what he wanted; if people did not like it they should ignore it. Others would say that his postings constituted harassment and intimidation of women on the basis of gender, and that such an instance is a clear form of harassment. As this case was discussed on USENET groups—mainly by the men who do 90% of the posting on the EFF newsgroups—the presumption was in favor of the student and his right to free speech, even when such speech effectively destroyed an electronic community. Such cases exemplify the tension between one individual's right to freedom of expression and another individual's right to be protected from harassment and intimidation based on personal characteristics of gender, race, religion, and other protected statuses.

There is yet another side to the problem, if we think back to the Akron case discussed earlier. Administrators and teachers might be ethically responsible or legally liable for offensive material stored on their computer systems or posted on their online conferences. The Electronic Frontier Foundation sees the Akron case as an instance of law enforcement gone wild—and uses it to show why we need to keep the government out of the business of network legislation. Yet I think it points to the fact that teachers might be ethically responsible and maybe even legally liable for the public actions of their students.

A test case has appeared concerning computer harassment at Santa Rosa Junior College. At the request of students, the college set up separate bulletin boards for men and women to hold discussions regarding gender. (That was the first mistake: Setting up separate lists based on gender itself is probably a civil rights violation). Some comments posted on the men-only discussion group contained "anatomically explicit and sexually derogatory remarks" about two women at the college. In April 1993, the women filed an harassment complaint with the Education Department's Office for Civil Rights. The male student chiefly responsible for initiating the discussion also filed a complaint that the University's response to the case threatened his right to free speech.

Now, one facet of the issue here is determining whether the computer conference is a public forum or an "educational program." DeLoughry and Wilson (1994) phrase the question this way: Do "students who use computer bulletin boards or conferences have the same rights of free speech that they would have on the campus quadrangle" (p. A26). If the conference relates to a specific class or instructional purpose, then the University has more responsibility (and authority) for what happens there. If the conference is more an open forum, then the free speech tenet probably holds more force. However, the gray area is huge here, and we are especially at sea because we do not yet have an established body of legal precedent to help our deliberations. Branscomb (1991) sees the question as not admitting to a simple answer: "Computer bulletin boards are an electronic hybrid, parts of which may be looked on either as public or private, depending on the desires of the participants" (p. 158; see also Kapor, 1991; Shade, 1996).

The end result: The College had to pay both women and the man $15,000 each to settle the claims. This is one of the dangerous side-effects of this kind of dilemma. Universities can be caught between the free speech principle, on the one end, and the problem of harassment and protection of the innocent on the other. The university is damned if it does and damned if it does not, seemingly, which can lead to a chilling effect. The more universities are caught in such dilemmas, the more their response will be to shut down resources or strictly monitor their use, and the less likely they will be to support a wide range of network activity.

We can get ourselves into some interesting dilemmas. The Prodigy bulletin board service was criticized by the American Civil Liberties Union for its restrictions on the content of postings, so it loosened some of those restrictions. Then some messages appeared saying that the Holocaust was a myth. At that point, the Anti-Defamation League of B'nai B'rith charged Prodigy with allowing its bulletin boards to be used to promote anti-semitism. Angry people responded with postings containing obscenities, which were automatically deleted by the Prodigy computer, which was programmed to delete messages containing obscenities. So then Prodigy really got into trouble for apparent inconsistency: allowing one group its say, but not allowing rebuttal. However, notice: Allowing all speech to be posted will not let them off the hook either.

Is the listowner or manager liable for what gets posted on a discussion list or bulletin board? According to Anne Branscomb (1994), such a decision rests on the question of whether the manager operates the forum as a "distributor" or as a "publisher" (pp. 102–104). If the forum allows network participants to post directly on the forum without any intermediary editorial control, then the list manager is a distributor and cannot, suggests Branscomb, be held responsible. A publisher, however, is someone who intercedes in some form or other (e.g., by screening messages, by collecting them and group posting them, or by accepting copyright) and thus takes on an obligation for the content of the postings. It might be a serious mistake, for instance, for a LISTSERV owner to place postings under his or her copyright designation, but then to allow free, unedited posting by list members.

A particularly interesting problem involving the ethics of responsibility was the case of YAM, the self-adopted persona of a student in a course I taught at Purdue in Spring 1991. In the class—a graduate theory course in audience—all the students received a University email account that they used for online discussions on PURWCLAS, a LISTSERV group created specifically for writing class discussions. (At that time, Purdue students could only get permanent computer accounts if they were sponsored by a faculty member. So the student's account was in my name. This was the computing center's way of avoiding liability, by passing on responsibility to faculty members—and accounts do not work this way everywhere. Purdue has since changed its policy and now assigns students their own lifetime accounts.)

Mostly, the student used the PURWCLAS group as intended. However, when YAM started posting messages on PURTOPOI—another rhetoric discussion list also maintained at Purdue—things started to get interesting. First, he posted a number of strange messages signed "YAM," the Babylonian god of chaos. The messages referred to all readers on the list—and indeed audiences of any sort—as "scum." This disconcerted some people and may have violated some notions of netiquette. However, I did not see such postings as causing any sort of ethical problem for me as teacher or account sponsor (I was acquainted with some expressivist rhetorics that pretty much held the same view of audiences; see Porter, 1992a), but his calling the list participants scum did cause some problems for the listowners (see Howard, 1992).

Next, YAM posted a long message on PURWCLAS ending with a demeaning anti-semitic remark about the ethnic heritage and character of a Purdue faculty member. At this point, I objected; I wrote a public message to the list protesting the "slanderous" nature of his remark. I also sent him a personal note saying that I regarded his comment as an inappropriate use of the account, and that I would consider revoking my *sponsorship* of his account if it continued. He followed this with a posting on PURTOPOI accusing me of threatening his right to free speech, but after that he pretty much stopped posting altogether.

Finally, in one last PURTOPOI posting, he published a copy of a letter he sent to the Dean of Liberal Arts charging the Purdue English Department and the rhetoric program with running a "fraudulent" operation. He directly and personally attacked individuals in the program by name. At the end of the letter he said that he would make a donation to the "Robert J. Lyon Defense Fund"—Robert Lyon being a dissatisfied Purdue employee who that spring shot and killed his female supervisor, on campus, over an employment disagreement. YAM went on to suggest that in certain situations such violence was the only way disputes could be resolved. Three other important points are worth noting about the situation: (a) The letter he posted did not directly threaten anyone on the PURTOPOI list, it was only a copy of a letter sent elsewhere; (b) this behavior occurred on a list and in a context that was only indirectly related to my class; and (c) the Robert Lyon incident created a climate of anxiety at Purdue, and so invoking that incident at that time created more consternation than it might have otherwise.

So how did the YAM problem resolve itself? YAM left the program and the University and in so doing ceased to have a right to an account. In this sense, the problem resolved itself—but even so I have to admit that I had made a decision. After checking through the resources of the Electronic Frontier Foundation (and other archives) and talking the matter over at some length with Purdue computing center personnel and with the listowners of PURTOPOI, I finally did revoke my sponsorship of the student's account—on the basis of its use of *threatening* language, not on its slandering of individuals. The particular technological and political context of the situation—that is, I was technically "sponsor" of the account—assigned me a certain kind of obligation and a responsibility. If we had been in a situation in which the student had his own unsponsored account, it would have been a much stickier problem from a legal standpoint, and at that point it would have been beyond my purview as teacher to do anything other than to exercise my own free speech right to denounce his behavior.

Am I certain about this judgment? No, but then certainty has nothing to do with ethical judgment. I think I was *probably* right in this instance, although absolute free speech advocates might be horrified at my decision. Yet I do not want to offer this story as what should or should not have been done, but simply as an example of the kind of issue writing we will face in the medium.

So what latitude should writing teachers take to control such discourse? Some say none; we should not try to regulate anyone's discourse. Yet at what point does expression of free speech become threat, harassment, or intimidation—especially considering these writings in context of hostile personal behavior to the people involved? It was a given of the situation that I had the *legal* right (at least with the university context) to revoke my sponsorship of the student's account. Do I have an *ethical* right to do this? Putting a little different spin on that, do I have the *responsibility* to do it? Whose rights need protecting?

When, if ever, should the faculty sponsor, the university, or some other agent pull the plug? The purists would say "never." A more conservative position says that when a student or staff member signs up for an email account that person is agreeing to abide by the guidelines governing the use of that resource. That access to these resources is a privilege, not a right, in other words. This argument is further extended to LISTSERV discussion groups: Does a group have the right to exclude a member who mondoposts 40 off-topic messages per day? Such an activity can destroy a discussion list—yet would it be ethical for us to make such a decision?

What if the policies themselves are conflicted? Obviously my policies themselves are constrained by law and ethics. I cannot make policies that discriminate on the basis of gender, race, and religion. I cannot apply my policies in a capricious manner. I cannot shut off others' legitimate right to express their views.

Revoking accounts is itself a tricky business. Some feel that there should be no censorship on the electronic network; some are arguing for a utopian medium that would be truly free and public, a truly public forum without restraint. Yet the interests that pay for the network constantly make technical decisions that intersect with political decisions. Do I pay for my site to receive USENET newsgroups? And if I do, do I then have the right to selectively censor newsgroups (such as alt.sex.bestiality)? Can I censor newsgroups on the basis of content? Can I censor newsgroups on the basis of format? Some sites have restricted newsgroups on the basis of the amount of disk space they occupy. Newgroups that ship graphics code typically take up a large amount of space; thus, censorship of alleged pornography is accomplished on the basis of volume rather than content.

As these cases demonstrate, electronic networking raises questions about social relations in online discussions. In the traditional writing class, the student's writing remains within the relatively secure confines of the course, shared only with the teacher and perhaps with classmates. In the era of online publications, wide-area networks, and synchronous conferencing, the once vast split between writing (as composing the text) and publishing (as printing and distributing the text to some public) has narrowed, maybe vanished. In many online conferences, for instance, the gap between writing and publishing has been reduced to that proverbial keystroke, and control of that keystroke is now in the hands of the writer, not (as formerly) the editor or publisher. In the realm of electronic networking, student text can be quickly distributed over a wide territory. This empowers students by giving their work potential for broad distribution—but with this potential comes added responsibility, for both students and teachers. Electronic writing multiplies the number of rhetorical and social, and hence ethical, relations possible in the classroom.

Internetworked writing has a spontaneous feel about it (the illusion of oral, face-to-face conversation, but without the physical presence of the other), and this spontaneity frequently leads to miscommunication, even to "flaming" ("Electronic mail," 1992; Seabrook, 1994). (*Flaming*, a common, although troubling, phenomenon on electronic mail systems, refers to messages that attack or disparage readers.) Discussion on electronic networks is governed by a general etiquette, known as *netiquette*. Such netiquette, whether articulated or not, provides standards based on the principle of respect for others. Of course, netiquette carries no legal authority, but such principles do have a social authority in defining parameters of acceptability and politeness, important forces shaping discourse conventions in electronic communities. Most network groups disallow or discourage flaming. Other rules of netiquette advise participants on matters such as relevance, frequency, and length of postings—advising members to keep their messages relevant to the group's purpose, to provide clear and descriptive subject lines for mail messages, to sign their messages at the end, to keep messages short (so as not to waste system space or user time), and to limit the number of messages posted (Howard, 1991).

Although the law is silent on many issues pertaining to computer use, educators and electronic writers can look for ethical guidance to acceptable use policies established by government, education, and private network lists. For instance, the National Science Foundation (1992) has established specific policies for acceptable use of the Internet, proscribing uses that violate U.S. or state law, that propagate computer viruses, and that violate or harass persons. The policy also stipulates that the network may not be used for "extensive" private or personal business or for for-profit activities. Numerous universities and schools have developed their own policies governing how students, faculty, and staff may use computer resources. Information about and examples of various acceptable use policies (as well as records of relevant legal decisions) are stored in an electronic database maintained by the Electronic Frontier Foundation.

Electronic discussion groups often develop their own acceptable use policies establishing guidelines on, for instance, netiquette, the relevance of message content, and the reproduction or redistribution of messages. Many lists have a ritual "no flaming" policy, for instance, although it is seldom made clear what "flaming" is, or by what process such a determination will be made, or what the penalty for flaming will be. The threat is palpable, however: If you flame (whatever that may be), you will be removed from the list—and in the world of LISTSERV the owner's rule is absolute.

There have been challenges to "no flaming" policies. Jesse Lemisch (1995), for instance, advocates an acceptance of flaming as a form of legitimate discourse, even on academic LISTSERV lists. He is afraid that cyberspace is "full of gatekeepers and fiefdoms, where those who would disagree must learn the oblique expression of the dissident under autocracy" (p. A56). He calls for others to join him in being a "dissenter in cyberspace," one who opposes the random censorship and "capricious rejection of messages" that he accuses many academic LISTSERV moderators of practicing. Lemisch is opposed to any editorial screening of messages on the basis of content, and this is a practice he sees as widespread on academic discussion groups. He is against "placing repressive limits on communications in the name of decorum and civility" (p. A56).

Lemisch raises the question of whether flaming is really so bad. We might see flaming as representing the willingness of writers to speak plainly and bluntly and angrily when the circumstances warrant. Here is where it might be helpful to distinguish between an angry reply and an offensive or insulting reply. An angry or strong response could be warranted, I would say, in certain circumstances. Anger is a form of protest, and Lemisch does not want to see protest muted in academic LISTSERV contexts. However, discourse that insults or demeans others is another matter. The personal attack or insult, the offensive "othering" of individuals on a list, the assault or dismissal that has as its aim the silencing or elimination of others, which constitutes a form of restricting their access, is certainly unethical. Yet most antiflaming policies do not make such a distinction, leaving open the important question of whether *any* strong or vigorous disagreements, or even sarcasm or irony, constitute flaming. If it does, then LISTSERV groups would be rightly faulted for muting an important aspect of dialogue.

The counterquestion, of course, is what about the individual who threatens the community? An individual can destroy an electronic community through offensive hostile postings, or excessive postings, or through repeated off-topic postings. As Howard (1993) points out, when an individual poster creates disturbances on a list, then membership decreases. This itself is not an argument for ousting the individual, but the listowner does have to balance the good of the list with the rights of individuals on the list and does have to balance the right of free expression against the issue of relevance of postings.

As co-listowner of the PURTOPOI discussion list in 1991, Howard pointed out in an email message to the list that "one abusive message" posted in 1991 led to

10% of the subscribers leaving the list in a four-day period. On the contrary, he noted, "serious disagreements and scholarly debates seem to produce higher subscription rates and greater posting activity." Again, the cyberspace ethic that insists on "no flaming" needs to carefully distinguish "abusive" and insulting or offensive posts from those that are genuinely serious, although perhaps angry and excited, substantive disagreements.

Does a LISTSERV manager have an absolute and unquestioned right to expel unwanted members from a list? Legally, it seems so, although that right may soon be challenged (DeLoughry, 1995). Partly, the issues hinge on whether the LISTSERV group is defined as an open, public space or as an exclusive club. Certainly the exclusion of members on the basis of race, creed, or gender would be illegal. However, can members be excluded on the basis of disciplinary status, rank, or other nonprotected factors? Can public institutions whose computer systems are supported with public monies maintain restrictive electronic lists? According to Mike Godwin, staff counsel for the Electronic Frontier Foundation, "the public does not have a right to join a chess club at a public university and does not have the right to participate in an electronic mailing list" (DeLoughry, 1995, p. A22).

This chapter has considered a few of the legal and ethical issues facing electronic writers and has begun the process of showing how a situated rhetorical ethics might help teachers and writers frame appropriate responses to these issues. Writers in the internetworked writing environment can get little guidance or solace from statutory law, which, in most cases, does not adequately account for the new kinds of communication events that computer technology generates. In fact, statutory law is still very much print based—and so, as Anne Wells Branscomb and John Perry Barlow both advise, it is necessary for us to work to develop a cyberspace ethic that can serve as a guide for constructing adequate and desirable law. Chapter 4 has identified some of the ethical resources that we might invoke in developing such a cyberspace ethic, and Chapter 6 will show how these resources can be deployed to provide ethical guidance for network writers.

6

The Exercise of Critical Rhetorical Ethics

> Bringing ethics into rhetoric is not a matter of collapsing spectacular diversity into universal truth. Neither is ethics only a matter of radical questioning of what aspires to be regarded as truth. Lyotard insists that ethics is also the obligation of rhetoric. It is accepting responsibility for judgment.
> —Faigley, 1992, p. 239

My perspective looks at the issue of ethics on computer networks from the point of view of rhetoric. In taking the perspective of the writer (or rhetor), rhetoric focuses on the issue of the writer's (and writers') responsibility toward readers. The questions of interest pertain not so much to what the writer *can* do (what is *legally permissible*) as to what the writer *should* do (what is *ethically obligated*). My primary professional role—that of writing teacher—places me in a specific ethical standpoint toward issues involving the rights of electronic citizens. What obligations do I have as the teacher of a writing class toward members of a class who can be victimized by the electronic speech of others? What obligations do I have as a teacher of writing to encourage members of my class to be responsible, fair, and ethical electronic writers?

My heart lies with postmodernist approaches to addressing ethics (as you can tell from my nomadic tendencies in the discussion of ethical positions in Chapter 4), but, like Lyotard and Thébaud (1985), I am nervous about the problematic politics of taking the postmodern *ironic* position. It is too easy to stand and smirk in the middle and point out that emperors and empresses have no clothes, but *then* what? What do you *do*? How do you justify any ethical or political stand? The issue for rhetorical ethics is to deal with the plurality and contingency of choices—and yet at the same time to be able to take a firm stand when it is necessary to do so.

So what do we do? Where do we position ourselves? Overall I am advocating a *critical rhetorical ethics* that is flexible and adjustable, but that is not a pluralist ethics. A critical rhetorical ethics does not generate specific answers. It suggests heuristics, tactics for exploring what "right answers" might look like in any particular case. (Figure 4.1 is an example of such a heuristic, a visual heuristic. See Sullivan & Porter, 1997, Chap. 2, for a discussion of the sources for critical rhetoric.) It offers procedural criteria for determining how ethical decisions might be made in the particular case. (Procedural criteria themselves are never innocent or neutral, of course; they should not pretend to universality. Procedural criteria are situated.) A critical rhetorical ethics is a *praxis* occupying the position on the border. It *inquires in a nomadic fashion*, but recognizes that at some level at some point *practical judgment is necessary*: the ability to inquire and then *to act in the manner necessary*. We might consider this position as that of *postmodern commitment* (as opposed to the kind of ludic postmodernism, which, in its extreme forms, can lack the capacity for decision and choice).

I do not think, however, that everyone needs to occupy the same position. There is simply not enough room for us all to stand in the same place, even if it were a good idea. We will inevitably have different inclinations based on our backgrounds, our passions, our characters as they have developed, and our life-world experiences, which lead us in different directions. We may have different positions when we occupy different roles: As a writing teacher using the network I have different responsibilities and obligations to students than I would have as a LISTSERV moderator or as a web site developer.

Personally, I tend to float in the lower right section of the rhetorical/ethical grid (Figure 4.1), with Paulo Freire and Iris Marion Young and, to a lesser extent, with Kenneth Burke: strong inclination toward the situated and the communitarian, but sympathetic to the postmodern critique and (with Irigaray) positing difference as a fundamental principle. My position is that problems are best worked out in terms of a situated and kairotic rhetorical ethics, which grants ethical authority to local practice and the conventions of particular communities, which accounts for the specific nature of the electronic medium, and which invokes a discourse ethic that is relatively pluralistic in its constitution and heuristic and rhetorical in its methodology. As I have discussed in Chapter 4, the sources of this discourse ethic can be found in various postmodern ethical systems: critical and feminist ethics, liberation communitarian ethics, and casuistic rhetorical ethics. Politically, this position can certainly be viewed as leftist, but it differs sharply from the political postures advocated by groups such as the Electronic Frontier Foundation, which promotes network policies based on legal principles of Enlightenment liberalism. Attempts to settle issues invoking some grand metanarrative of the self or of Universal Principles alone (e.g., Habermas) are not likely to address either the pluralistic nature of electronic communities or the situated nature of writing acts and so will be unlikely to settle the sorts of practical problems that are now arising on the networks.

Occupy the border, and be ready to move, nomadically, when necessary. At some level, *phronesis*, or practical judgment, is required to do what is necessary and just. As a writer or writing teacher, you have to recognize that your rhetorical action of taking a position involves an authority and responsibility and, yes, a power that *cannot* be evaded or redistributed. What you can do is use that power wisely and responsibly—or try. As Foucault (1987) says, the power cannot be dissolved "in the utopia of a perfectly transparent communication" (p. 18); rather, we can work to develop in ourselves and to encourage our students to develop "the rules of law, the techniques of management, and also the ethics, the *ethos*, the practice of self, which would allow these games of power to be played with a minimum of domination" (p. 18).

The message here is that teachers should not try to control their students' writing, but that in their effort to avoid control they should not give up their role as interveners, their role as teachers of commitment. Of course, writing teachers should not presume to dictate absolutely what ethical writing practices consist of in every given case, but they should also not surrender their responsibility to promote ethical writing practices. Foucault (1984e) himself warns against the danger of opposing consensuality: "Perhaps one must not be for consensuality, but one must be against nonconsensuality" (p. 379). The danger of consensuality is that it can threaten difference, but the far greater danger is that in the fear of obliterating difference we become advocates of nonconsensuality—that is, we fail to recognize the importance of common ground, of judgment, of commitment, of responsibility. As Faigley (1992) says,

> Bringing ethics into rhetoric is not a matter of collapsing spectacular diversity into universal truth. Neither is ethics only a matter of radical questioning of what aspires to be regarded as truth. Lyotard insists that ethics is also the obligation of rhetoric. It is accepting responsibility for judgment. (p. 239)

A postmodern rhetorical ethic, of course, opposes any effort to insist on the absolute dominance of rules (what Faigley refers to as "collapsing spectacular diversity" into universalist hegemony), but in this opposition it does not satisfy itself *only* with celebrating the absence of rules (in the kind of "radical questioning" that can lead to uncommitted pluralism or relativism). A committed postmodern rhetorical perspective focuses, rather, on the "invention of rules" (Steuerman, 1992, p. 112); *what* rules—and how constituted?

CASE 1: NEWSGROUP INTERVENTION, OR BEING COMMITTED WITHOUT BEING A BULLY

Let us start with some actual cases and use them to work toward an understanding of what I mean by the praxis of critical rhetorical ethics. Several years ago, a graduate teaching assistant at Purdue set up an electronic newsgroup for his technical writing class discussions. Because of my interest in the course, I read the postings on that newsgroup from the beginning of the class.

During the first week of class, a male computer science student posted a list of jokes, some of them anatomically and sexually explicit, about what he called "dumb blondes" (by which he meant women with blonde hair). The posting was written assuming as implied audience a set of like-minded male fraternity brothers who could appreciate a good joke about dumb women, but in fact there were several women, and several blonde women, in the class. Before any of them had a chance to post, they were already typecast on the newsgroup as occupying a subject position as ignorant sexual toys. If you are familiar with newsgroups, then you know that this sort of thing is fairly common, if not endemic. However, this was not a typical newsgroup, as it was tied to a nonvirtual academic community.

So what do *you* do if you are the teacher or a lurking faculty member reading this newsgroup? To write or not to write?—that is the question.

I will tell you what I did, *not* because I think it represents *the right answer*, but because it represents *the answer that was right for me at that time in those circumstances*. I predict that many will disagree with the response I took to the case, deciding either that I made a big deal out of nothing, was too impulsive, or lacked political conviction. Yet the right or wrong of the ultimate decision is not the issue here, and I do not think that rhetorical ethics answers that question anyway. What I am interested in, and what I hope to illustrate, is *the process of rhetorically interrogating the writing situation from a rhetorical ethical standpoint*.

I applied a kind of ethical stasis procedure to the problem. The first determination was "How important is this"? Is a list of jokes something to get angry about, or should I simply do what Howard Rheingold and others in the Electronic Frontier Foundation say is the right thing to do in cases of electronic boorishness: Ignore it? That was an easy question for me: I see the electronic network as an ethical frontier where it is particularly important for people (and maybe especially people with some measure of power) to step forward and actively participate in constructing the network as a place that encourages open discussion from diverse participants. Yes, it is worth countering messages that dominate and exclude, that make the network a hostile place.

OK, this kind of stupidity should be opposed, but the second question is: Should *I* be the one to do it? I contemplated my several selves. As a lurker and an outsider (in the class), I wondered if I had the *right* to say anything. As a faculty member at Purdue, as a teacher, and as a concerned electronic citizen, I wondered if I had the *obligation* to say something. Like a good sophist I found compelling arguments for both sides. I decided to wait (sophists end up doing a lot of waiting, the problem with having an overdeveloped sense of irony) to see if the teacher or others in the class would do anything, thinking that my position as an outsider and possibly an intruder made my *ethos* in the matter suspect. Clearly it would be preferable if the teacher responded, or the women in the class. Being a white male faculty member further disabled me: Would this be an unfair use of power? The big faculty bully coming in to lay the law down to students and a graduate teaching assistant? Or worse, white knight syndrome—that is, hero knight saving damsel in distress—not roles I coveted.

Could this constitute interference on my part with the teacher's authority in the class? (I decided that this would not be a particular problem with *this* teacher, as he and I had participated on each other's class discussions before. It would be with others.) Could my intruding in the group create a chilling effect on the discussion? (Well, actually, I did want to have a chilling effect on blonde jokes.)

Partly my response to the case was situated in the material fact that this was a newsgroup rather than a LISTSERV or other more private electronic forum. A newsgroup is a relatively public forum (it does not have a subscribed membership as such). It is a more free-wheeling forum. Its membership is not closed or private. Given its more public nature, I would say that comments from those outside the class are far more appropriate than they would be on a LISTSERV class group where I might be an invited member.

I waited two days, but since no one else responded to the jokes, I decided to.

Part of figuring out *whether* to become involved is related to deliberations about *what* to say and *how*. How do I construct myself and my relations with the others in the newsgroup? Do I identify myself as a Purdue faculty member—or simply respond as a reader? Do I give a long and elaborate apology, post a rude flame, or give a short personal reaction?

I finally posted a two-sentence remark that did not identify me as a faculty member, saying in effect that I thought the jokes were not harmless fun, but were rather an instance of promoting an unfair stereotype. I said that the jokes were offensive and "demeaning" and that others might think so, too, particularly women.

At this point two things happened, one of them predictable, one of them perhaps not. In response to my implied advice to "get a sense of audience," the student replied back with a post that said, in effect, "get a sense of humor." (I decided to let that one pass—but I was also relieved: I need not have worried about intimidating anyone with my writing.) Then, a woman in the class wrote to me privately thanking me for saying something because it encouraged her to post something to the newsgroup, which she did a day later, telling the joke poster that his message made the class environment less comfortable for her. After this point, there was no further response or discussion of the issue on the newsgroup, and no further blonde jokes. Discussion moved in other directions.

My guess about this incident is that the computer science student had learned a style of locker-room conversation from his male peers that was also probably reinforced on the mostly male technology newsgroups he inhabited. He carried this style into a forum where there were women (surprise), and he did not think carefully enough about a basic rhetorical/ethical principle—"know your readers, and respect them"—or else he just did not care. Should his email account be revoked? Of course not. Should he be ignored? No, because ignoring such acts constitutes tacit approval of them. Should he be challenged? Yes, I strongly believe so. Here is an instance that points up the difference between ludic post-modernism (which would have a hard time justifying any such intervention) and the postmodern *commitment,* which I am advocating—which is not "rule bound," but which does make some attempt to construct a negotiated position considering the competing ethical principles and rules that comprise the situation.

Should I have spoken at all? Am I guilty in this instance of what Spivak (1988) cautions against as an act of imperialism: white men saving women from other men. Well, perhaps. But then I am a white man. What am I supposed to do? Silence is tacit approval, collusion; speech is imperialism. Take your pick.

To see this as an either-or choice is to simplify the rhetoric of the scene. Rhetoric points out in the first instance that there are different ways to speak and different forms of silence. The *how* is complicated. Looking at the scene from a rhetorical frame (something Spivak does not do) can be helpful here. There is a way in which effecting political action/change in this scenario calls for a man speaking to other men. Would the oppressor males even hear the lone female student voice? Cannot a man speaking to other men make some difference here? It might perhaps take someone from within the oppressor group to effect the change—or at least to serve as a catalyst for eventual change. The oppressor group will not see or hear the subaltern speaking. As a stage in a process of change it might require an insider "speaking for" the subaltern. Spivak dismisses such a subject position out of hand (in her critique of Foucault, for instance). But I am suggesting here that such a subject position might serve a pragmatic purpose, might in fact be required as a stage in a process of change.

CASE 2: FREE SPEECH ON THE LISTSERV GROUP

In the early 1990s, Paul Trummel was infamous on LISTSERV groups in rhetoric and professional writing for distributing an online publication, CONTRA CABAL, in which he excoriated a rhetoric/writing doctoral program he was formerly enrolled in. He accused administrators at the university of gross malfeasance and the faculty of drunkenness. He argued that this program trampled on his rights as a student—and has continued to threaten his right to free speech, by which Trummel meant his right to distribute electronic attacks on the program.

The ethical issue of interest to me is not Trummel's grievance against his former program, but rather his insistence on posting CONTRA CABAL to numerous electronic groups in rhetoric and professional writing, even though these groups have made it clear to Trummel that they are not interested in his postings and do not see CONTRA CABAL as relevant to the themes and topics defining the groups. However, if a particular LISTSERV group does not exercise an editorial screening of messages—and many do not—then there is nothing from preventing Trummel's postings from going out to all members of the list. Trummel can be refused as a subscriber, but he can still post to these lists.

A consensus that seems to be emerging on the nets and in discussions of network freedoms is that indiscriminate "mondo posting" is unethical and should be discouraged, if not disallowed. The "Yahweh is God" message, which went out to thousands of lists in 1993, is one example. An advertisement for replacements for the pentium chip (posted in 1994) is yet another. Generic messages, advertisements, lists of jokes, and off-topic stupidities waste bandwidth—and are clear examples of unethical mondo posting.

Do Trummel's postings fall into the same category? From one viewpoint, they are slanderous and unsupported attacks that damage the reputation of a university. However, Trummel casts these attacks in the form of a political questioning of an entire set of academic and institutional practices, representing them as a set of secret and powerful efforts to defraud students and taxpayers. Trummel's postings are not "mondo" in one sense, they are directed specifically at rhetoric and writing groups.

CONTRA CABAL is clearly unwanted on most of these groups, and the question is: What should the response to this be? Some LISTSERV administrators complained to the systems administrators of the university to which Trummel transferred to see if his activities violated that university's acceptable use policy. (Apparently they did not because the university was unwilling to act in the matter.) Other LISTSERV owners wrote Trummel personal messages asking for his cooperation: In one case, the manager said that Trummel could certainly advertise CONTRA CABAL on the group, but she asked him to please stop posting it directly to the group. None of these avenues effected any change: In 1994 and 1995, Trummel continued to post CONTRA CABAL.

The rhetorical and pragmatic viewpoint I am developing here would not begin by invoking a rights First Principle—such as "free speech" or "the good of the community"—to be applied algorithmically as a formula to solve the problem; rather, it would begin by looking at the rhetorical and technological circumstances of the case. It is not possible for LISTSERV listowners to stop Trummel from posting to their lists unless they are willing to implement an editorial screening procedure. Personally, then, I would advise LISTSERV owners to balance the furor over and inconvenience of Trummel's postings versus the trouble involved in setting up editorial screening. Editorial screening of messages will also have the side-effect of changing the personality and dynamic of the list: No matter how quickly the editor works, the spontaneity of postings will be lost.

How much trouble is Trummel? That is a question that can only be answered in terms of specific lists. Trummel posts to several lists of which I am a member: His postings might amount to one per month per list, but the postings by other members protesting his postings frequently quadruple that. (There are no doubt numerous personal postings to the LISTSERV moderator as well; see Howard, 1992, 1993.) LISTSERV managers have to balance the trouble of Trummel's presence against the trouble of ridding the list of CONTRA CABAL.

The response to the question of what to do is also determined by one's particular role in the case. A LISTSERV manager has a certain obligation to the members of the list: to serve their interests. He or she also has some obligation to protect innocent parties from unwarranted attacks. (Legally, of course, the LISTSERV manager might also incur some liability for libel.) Yet the issue for any LISTSERV manager in this case is to balance the needs of the many and the few. What if the desires of the many threaten the legitimate rights of a single member?

What if I am not the LISTSERV manager, but am simply a participant on the list? Should I write a message of complaint or stew quietly at home? At what point do I decide that I should write something? And if I decide to write, to whom? If Trummel's lengthy messages cost me download time, then I am likely to take a far less tolerant view of unwanted mail. I could write a private note of complaint to the list manager or to the systems administrator at Trummel's home university. I could write a private note to Trummel. I could write a public note to the entire list. (I could write a book using the Trummel case as a case involving the ethics of electronic writing.) The choice of whether to write, and where to post it, is part of the rhetorical ethics of the situation. What if I am a faculty member at the university that Trummel attacks? Should I defend my program and myself against his unfair assaults? Or would such an act simply call further attention to Trummel's slanders—and perhaps even serve to instantiate his self-proclaimed status as victim? Is ignoring him the best policy?

There are different writing roles and relations vis-à-vis Trummel and distinct members of particular lists. A "one-size-fits-all" approach to network ethics fails to account for the distinctness of these particular roles and relations. A rhetorical ethics *begins* with this distinctness, with the differences in rhetorical situations—that is, with the particular alignment of sites, writers, and readers.

Complaining to the list compounds Trummel's off-topic postings by adding more off-topic postings. Writing Trummel himself would seem to be a reasonable ethical starting place, as the one LISTSERV manager realized. That response gives Trummel the benefit of the doubt and asks for cooperation (rather than merely demanding it or expecting it). It is a response that assumes a dialogic ethic of caring, that is, it respects the personhood of the Other, essentially by turning the Other (the interloper, the intruder, the irritant on the list) into a Thou. The strategy apparently did not work in this instance, but that is not to criticize the strategy as a starting point for rhetorical/ethical inquiry.

CASE 3: HARASSMENT IN CYBERSPACE

Let us up the stakes a bit. Let us look at what might be the most famous piece of electronic student writing ever: the story written by University of Michigan student Jake Baker and posted on January 9, 1995, on the Internet newsgroup alt.sex.stories. Baker's story described in vivid detail the torture of a woman with a hot curling iron and her mutilation and sodomization while gagged to a chair (Lewis, 1995a).

The story itself would have probably passed into oblivion, but for two extenuating circumstances: (a) the woman's name in the story was the same as that of a University of Michigan woman who was in one of Baker's classes—and her name was actually used in the subject line of the posting; and (b) in an email exchange with a virtual friend, "Arthur Gonda" (whom authorities were unable to locate), Baker said that he was ready to "really" do what he describes in the story, that writing about it was not good enough anymore. These two points moved the story out of the realm of fiction—at least as interpreted by the courts and by the University.

For this offense, Baker was jailed and held without bond for 29 days, charged with the federal crime of transporting threatening material across state lines (because Internet postings cross state lines). He was also expelled by the University of Michigan (Branam, 1995; Branam & Bridgeforth, 1995).

After Baker was released from jail, the government dropped the charges related to his writing the fantasy story on alt.sex.stories. The prosecution's case against Baker will be based entirely on the e-mail exchange with "Arthur Gonda," which, they will argue, constitutes a specific threat (Cain, 1995).

Baker's defense lawyer tried to present his client's position in these terms: Big Government and a Powerful State University are in collusion to censor the individual expression of an individual. Baker's lawyer calls the story and the email exchange with Gonda as simply a "fantasy," the act of an "active imagination." The ACLU and the Electronic Frontier Foundation are defending Baker's writing as a type "acceptable under the community standards" of alt.sex.stories (Lewis, 1995a; see Shade, 1996).

We can look at Baker's original act in another light. Catharine MacKinnon sees his rape/torture fantasy as *itself* an act of aggression and intimidation against women as well as against a particular woman (the University of Michigan student whose name Baker used in the story). From this view, the law's entrance is not designed to stifle an individual, but rather to protect a student who is also a member of a group that has been historically marginalized.

The legal judgment in such a case has to consider the degree of harm involved (in this case, how much aggression? how much intimidation? how likely is the suspect to commit the acts he describes in his story?). Aside from that determination, MacKinnon would argue that the act itself constitutes a harm: The posting is not "only words," but is itself an act of aggression. The First Amendment is not a First Principle: It is rather one principle to be balanced against many others and to be applied with consideration of the particular circumstances that comprise each and every case (including the relational status of the parties involved).

I believe, based on what I have read about the case, that Jake Baker did not understand the complexity of his writing situation—and this is an indictment of an educational system that never helped him to understand it. Baker did not understand that writing has *force*, that it has the capacity for harm, and that his writing mattered in a way that he could not imagine *for readers* that he did not think about. He is rhetorically and ethically illiterate, although maybe after his 29 days in jail that is no longer true.

A mitigating circumstance in the case is that the story he wrote was well within the standards of the electronic community he inhabited. Part of his ethical illiteracy, however, was not recognizing that such a newsgroup is not a closed and isolated community. What he posts there is public: It can be read by people not in agreement with community standards; it can be copied and reposted in communities with a less tolerant view of his writing; and it has real implications for people outside that closed community. This failure to be aware of "audience," his failure to understand the rhetorical dynamic of the technology; and his blurring of the fiction/nonfiction boundary are all components of his particular brand of ethical illiteracy. (In fact, the Internet and the World Wide Web may blow apart the entire notion of a selective audience; although electronic documents might *address* one or another particular audience, in terms of distribution potential, anyone with Internet access could potentially read the posting. In other words, the vast distribution potential of the electronic network poses something of a problem for print notions of audience, which tend to be more exclusive constructs tied to more limited distribution potential.)

In *Only Words* (1993), Catharine MacKinnon points out that the First Amendment was originally developed to protect the powerless from the powerful (the U.S. government or Government generally). Increasingly, the First Amendment is being used in defense of continued discrimination against the less powerful, as both MacKinnon (1993) and Stanley Fish (1994) have noted.

MacKinnon implies that the free speech principle should have built into it a preferential option for the marginalized. That is, it should allow the marginalized, oppressed, or silenced a chance to speak against the majority, the dominant, the hegemonic, but it should not be applied to further discrimination against the marginalized, oppressed, and silenced (p. 39). In any particular case, of course, one has to determine the degree of possible harm to those involved. Usually it is the weaker, the oppressed, and the marginalized who bear the greater burden of risk in such cases—although not always. (Acts of terrorism—for instance, the bombing of the federal building in Oklahoma City—show quite vividly how any individual or small group can, through an act of ultimate extremity, cause some harm to the more powerful. The futility of such acts, however, is that the terrorist attempt to harm the powerful usually ends up harming individuals while leaving the system of domination intact.) Essentially, MacKinnon is urging us toward a kind of affirmative action ethic in such cases.

The other implication—more mine than that of MacKinnon—is that the First Amendment is not a rule, but a principle to be applied heuristically. Yes, it represents a deeply held value—but in any given case it may conflict with other deeply held values, in which case some kind of careful judgment is necessary. (MacKinnon argues that in cases such as Baker's, the First and Fourteenth Amendment, which mandates equal protection for all citizens, ought to be placed in a kind of binary tension—although the courts typically do not do that.)

The Electronic Frontier Foundation takes the position that all network discourse should absolutely be protected by the First Amendment (Rheingold, 1994). I consider this as a presumptive position, but they advocate it as an absolute rule. To advocate such a position is, to me, to underestimate the power of an individual's use of language, its capacity to do harm, and, especially on electronic networks, its capacity to shut down communities. Yes, the presumption lies with the individual because the individual is usually the weaker entity, but the controversy of the position I am advocating is that it says that in some situations it is the community that needs protection (Riddle, 1990).

There is yet another position that says that teachers are responsible for promoting, and maybe even legislating, ethical writing practices. Should not respect for audience be a requirement of "good" writing?

TOWARD A CRITICAL RHETORICAL ETHICS

So what are we left with? Where is this critical rhetorical ethics of internetworked writing?

Developing his theory out of the framework of liberation theology (a frame of reference he shares in common with Paulo Freire, 1970/1993), Enrique Dussel (1988) draws a sharp distinction between the legal and the ethical. He sees the legal as representing the minimal norms of behavior established by the consensus of society. These norms are by no means adequate in guiding human action because the consensus of society can be, and often is, oppressive, stultifying, unfair, and just plain wrong. Do not look for morality in inscribed law, in the social order, in majority consensus, or in governmental strictures and institutions (Althusser, 1971). Dussel, instead, argues the necessity of developing an ethical/ moral counterauthority, which is necessary to critique social norms and conventions as established through law. This counterauthority is, for Dussel, a higher authority—and no resistance is possible without the existence of some ethic that provides criteria for challenging the domination of law. Maybe U.S. law grants you the right to read your employees' private e-mail and electronic files under the aegis of system administration. That does not mean it is ethical to do so.

The cyberwriter must negotiate a position among at least two competing frames. One frame, the legal frame, derives chiefly from a world of modernist assumptions and print expectations. In saying this I do not want to suggest that this world has no value, is impotent, or can be safely ignored—hardly. This set of assumptions constantly insists on affirming its value and its power (if not domination) over the realm of electronic discourse. It is a force to be reckoned with.

Yet it might also be a force to be resisted. A second frame, what I am constructing as a rhetorical ethics for internetworked writing, is a set of assumptions and practices that constitute a kind of cyberspace common law whose contours we can only dimly see. To negotiate this second frame, I am suggesting that the cyberwriter must develop a *critical rhetoric* that is also an ethical rhetoric. I am calling for an electronic ethics, a critical positioning that serves as a place for critique of the dominant legal realm. But what is meant by a *critical* rhetorical ethic (Porter, 1997)?

When I use the term *critical* I am invoking Horkheimer's distinction between critical and traditional theory. Horkheimer (1972) criticizes the traditional approach to theory because it *decontextualizes* (Feenberg, 1991), it separates knowledge and action in the pursuit of knowledge for its own sake. Critical theory, on the contrary, articulates a liberatory aim—"emancipation from slavery" (Horkheimer, 1972, p. 246). Critical theory *contextualizes*, considering the relationship of the individual to the society in terms of a situated web of relations, including historical factors, the system of labor and production involved, and the class implications of such relations (Deetz, 1994; Geuss, 1981; Hoy & McCarthy, 1994; Luke, 1991; Poster, 1989; Simons & Billig, 1994).

In invoking the term *critical* I am invoking a particular tradition—that of the Frankfurt School—but Patricia Sullivan and I (Porter, 1996; Porter & Sullivan, 1996; Sullivan & Porter, 1997) are moving toward a version of *critical* that merges more conventional critical theory with several other areas: the social postmodernism of Foucault (1979, 1984a, 1984b), postmodern geography (e.g., Soja, 1989; Sullivan & Porter, 1993a), and feminist theory, especially as regards methodology (e.g., Lather, 1991; Stanley, 1990a, 1990b; Stanley & Wise, 1990) and ethics (e.g., Benhabib, 1992; Card, 1991; Young, 1990). Of course, "critical" does not simply mean attack, negative commentary, undermining, or ludic deconstruction of, but critical in the sense of critical reflection on, challenge, and then positive action. It is closer to what Lather (1992), Ebert (1991), and others have referred to as "resistance postmodernism." It may, in fact, be more appropriately described as "postcritical" (Lather, 1992; see also Luke & Gore, 1992).

This rhetorical ethics borrows from diverse theoretical positions, including critical Marxism (Feenberg, 1991), feminist communicative action (Benhabib, 1992; Young, 1990), and rhetorical casuistry (Jonsen & Toulmin, 1988). This ethic focuses particularly on ethics as situated praxis, as central to human relations, and as particularly sensitive to the role of rhetoric (and language) in determining ethical action. It is an ethic of situated relations, that is, of situated rhetorical relations and of composing processes. It draws on both feminist and neopragmatic discussions in focusing on ethics as a rhetorical process and on rhetoric as an ethical process of constituting relations given the spatial and material conditions that define power

The realm of cyberspace can become a realm of domination, unless writers are willing to adopt the role of "cyborgs" (Haraway, 1991) and resist the rigid formulation of legal realities. Timothy Luke (1991) calls for a critical theory that "must be essentially reflective, reflexive and ironic rather than positive, objective and methodologically formalistic" (p. 21). The goal of this critical theory is "human emancipation." Luke uses this theory to articulate a critical agenda for cyberwriters:

> Power in hyperreality derives from controlling the means of simulation, dominating the codes of representation, and managing the signs of meaning that constitute what hyperreality is taken as being at any particular time. By setting the limits of what is hyperreal, and therefore at least temporarily "real," the managers of media, movements, and displays can set agendas, determine loyalties, frame conflicts, and limit challenges to the prevailing organization of what is or is not taken as being real. (p. 20)

The central aim of critical rhetoric is clear: It posits as its goals liberation of the oppressed (Dussel, 1988; Freire, 1970/1993); improved communicative relations (Habermas, 1990); the improvement of social conditions, including the quality of work life (Zuboff, 1988); and, in academic contexts, the improvement of learning conditions. For cyberwriters, this critical rhetoric translates into an ethic of advocacy for one's electronic audiences—users, browsers, electronic readers—that aims to improve their conditions of learning and ease their conditions of oppression or dominance within institutional settings (see Cushman, 1996; Kleinman, 1995).

Critical rhetorical ethics has several emphases: First, the dominant views of writing have tended to see writing as mainly or only a product, that is, a text that floats in cyberspace. The first step in taking a critical point of view is to recognize writing as a social action with legal and ethical implications. It is a doing as well as a making. So critical rhetoric is conscious of how acts of writing constitute acts of *power* within an already dynamic set of power relations; it raises the political and ethical questions pertaining to the nature of power relations: To whose benefit am I working/writing? To whose advantage/disadvantage?

Second, critical theory reminds us that writing resides in an economic system (Eagleton, 1976). Writing is a commodity, and U.S. law seems to be increasingly viewing writing, and especially internetworked cyberwriting, as *private property to be protected*, rather than as *social resource to be shared and distributed* and, therefore, as a *means of enabling broader, more active citizen participation*.

Third, critical theory points to the necessity of "rhetoricizing" one's writing actions, understanding them as situated in a network of human relations involving multiple writers and multiple readers engaged in overlapping communities of discourse. It is politically dangerous to hold to a simplified view of the writing process as I Writer producing My Text to be read by You Reader. It is dangerous, especially in cyberspace writing, to presume that your writing will have a limited and well-defined audience. (When Jake Baker was indicted for posting a pornographic story on the newsgroup alt.sex.stories, his story was "appropriate" given the standards and conventions of that newsgroup; however, what he failed to appreciate was that a newsgroup, although existing as a community with its own standards, is not totally sealed off from other communities, including the U.S. legal community.)

"Being rhetorical" means attending to situated contextual features that form, maintain, and constrain discursive relations, such as examining one's position as a participant in a network of relations in which the goals of liberation and freedom must be situationally negotiated through discourse; recognizing the role of power in human relations (including but by no means limited to the variables of class, gender, sexual orientation, race, economics, and labor status); and acknowledging the role of technologies, institutions, disciplines, and other modes of system and production in constituting and constraining human relations.

THE SECOND CYBERNETIC AND WRITING THE INTERFACE

On a daily basis, the cyberwriter will be working at the point of the technological interface, working *at* the interface and also working *at the design* of interfaces. By *interface* I am not talking about screen design elements only (trash cans and such), but rather larger space (what Foucault, 1986b, might call a heterotopia) in which the screen intersects with situated uses of the technology in the classroom, community, and workplace—a contextualized interface, in other words.

Unlike the rationalist and systems-oriented approach, a critical approach to cyberwriting is against viewing computer technology in a detached, decontextualized way and in favor of seeing technology as created by, situated in, and constitutive of basic human relations. This critical view of technology is affiliated with the so-called "second cybernetic," a philosophical movement in computer theory that "looks at the world [and technology] from the standpoint of the involved subject rather than from that of the external observer" (Feenberg, 1991, p. 106; see also Johnson-Eilola, 1995; Lyytinen, 1992; Suchman, 1987; Winograd, 1995; Winograd & Flores, 1986). It sees technology not as abstracted or decontextualized systems, but rather as involving real people using human-designed machines for situated purposes.

Andrew Feenberg (1991) is one of the leading theorists of this second cybernetic. Feenberg's "critical theory of technology" aims to counter the modernist notion of technology that ends up installing in technology "the values and interests of ruling classes and elites" (p. 14). Far from seeing technology as a neutral tool (which the rationalist supposes) or as inherently bad (which the Romantic "substantist" supposes), Feenberg argues for viewing the tool in its context of design and use. He rejects the decontextualizing move of High Theory and philosophy toward formal abstraction and offers instead the contextualizing move of critical theory, which historicizes, situates, and personalizes technology: "Critical theory shatters the illusion [of neutrality] by recovering the lost contexts and developing a historically concrete understanding of technology" (p. 181). (For a fuller discussion of Feenberg's critical theory, see Sullivan and Porter, 1997, Chap. 5.)

Feenberg's theory is affirmed by Zuboff's (1988) distinction between uses of technology that "informate" versus those that "automate." Automation "displace[s] the human presence" (p. 10) by computerizing activities in a way that either eliminates the human presence altogether or reduces it to a lesser status (cognitively, institutionally) in some production process. However, computer technology that "informates" enhances the status of the human presence in the production process, perhaps by engaging people in new ways or by allowing them to collect new types of information or in some cases actually producing a new "quality of information" (p. 10). Informating "sets into motion a series of dynamics that will ultimately reconfigure the nature of work and the social relationships that organize productive activity" (p. 10–11). Thus, Zuboff's distinction calls attention to the importance of social relations in network space. She says that better relations, enhanced status for workers, should be the primary goal of technology applications in the workplace (i.e., as opposed to reducing worker status or eliminating workers altogether). Zuboff's goal of informating provides a criterion for cyberwriters who are developing interface designs and web sites.

Selfe and Selfe's (1994) study of "The Politics of the Interface" is an example of research that applies critical theory directly to interface design. Their study articulates a clear agenda for technological change in the direction of liberating users. They notice, for instance, that the Macintosh interface, which represents the virtual world in terms of a desktop metaphor, presents "reality as framed in the perspective of modern capitalism, thus, orienting technology along an existing axis of class privilege" (p. 486). Furthermore, they note how this metaphor aligns with "the axes of class, race, and gender" (p. 487). Entry in this interface signals to users that they are entering a certain world, and that to attain the power that this world represents requires adopting the "values of white, male, middle- and upper-class professionals" (p. 487). The hypothesis that Selfe and Selfe develop is that computer interfaces are not neutral, but assert cultural value and in so doing practice a power.

Selfe and Selfe are speaking to teachers, but their call applies to cyberwriters as well: They want teachers and writers to move in the direction of influencing the design of computer spaces, certainly the design of the screen, but also the design of computer classrooms, workspaces, and other technological arrangements. In this respect, their political agenda instantiates the proactive goals of the second cybernetic, which calls for more active advocacy of users (see Johnson-Eilola, 1996; Kleinman, 1995; Mirel, 1996). A critical rhetorical ethic calls for writers to take a direct stand in constructing a less oppressive and more liberated electronic network.

7

Framing Postmodern Commitment and Solidarity

> I am arguing for politics and epistemologies of location, positioning, and situating, where partiality and not universality is the condition of being heard to make rational knowledge claims.
> —Haraway, 1991, p. 195

The position I am developing is a postmodern pragmatic one that involves a lot of deliberation and balancing of competing perspectives. You might consider it a kind of neo-Aristotelian brand of postmodernism because of its revival of *phronesis* as an important faculty of the art of rhetoric—and yet it is also very much sophistic. I am less interested, however, in naming it than I am in describing its operation.

This rhetorical ethics begins by seeing values and language use as inextricably bound. It sees writing as an act fraught with ethical issues. The stance I am advocating is respectful of law, but does not see law as a determining or ultimate authority. It puts a high value on community customs, conventions, and beliefs (*nomoi*), but recognizes that communities can be wrong, hegemonic, or oppressive. It puts a high value on the right of individual free expression and the importance of protecting that right, but also notes that individuals can wreck havoc on communities, and that, ultimately, the individual is not a very solid or trustworthy ground for moral authority. It places a high value on the spirit of caring, of brotherly and sisterly love, of friendship—of a number of related principles that have status in numerous religious and cultural traditions, which we might sum up with the phrase "love and respect for others" (although that notion admits to a wide range of interpretations). It assigns a preferential option for the poor, oppressed, and marginalized, saying in effect that any ethical system based mainly on the principle of operative equality will fail to account for systemic inequities and, thus, will risk perpetuating those inequities. It places a high value on involvement and collaboration with others (and with The Other) and on developing moral positions within a collaborative and cooperative framework of dialogue. It places a high value on deliberation (a key principle in Aristotle's [1976] *Nicomachean Ethics*), the importance of carefully considering each situation in an antilogical manner before pushing ahead. It places a high value on action: Deliberation is necessary, but to overindulge in it is to defer action and, ultimately, to freeze oneself into inaction. It stresses the operation of *phronesis*, the quality of being able to determine what one should do, how one should act, and what one should be even when the circumstances are murky, the issues complex, and the right action hard to determine. It places a high value on the constraints of the particular case.

A list of counterprinciples is not very satisfying, I realize, because such an approach does not generate clear and concrete answers to pressing problems. What it does is suggest a process by which problems might be addressed. It does suggest some key principles one should bring to bear on rhetorical/ethical problems, as suggested earlier. It does not, however, tell us which principle ought to control a decision in any given case or how to reconcile opposing principles. It does suggest criteria for judging the process—and in that sense is Habermasian.

The whole point of my position is that we should not attempt to develop a moral geometry—a scientific, rigorous, rules-based approach to settling ethical decisions. In this respect, my rhetorical ethics differs sharply from the approach of Kantian-type ethical theories (like Rawls', 1971). My approach is closer to Aristotle's in its insistence on the necessity of developing "the art of moral judgment" (Benhabib, 1992, p. 53). This art of moral judgment requires a strong sense of values and priorities and principles, but does not leverage those values and priorities in a top-down, rules-oriented procedure. It places a high value on reflection, deliberation, and "theorizing," but does not place much value in Theory, as the abstract formulation of determining rules and principles. Rather, it places values and priorities into a heuristic tension (a) with competing values and priorities, and (b) with the concrete particulars of ethical and rhetorical situations involving real people and particular technologies.

My approach is also an effort to develop a procedural heuristic that will assist the rhetorical ethical *process*, that is, that will help writers and writing teachers in the act(s) of producing discourse. Too often ethical systems of the philosophical sort fall into a backward-looking hermeneutic rut: they focus too much on post facto moral justification (or critique) of past action and do not provide us with much help figuring out what to do *now* as we write *today*. When one writes, one decides. Writing is an action involving an ethical choice about what one is to be and what one is to do. At the point when you begin to write, you begin to define yourself ethically. You make a choice about what is the right thing to do—even if that choice is a tentative and contingent one.

As I argued earlier (in Chapters 2 and 3), adopting this point of view requires seeing rhetoric *as* both productive and practical art, not merely as one or the other. It requires seeing rhetoric and ethics as distinct yet also overlapping arts. Writing is not only a making (*poesis*), but it is also a doing (*praxis*). Writing is an action with ethical and political consequences. Writing is a praxis that is both an act and a relationship (Dussel, 1988), that is, it does something to someone, one part of which is establishing power relations (e.g., between writers and readers, among various audiences).

Paulo Freire (1970/1993) echoes this important point as well in his description of the two dimensions of the word: reflection and action. He argues that:

> When a word is deprived of its dimension of action, reflection automatically suffers as well; and the word is changed into idle chatter, into *verbalism*, into an alienated and alienating "blah." It becomes an empty word, one which cannot denounce the world, for denunciation is impossible without a commitment to transform, and there is no transformation without action. (p. 68, emphasis in original)

The view of language and writing as *poesis* only ("verbalism") renders language into impotent, "idle chatter." Viewing language and writing as also action allows for commitment and transformation. The praxis that my rhetorical ethics promotes is the coordinated and dialogic view that Freire espouses: viewing the full capacity of language/writing as both reflection and action in dialogic tension, as both a making and a doing.

So what does all this mean on an operational level? I mention now several procedural principles that I see deriving from this approach. Despite the many deep and murky ethical problems we seem to face on electronic networks, we can cull some principles and advance some arguments for a critical rhetorical ethics for internetworked writing, that is, we can make some positive statements about how one ought to act as a writer (and secondarily as a reader). I divide these principles into two categories: writer posture toward audience and procedural strategies.

The question of whether these principles do, or should, have any legal force is a legal question that I do not address here—although, of course, several of the discussions here have become intertwined with legal issues. The ethical cannot ignore the legal, nor the legal the ethical.

THE WRITER'S RELATIONAL FOOTING VIS-À-VIS AUDIENCES/READERS

Respect Audience/Respect Differences

If there is a single main principle of postmodern ethics, it is probably this— acknowledge differences. Postmodernism's primary critique of modernism is that in its move to rationality, impartiality, and objectivity, modernism obscures difference, and difference as an operating principle is seen by many postmodernists as fundamental. Show respect for—care for—others. Respect their differences. Heed the values of your audience, both the values of the community/culture at large and the differences among individual audience members.

What do we mean by "audience"? The postmodern injunction to show respect for difference extends beyond audience in the limited sense (that is, those whom one directly addresses in a discourse) to pertain to all those who are represented in or affected by such discourse as well. Audience in this broader sense refers to an entire community, not simply to a physical flesh-and-blood assemblage, not simply to the evident or immediate readers or listeners of a discourse (see Porter, 1992a). When we start thinking about the vastness and diversity of the potential audience(s) involved in the Internet and World-Wide Web, then we can see that internetworked writing poses a challenge for conventional (and more constrained) print notions of audience.

A postmodern rhetorical ethics says that differences among audiences must not be obliterated. Distinct identities must be recognized. In a moral discourse readers should not be treated as an homogenous whole or as if they were all members of a universal collective. Difference must be respected, but we should move beyond merely "respect" for difference, which could be seen to promote a kind of distant, begrudging tolerance. Luce Irigaray (1984/1993) suggests that we should move actively to *embrace* difference and to *celebrate* it, and that we should certainly be in awe of the mystery of difference. When I was first joining academic LISTSERV groups in the late 1980s, I remember how such groups had to adjust to the presence of "outsiders," that is, people from other fields and disciplines would frequently participate in such groups and would occasionally invite the ire of the "insiders" by doing so. The insiders in the field would sometimes wave the flag of disciplinary expertise as a way to stifle the contribution of those contributing other viewpoints or working out of alternate disciplinary paradigms. (For example, sometimes lawyers on the CNI-COPYRIGHT group would express impatience with the nonlawyers. One speech communication theorist on the IPCT list, Interpersonal Computing Technology, would trot out his academic credentials whenever the discussion was threatened by a nonacademic viewpoint.) What I have noticed more recently, at least in the academic electronic groups I belong to, is that there is greater tolerance for disciplinary difference and often even an appreciation for multidisciplinary difference. I cannot say, however, that such a respect for difference extends much beyond academic notions of multidisciplinarity.

The importance of differences among audiences is a key, although seldom discussed, principle in Aristotle's *Rhetoric*. Yes, Aristotle's conception of audience is exclusively male, but what Aristotle builds into his art is the essential fact of difference: Considering differences between audience types (e.g., age, gifts of fortune, emotional disposition) is a crucial part of the art (Book 2). Unless the rhetor knows quite specifically the various characters and positions of his audience, he cannot begin to understand how to talk to them. Furthermore, Aristotle posits that rhetorical argument begins with audience belief, the basis for enthymemic reasoning. So in this sense, respect for audience standpoint is integral to Aristotle's conception of the art.

Irigaray (1984/1993) provides a direct critique of Aristotle's sexual monism. In her deconstruction of Aristotle's *Physics* (in *An Ethics of Sexual Difference*), she argues for physical sexual difference as the foundational ground for ethics. Both Irigaray (1984/1993) and Iris Marion Young (1990) point to difference as a foundational principle. For Irigaray, sexual difference is the foundation of a relational ethics. For Young, acceptance of the validity of differences among social groups must be the basis for political justice. Irigaray and Young both point to how traditional philosophy—or what Young calls "normative social philosophy and political theory" (p. 149)—has worked to obscure difference. The result of such an obfuscation is domination by a privileged group that hides its "groupness" (e.g., whiteness, masculinity) under the coordinated claims of objectivity, impartiality, neutrality, and universality. The first step, then, in achieving political or ethical justice is the process of acknowledging differences, including exposing the hidden or obscured differences that often end up dominating. The critical turn that Young makes is to view differences not as undesirable, or alien, or the Other (p. 170), not as the subordinate second term of a deconstructed binary, but as a value in its own right—that is, as "specificity, variation, heterogeneity" (p. 171). The turn Irigaray makes is a theological one: Embracing and celebrating difference brings us to a transcendent spirituality.

Charles Scott (1990) reminds us of the importance of being "alert to exclusions and to forgotten aspects in a people's history" (p. 7). Our uses of discourse must work to insure that the values we invoke do not drown out alternative voices. Thus, a critical rhetorical ethic does more than merely "respect" audience in a passive or detached way. It works to liberate the Other by naming and making space for that which is taken for granted or "routinely excluded and silenced" (p. 8).

Care for Audience/Care for Concrete Other (Versus Generalized Other)

In Book 2 of *Rhetoric*, Aristotle introduces several characteristics of speakers/writers as ethical principles. These are especially powerful principles, as Aristotle articulates them, because they combine *ethos* and *pathos*: They are feelings as well as elements of character. Aristotle emphasizes the importance of expressing kindliness, of having good feeling toward others (*karis*) (see Grimaldi, 1988, pp. 127–128). Also important is entering discursive relations in a spirit of friendship and mutual caring (*philos*) as well as a generosity of spirit (*caritas*). Cicero (1942) pushes "respect" for audience even further, into the realm of emotional and psychological commitment, into what we might consider the realm of *caring* for audience (*De Oratore*, 2.44.189). We see the principle of "commitment to other" as a principle in Greek culture as well as classical rhetoric. The "guest friend" relationship is an important ethic, perhaps the most important, in Greek tragedy: The principle says that as host or hostess you have a sacred duty to protect and care for the Other, the visiting alien. In Greek tragedy, violating this ethic leads to war, death, destruction, and chaos. (Usually only the intervention of the gods, *deus ex machina*, can restore order.) If we think about such a principle as applied to the management of LISTSERV groups, we can see that it would call the listowner to take on some responsibility, as host or hostess, for those "guests" participating in any particular electronic community.

The caring ethic, as we saw in Chapter 4, gets its most thorough treatment in the feminist ethical articulations of Nel Noddings (1984) and Carol Gilligan (1993), who view the ethical stance of the "caring one" as a distinctly feminist position that has been historically subordinated to the masculine deontological and abstract ethic of rights. Rather than viewing abstractness and impartiality as the revered characteristics of the ethical stance, the caring ethic views personal and emotional concern for the distinct person as a superior ethical posture.

In her critique of the abstract impartiality of Habermas's discourse ethic, Benhabib (1992) stresses this point in particular. One must avoid "generalizing the other," but must engage the concrete and particular features of one's audience, who is actually "there," as far as that can be determined (although that becomes particularly difficult in electronic discourse): "The standpoint of the concrete other . . . requires us to view each and every rational being as an individual with a concrete history, identity and affective-emotional constitution" (p. 159). Stereotyping of audience differences—for example, referring to "women" as a political or social collective—is what Benhabib means by treating the other as a generalized type (see hooks, 1990; Rorty, 1991). Benhabib critiques Habermas's discourse ethic for not stressing the importance of "the concrete moral self" (p. 146). Similarly, Feenberg (1991) sees the kind of formal abstraction represented by Habermas's ethic as too remote, both from specific material technological settings as well as from the experiences and identities of real people.

We see a theological take on this principle expressed in liberation theology. The ultimate sin, according to liberation theologian Enrique Dussel (1988), is instrumentalizing people as things: "Sin is domination over the other" (p. 61); it is failing to take into account distinct personness (needs, identity, character, gender, background, experience). From this perspective, formal abstraction does not simply result in bad theory or bad rhetoric, it is unjust and sinful.

Do Not Oppress/Do No Harm

The negative corollary of the principles "respect audience difference" and "care for audience" is do not oppress them or dominate them. Do them no harm. But what exactly does this common ethical principle mean in terms of discourse?

Invoking Habermas's discourse ethic, Benhabib (1992) identifies two key principles of communicative ethics that provide some criteria for determining whether a discursive setting is indeed "doing harm"—the principle of universal moral respect, and the principle of egalitarian reciprocity:

> The "universal and necessary communicative presuppositions of argumentative speech" entail strong ethical assumptions. They require of us: (1) that we recognize the right of all beings capable of speech and action to be participants in the moral conversation—I will call this *the principle of universal moral respect*; (2) these conditions further stipulate that within such conversations each has the same symmetrical rights to various speech acts, to initiate new topics, to ask for reflection about the presuppositions of the conversation, etc. Let me call this *the principle of egalitarian reciprocity*. The very presuppositions of the argumentation situation then have a normative content that precedes the moral argument itself. (p. 29, ital in original)

These principles extend from Habermas's (1990) distinction between strategic action and communicative action. Strategic action is manipulative persuasion or public speech acts that attempt to coerce or manipulate audiences. Communicative action is Habermas' ideal ethical discourse action, the criteria for which are expressed in the two principles stated earlier. In ethical communicative action, the audience is treated not as a passive decoder or receiver, but as an equal interlocutor with reciprocal rights. In this sense, Habermas sets up a discourse ethic that reaffirms the old rationalistic privileging of dialectic (and argument) over rhetoric (and persuasion). The limitations of this ethic are: (a) it does not provide us with pragmatic criteria, as almost no real public discourse are capable of meeting these criteria; and (b) it is not sensitive enough to the inequities of discursive arrangements or to the presence of power and oppression in discursive settings. (In her revision of the Habermasian discourse ethic, Benhabib recognizes these limitations and works to address them.)

For alternate criteria, we can look to postmodern political commentary that begins with the consideration of power and oppression. Foucault (1987) makes a crucial distinction between "relationships of power" and "states of domination." Although all acts of writing or rhetoric might be said to be acts of power, they are not all acts of domination. Power is more general. Foucault says that relationships of power "have an extremely wide extension in human relations. There is a whole network of relationships of power, which can operate between individuals, in the bosom of the family, in an educational relationship, in the political body, etc." (p. 3). Domination, on the contrary, refers to invariable relations of power, that is, to "firmly set and congealed" settings that "block a field of relations of power" and "render them impassive and invariable" by preventing "all reversibility of movement" (p. 3). Both individuals and social groups can dominate.

This distinction is important for an ethics of rhetoric as it provides a criterion for critiquing rhetorical acts. When we write electronically (or otherwise), we are engaging in an act of power, according to Foucault's notion of power: Our effort to inform, persuade, or entertain is an effort to establish an authority vis-à-vis some reader(s). Rather than wring our hands in dismay over the arrogance of wielding this power (what I think of as a spasm of postmodern liberal guilt), we should see the exercise of discursive power as common, frequent, unavoidable, and not necessarily unethical. The distinction that is important pertains to acts of domination and oppression. For Foucault, domination refers to those acts of visible or invisible power that block "reversibility of movement," that is, they prevent a group or individual from expressing alternatives or exercising alternate choices. Although we cannot avoid the obligation of power when we write, we can try to avoid writing that dominates or oppresses.

Young (1990) further distinguishes between domination and oppression, viewing both as institutional forms. Domination refers to "institutional conditions which inhibit or prevent people from participating in determining their actions or the conditions of their actions" (p. 38). All of us are subject to various forms of domination, but that does not mean that domination affects us all in the same way: "[N]ot everyone subject to domination is also oppressed" (p. 38). Domination, in fact, may work to the advantage of some social groups. A social group is oppressed, however, when the domination works to systematically inhibit people's abilities, freedoms, choices (p. 38). Thus, domination means that people are excluded from participating in the systems and institutions that guide or determine their actions. Oppression means that, because of this exclusion, a people's freedoms are inhibited. This distinction is important for an ethics of rhetoric as it provides a criterion for distinguishing competing social groups' claims to being "oppressed." (See Sullivan & Porter, 1997, Chap. 5, for further discussion of the implications of oppression.)

Does your act of rhetoric allow for what Foucault calls "reversibility of movement" and Benhabib (1992) refers to as "reversibility of perspectives" (p. 146)? If you are a LISTSERV manager, for instance, are you autocratic in terms of how you exercise your authority on the list? (The liberal individual theory of property supports such autocracy, preferring to focus on the question of who "owns" the list rather than assigning at least some communal ethical authority to participants.) Or do the members of the list have some say in determining the status of their condition? Does the list operate by a "love it or leave it" philosophy, which says in effect that if you do not want to abide by the owner's rules, then your only choice is to leave the list? This is an act of domination and exclusion, and the presumed "choice" to leave a list is a forced choice and maybe a professionally harmful one for an academic whose area of specialization is represented on the list.

Again, the issue should not be reduced to this kind of either–or false dilemma: If the listowner does not establish authority (i.e., create and enforce strict rules), then the list participants will endlessly debate what the rules should be, and chaos will result. Certainly, with the way LISTSERV operations work, the listowner has every right to set up a list as he or she sees fit. The listowner has power, but with that power comes the obligation and responsibility to list participants. The problem, of course, for listowners or for writing teachers who sponsor electronic conferences is addressing the dilemmas that can arise (as we saw in Chapter 5) between competing interest groups or between individuals and the majority.

THE WRITER'S PROCEDURAL STRATEGIES

Consult Dialogically With a Diversity of Sources

The law should always be considered very seriously in decisions about the status of intellectual property, but the law cannot be relied on, in every instance, to provide clearcut advice or protection. The law is a complex and diverse set of decisions, statutes, opinions, and judgments that intersect with a wide range of human practices. The ethical writer has to consider a plurality of choices, including diverse and often conflicting laws, policies, and theories. The principle of ethical pluralism does not say that "everybody is right," but it does say that there are competing ethical standards that may have application and validity in a given situation. How do you choose among them? First, you do not do it alone. In rhetorical ethics, decision making is social, collaborative, and dialogic. Numerous theorists have recognized openness to dialogue (Haynes-Burton, 1990) and "tolerance for differences" (Lang, 1991, p. 5) as important qualities of ethical writing. Rorty says that responding to ethical dilemmas often involves "interweaving" opposing principles.

This process resembles what Jonsen and Toulmin (1988) describe as the key operating procedures of *phronesis* in Aristotle's *Nicomachean Ethics* (1976). The ethical person/writer must apply *circumspectio* ("looking around") in order to determine options and choices. He or she must be careful to judge *circumstantiae* ("what is standing around"), that is, the current conditions. He or she must apply *cautio* (carefulness) in making any decision, because human action is *multiforma* (takes many forms) (pp. 130–131). In short, ethical writing requires some careful deliberation, some marshalling of options and alternatives, some care in determining the conditions of one's rhetorical setting, and some respect for the variances of human action: We might regard such principles as the basics of an ethical approach to rhetorical invention.

You start this process by collecting a range of authoritative principles from a range of sites. Rhetorical ethics does not assign a priori authority to any site or source, but rather places competing sources of authority in dialectical tension. The list of resources in the Appendix includes a number of online discussion group that consider ethical and legal issues in electronic networking. Writers and writing teachers can use this list both to collect sources of authority and as a forum for ethical dialectic. They can look for ethical guidance to acceptable use policies established by government, education, and private network lists. Information about and examples of various acceptable use policies (as well as records of relevant legal decisions) are stored in an electronic database maintained by the Electronic Frontier Foundation. In short, these network sites serve as a concrete basis for dialogic exploration of rhetorical/ethical issues.

If I have a question about the ethics of the use of electronic text, for instance, an electronic copyright question, I know that there are several sites of authority I can consult. For legal authority and for publishers' and librarians' perspectives, I would consult the CNI-COPYRIGHT electronic list. For a discussion of these issues from the point of view of writing teachers, however, I would consult participants on ACW-L, the list for the Alliance of Computers and Writing. Different lists provide different disciplinary viewpoints and different forms of expertise. For truly problematic cases, I might consult several lists by posting my dilemma in the form of a question to each list. Thus, the electronic network provides the technological mechanism for heuristic invention of rhetorical/ethical issues.

Reading is obviously important. Read suspiciously, read critically, but nonetheless read. Consult a variety of sources for guidance when necessary, especially electronic sources. Cyberwriters can learn more about copyright law, for instance, by consulting print sources on intellectual property law in general and on how it applies to cyberspace in particular (e.g., Branscomb, 1994; Ermann, Williams, & Gutierrez, 1990; Forester & Morrison, 1994; Miller & Blumenthal, 1986; Oz, 1994; Woodmansee & Jaszi, 1995). Cyberwriters should consult electronic publishing guides that develop policy for use of electronic text (e.g., American Library Association, 1971; Association for Computing Machinery, 1995; Bill of rights, 1993; Corporation for Research and Educational Networking, 1993; Duggan, 1991; Kadie, 1991; Kahin, 1992; National Science Foundation, 1992; Oakley, 1991). The work of Paula Samuelson (who writes a regular column for the *Communications of the ACM*) addresses issues of intellectual property in the digital age—in fact, Samuelson (1996) is one of the leading authorities on electronic copyright. The network itself is a useful source for collecting up-to-date information. The internetworked writer can browse some of the intellectual property web sites listed in the Appendix and participate in LISTSERV discussion groups that focus on copyright and other legal/ethical issues.

Figure 4.1, the shot chart of ethical positions, can also serve as a rhetorical/ethical heuristic for writers. The diagram problematizes ethical positions. If anyone is inclined to rely on simplistic ethical pronouncements, that diagram serves to identify a range of competing ethical frameworks that can serve to critique and problematize such pronouncements.

Situate and Contextualize at the Local and Particular Level

A postmodern rhetorical ethics emphasizes the authority of contextualized elements and of the situated moment (*kairos*). It says that the particular historical and situated moment and the particular details and circumstances of that setting (the "facts," values, audiences, timing, historical circumstances, technologies) are critical. In their neocasuistic rhetorical ethic, Jonsen and Toulmin (1988) stress the importance of authorizing the details of the case, as well as the particular situated circumstances in which any ethical issue resides.

The situated side of critical rhetorical ethics requires that we make judgments sensitive to the constraints of local policy and practice, particular settings and cases, and, in the case of electronic writing and publishing, to the particular technologies and customs of use for those technologies. Feenberg (1991) in particular says that we have to avoid "the *decontextualizing practice* of formal abstraction [which] transforms its objects into mere means" (p. 170), by which he means, in part, the kind of rationalistic, philosophical approach to ethics and technology advocated by those in the Western deontological tradition of philosophical ethics (including Habermas). Contextualized awareness is sensitive to the constraints and norms of the particular form of technology. In concurrence with Feenberg, Martha Cooper (1991) says that a postmodern ethics must consider (a) "rhetorical situation" more broadly than in the conventional sense to include the medium and the effect of the medium on power relations (questions about access, for instance, and who controls and maintains the medium), and (b) the institutional bureaucracies and professional settings in which political advocacy and decision making occur.

A position sensitive to a technological setting would notice, for instance, that notions of netiquette on LISTSERV groups are different from that on MUDs or newsgroups. LISTSERV groups that have a designated "owner" tend to be more orderly and academic in the way they carry on discussions. Participants know (or should know) that their presence there depends on owner tolerance. In this respect the ethical "law" of the LISTSERV group is fairly absolute and undemocratic: The owner rules. (Even though enlightened owners can choose to share their power if they wish, the choice is that of the owner). Newsgroups and MUDs are much more freewheeling forums that do not have owners in the same sense (although they may have initiators and moderators).

Notions of ownership for print publications are different than for electronic archives. To questions about the ethics of reposting electronic messages, a rhetorical ethic would inquire about the conventions of the specific community, about the nature of the message, about the norms for reposting that may not be articulated, as well as about explicit policies and laws that may have relevance to the case. In other words, such an ethic would grant authority to the specific situation, to the specific technology, to the exact nature of the message, and to the norms and conventions (*nomoi*) of the electronic communities involved. It is, however, also aware of the danger of letting any single community isolate itself from principles outside that particular community—principles of universal human respect and reciprocity, for instance, from discourse ethics.

Figure 7.1, which served to identify the various agencies influencing the act of electronic writing in the composition classroom, can also double as a visual heuristic to identify the agencies involved in rhetorical/ethical writing situations.

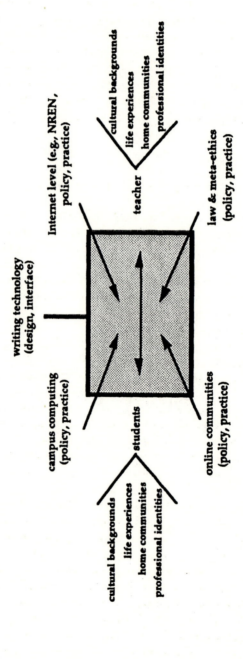

writing technology
(design, interface)

Internet level (e.g., NREN,
policy, practice)

campus computing
(policy, practice)

cultural backgrounds
life experiences
home communities
professional identities

teacher

law & meta-ethics
(policy, practice)

cultural backgrounds
life experiences
home communities
professional identities

students

online communities
(policy, practice)

FIGURE 7.1. Sites influencing internetworked writing.

That is, the diagram represents the matrix of forces that one might consider as operative in the act of internetworked writing. The answer to the question of "what policies should guide my writing in this electronic group?" lies not in one place but in several: There are likely to be competing policies and guidelines to be negotiated and reconciled. The visual serves as a prompt to writers to "look in several places" and alerts them to the need to reconcile possibly competing sites of ethical authority. The heuristic is general enough to function across a spectrum of electronic writing situations, yet its terms focus the writer on concrete agents and sites. (This is the challenge facing the designer of any heuristic: designing the heuristic for application across a relatively wide range of writing situations, yet not making the terms so general and abstract as to lose pragmatic and situated value in prompting writers.)

Acknowledge Ethical Complexities and Ambiguities

If I offer an "answer" in this book it is that problems (real problems, that is, not just inconveniences, but real problems of incommensurability and ethical dilemmas) are best worked out through the operation of a local and patient rhetorical pragmatism that is deliberative and reflective and that pays some attention to the processes involved, to the particulars of each case and its material conditions; and to the individual persons affected. I admit that at points we may have to resort to abstractions and slogans—yes, by all means, Free Speech! and hurrah for Democracy!—but remember how easy it is to misuse such slogans. Do not use them to shut off or polarize discussion. Be aware of how resistant the really difficult cases are to simple solutions by abstraction.

As I say, this is not the answer that most want to hear. As Stanley Fish (1994) says, "Complexity does not play well in Peoria or anywhere else" (p. 58), including Washington, DC. But then, that leaves something for educators to do, does it not?: to acknowledge the complexity of public issues, to promote careful thinking and deliberation, to promote fair consideration and representation of all sides, to resist the "single story" approach that the newspapers and television media and, increasingly, the electronic networks promote—and that both right- and left-wing demagogues favor.

As soon as you make claims like the ones in the previous paragraph, you run into trouble, of course, especially with postmodern ironists. The abstractions you casually dismissed, then yourself used, double back to trip you up: Whose idea of "careful thinking"? Which notion of "fair representation"? You can never completely evade the abstractions (a.k.a. theorizing), but you can be wary of them and alert to their operation. You can be an advocate of "free speech," but be wary of those cases that push the free speech principle to its limits and be capable of asking the critical questions ("free" for whom? at whose expense?).

Jonsen and Toulmin (1988) remind us that complexity is the nature of ethics. For some difficult cases and situations there will *never* be clear and easy answers—and to shout at each other as if there were, or could be, is the ultimate act of stupidity. For tough cases there will always be moral ambiguity (this is the de facto nature of tough cases). It is in the nature of human experience to be *multiforma*, complex to the degree that it in its distinct situatedness it will always manage to remain one step ahead of our theorizing and our categories for talking about it. Rather than being dismayed by this complexity, we might try to appreciate it.

MOVING TOWARD SOLIDARITY

There is a point at which continual open-ended heuristic thinking is dangerously disabling. Reflection, deliberation, careful interrogation, practiced skepticism—all are valued postures in this critical rhetorical ethic. At some point, however, the questioning process has to stop to make a commitment, even if only a contingent one. (If you deconstruct the idea of "computer classroom" to death, you just are not gonna have a computer classroom to teach in.)

If the position I am advocating tips in a direction, it tips in favor of solidarity—in favor of the position that we have to use rhetoric, ultimately, to enable solidarity: a solidarity that does not build itself on a rockbed of universal strictures, but that is a symbolically constructed solidarity of opinions that we build for our common good because we need a common good. This position tips in the favor of solidarity and the communal, too, in part for an ironic reason: Because in U.S. society the liberal-individualist position has for so long been dominant, I adopt the communal standpoint because it provides the most direct counter to the dominant—and often, at times, oppressive—liberal-individual ethic.

The great fear is that communal identification represents a return to a Western logocentric masculine rhetoric. Critics worry about solidarity and community as operating principles. They say we have been "identified" for too long and that it is time to recognize diversity. Steve Katz (1992, 1993) and others warn us about the problem of the common good becoming a totalitarian evil or a majority oppression. Yet my worry is that we are circling back to a place we have already been. Are we teaching writers to hurl their differences at one another, just like rhetoric used to teach its practitioners how to hurl arguments at one another, without actually *listening* to one another? (This is what appears to happen frequently in newsgroup arguments and on the floor of the U.S. House of Representatives.) Are we returning to a debate model assuming equal and opposite participants in a world where equality is not the common condition? Does the resistance to a community or solidarity model lead us to another version of the old liberal model, perhaps a postmodern version of it? In such a model—what we might call the rock-hurling, debate model of public discourse—the more powerful are bound to win, because they can afford more and bigger rocks. Young (1990) warns against the dangers of interest group pluralism that in its stridency can disable dialogue and, thus, block effective change. If interest groups do not work toward solidarity, then they will diffuse political potency and leave untouched and unchanged the systems and institutions that dominate us all.

The community I have in mind is not a melting pot or blender. The solidarity of this community does not require the effacement of difference, but rather builds on difference in the manner suggested by both Irigaray (1984/1993) and Young (1990). This community requires both feminine and masculine modes of thinking. For Irigaray, we achieve transcendence, spiritual fulfillment, in the mutual embrace that is a celebration of our difference. This commonality achieves its strength through and celebrates diversity. For Young, diversity and variation in a society should be viewed as a source of strength (although I do not share her optimism in the city as the ideal model of communal diversity).

There is a tendency in the field of rhetoric/composition, especially in cultural studies discussions, to mislabel community metaphors mainly in a negative way (e.g., as hegemony, exclusivity, the dominant culture) and to set up a straw binary: diversity as hero, hegemony as villain—which is an unassailable position, like saying "good" and "bad," and so is ultimately not very helpful.

There is another set of terms one can invoke to stress the positive notions of community and solidarity: unity, identification, alliance. Rather than throwing our competing sets of god terms at one another, take an ironic viewpoint and, like Kenneth Burke, see these two sets of terms as operating in a kind of binary tension. Burke saw all rhetoric as always involving both Identification and Division: As we strive for likeness and similarity (consubstantiality) we also affirm our differences, and the two notions are in constant oscillating tension. Any act of writing involves an identification—a positioning of a "we" and an establishing of a set of values that are over here, with "us." There is always an embracement: The writer engages an audience, identifies with an audience, and in that process a community is formed or changed. In the best of worlds, we always hope the writer's hug is an embrace, not a strangulation. We hope the embrace is mutual—dialogic if you like. However, you can not have rhetoric/writing without it, or without its counterpart—division.

Thus, the exercise of rhetoric is always at its core ironic, and the trick from the point of view of rhetorical ethics is to not let the irony freeze us into inaction, but to try to negotiate a nonoppressive committed standpoint in the midst of this irony.

At this point, my position may sound like Richard Rorty's (1989) description of "liberal irony" in *Contingency, Irony, and Solidarity*. Rorty assumes an ironic stance through most of the book, yet argues at the same time for liberalism as a utopian ideal. He explicitly situates himself between Foucault ("the ironist unwilling to be a liberal") and Habermas ("the liberal who is unwilling to be an ironist"; p. 61).

The stance Rorty advocates is that of the "committed ironist," who looks at all sides of an issues but then takes a stand. The stand may have doubts; it may be contingent, but for the time being it is a strong stand. Like me, Rorty is suspicious of the use of common-sense god terms (e.g., *democracy* and *liberalism*) to address problems: Too often they are instruments used to end dialogue by shutting off the Other. Like me, Rorty does not see much promise in extreme postmodern ludicism as a way to address social problems. This will lead to too much self-doubt and lack of action and character on the part of the community.

Unlike me, Rorty views irony as something private, to be carried out among expert philosophers and literary critics of irony, who effect change in small increments within disciplinary groups (e.g., Nabokov). This is where I have trouble with Rorty's conception of the "committed ironist" or "liberal ironist." Such a position ends up reinstantiating the academic male philosophical liberal humanist, the elite intellectual who publicly advocates what he privately and ironically despises. This posture is, ultimately, one of despair that public discourse can ever be anything other than stupid and rhetorically useless. Rorty's position ends up splitting academic from public, as well as private from public. It also ends up despairing of any productive role for mass education in public life. The best that education can aspire to, in Rorty's model, is to train a few elite and aesthetically sensitive ironists, who will celebrate their critical acumen in isolated academic enclaves—the ethical ivory tower.

My position on irony owes more to Burke and especially to Lyotard and Thébaud's (1985) discussion of rhetorical ethics in *Just Gaming*. It views certain paired opposites as having a rhetorical/ethical value in helping us construct writing stances. (Such pairs include individual/community, cooperation/competition, critique/construct, and static/dynamic.) Rorty falls victim to the philosophical temptations of ironic formal abstraction: He never contextualizes his discussion. However, the Lyotardian position, although ironic and theoretical, is a casuistic one that advocates a pragmatic case-by-case basis. It is ironic because it is constantly questioning the commonsensical, overturning the expected, saying "no" when everybody else says "yes." However, it does manage to locate commitment at a situated case level. Lyotard accepts, finally, the inevitability of *phronesis*, a concession that Rorty is not willing to make.

My cautious endorsement of solidarity also contrasts with Victor Vitanza's (1991a) rejection of Aristotelian pragmatics, which he views as a system advocating a strong view of consensus. Although I agree with Vitanza's critique of strong consensus, I cannot ultimately endorse his construction of ethics as "drifting." To me the ethics that Vitanza ultimately affirms embodies two constructs. One construct is the free-floating individual system resister, which is simply an angrier, more radical version of liberal individualism. The other construct is itself a system: Although Vitanza says he wants to resist all systems, he also clearly wants "to drift toward some notions of a Third Sophistic" (p. 121; see also Vitanza, 1991b, 1994).

The chief components of this situated ironic communalism are pursuit of the common good; respect for individual *and* community, for diversity *and* unity;

and constant questioning and revision. I see the community versus individual, consensus versus dissensus, controversy as a false binary. Why not hold both together? In *The Politics* (1962), Aristotle makes an important point about unity versus diversity:

> Certainly there must be some unity in a state, as in a household, but not an abso-
> lutely total unity. There comes a point where the state, if it does not cease to be a
> state altogether, will certainly come close to that and be a worse one; it is as if one
> were to reduce concord to unison or rhythm to a single beat. As we have said
> before, a state is a plurality, which must depend on education to bring about its
> common unity. (2.5 1263b29)

Aristotle says, in effect, that in developing unity we must not obliterate difference, we must not "reduce concord to unison or rhythm to a single beat." Other
unity metaphors are more problematic, insofar as they do not so readily grant
diversity its due. For instance, in 1 Corinthians 12, Paul talks about the relation of
parts to whole and gives us the metaphor of the faithful as one unified body:
"There are many parts, yet one body." Postmodern ethics has expressed strong
reservations about this kind of single body image (as numerous feminists have
said, whenever there is just one body it is bound to have a penis). Irigaray (1984/
1993) offers us an alternative scriptural metaphor in her consideration of the two
bodies, of the sexual difference that she constructs as the foundation for an ethic
of relations. Her account, in fact, shows us how, through embrace of the Other
(mutual embrace, not a "disguised version of the master–slave relationship," p.
17), we can achieve a kind of celebratory transcendence.

Is it possible to have a postmodern view of community? Carolyn Miller (1984/
1993), Iris Marion Young (1990), and Lester Faigley (1992) have all pointed the
way to such a vision of community. In a discussion linking communitarian and
rhetoric theory, Miller (1993) develops a vocabulary for talking about community in a way that highlights difference: Concepts like "the bazaar, the collage,
the carnival, bricolage, pastiche, eccentrism, nomadism, diaspora, migration"
(pp. 89–90) all suggest ways of thinking about social/communal events in a postmodern light. The community does not have to be a Governing State, or a Majority Consensus, but can be a gathering for the purpose of festival and play, a
celebration of difference. The Internet could potentially be the site for such electronic communities, but only if we begin the process of constructing a cyberspace
ethic that promotes it as such a site and recognizes that such a festival cannot proceed without some regard for the ethical.

Miller (1993) does worry that a postmodern conception of community might
"leave us with a community that is so fragmented, perforated, intermittent, and
attenuated that it no longer performs any rhetorical work" (p. 91), but the answer
to that is to work to construct, and reconstruct, communities (plural). The effort is
ongoing. She thinks that rhetoric must foreground community because it "is nec-

essary both for emotional solidarity and for political action" (p. 91). I very much agree.

Aristotle's musical metaphor is a significant one. The terms *community* and *unity* suggest consensus, but that consensus should not be conceived as homogeneity. Consensus is to be understood here in the sense of harmony: The different sounds aligned and blended in a particular way will produce a pleasant sound, a more aesthetically pleasing state than any of the individual parts. This kind of harmony is not the same as everyone playing the same sound, the same note, in the same key. All that produces is one loud blare, not music. Harmony is not homegeneity.

So, let us work toward this: an electronic network promoting a social harmony that values the diversity of sounds, that celebrates differences for a common good we have to work to construct. If we can use writing to design a network that achieves the spiritual transcendence that Irigaray (1984/1993) hopes for, the third age of the "incarnation of the spirit . . . the era of the wedding and the festival of the world" (pp. 148–149), let us do it.

Appendix

Electronic Resources for Ethical Inquiry

The rhetorical/ethical inquiry process that I am advocating calls for situated dialogue, for participation among diverse members of the electronic community in the process of making decisions about the common good (see Chapter 7 for discussion). No significant ethical decisions should be made by the individual alone, unless he or she has first sought out and engaged a diversity of views. The network itself provides the means for such a dialogue.

In fact the network—the Internet and World Wide Web—is an indispensable resource. Because of the lag time involved in traditional publishing, print resources other than newspapers or news magazines seldom reflect current thinking on critical problems. Networked discussion groups and newsgroups provide a means for live rhetorical/ethical interaction and discussion of new topics; online archives (available through FTP, gopher, or HTTP) provide relevant documents such as acceptable use policies, news about government legislation, and, frequently, electronic versions of print publications.

Cautionary note—Producing a print list of web URLs is a little like carrying water across a desert using a sieve: If your trip is long, there will not be much of it left. The exponential growth and dynamic change of the World Wide Web means that any print listing of resources, especially in a book, is bound to be out of date in a matter of months. New electronic groups and online archives are frequently created, moved, or reorganized; many have a relatively short life span.

The groups and web sites mentioned here were all active and healthy as of August 1996, but by the time this list appears in print some will no doubt have vanished, and new ones relevant to ethical inquiry will have emerged. There is no guarantee that the lists and archives mentioned here will exist in another six months, or will be located at the same site. The best strategy is to know how to work whatever search engine or navigational tool is available to you in order to find what you need using a keyword search. The lists that follow should, however, serve a suggestive purpose, providing examples of the range of groups and archives available to support ethical inquiry.

The rapid changeability of the Internet also supports the argument made in Chapter 7 for *phronesis* and for a procedural and rhetorical approach to network ethics. Although the informational content and structure of the Internet will no doubt change, the heuristic and procedural approach have a flexibility that should accommodate such changes. The ability to "theorize" across rhetorical situations and changing technological circumstances, to accommodate changes in law and ethical normativity, is an important facet of *phronesis*. To make good ethical decisions about internetworked writing events, the writer needs adaptability and situated critical judgment, not a set of rules or an armload of generic principles.

The LISTSERV groups mentioned here tend to take a disciplinary and professional approach to discussing ethical and legal issues in cyberspace. (They also tend to be tamer, less volatile, and more focused on professional academic and work issues than their newsgroup counterparts.) MegaByte University, or MBU-L, is one of the two principal online groups focused on issues related to computers and composition. To find out what writing teachers working in computer classrooms think, MBU-L is a good source, because its membership is comprised of about 300 writing teachers (as of May 1995), almost exclusively from the university level. The other group is the Alliance for Computers and Writing, whose online discussion group (ACW-L) also comprises over 300 members (as of May 1995). Although neither group focuses primarily on legal or ethical issues involved in the use of computers for writing, ethical issues are occasionally discussed on both lists. The CCCC-IP discussion list focuses on intellectual property issues affecting writing and communication teachers and scholars. This list focuses on both ethical and legal problems pertaining to copyright, fair use, the status of electronic text, the ethical use of student writing, and so on. The list also serves as an electronic forum for the Caucus on Intellectual Property and Composition Studies, a group that meets yearly at the Conference on College Composition and Communication (CCCC) to consider legal and ethical issues pertaining to copyright and intellectual property.

It is ethically risky and critically suspect to seek out views *only* from within a particular field. It is important to develop a multidisciplinary perspective, and electronic groups are a particularly effective means of doing that. Several online conferences consider ethical issues related to computer use, for example, the LISTSERV list "Discussion of Ethics in Computing" <ETHICS-L@vm.marist.edu>. The Coalition for Networked Information (CNI) maintains the <CNI-COPYRIGHT@cni.org> list; discussants include librarians, educators, lawyers, computing center administrators, and publishers (Yavarkovsky, 1990). The Electronic Frontier Foundation (EFF) sponsors an online USENET newsletter, *Computers and Academic Freedom News*, available at <alt.comp.acad-freedom.news>, and a discussion group <alt.comp.acad-freedom.talk> considering ethical and legal issues related to Internet policy, school and campus computer use policies, and First Amendment matters generally. Other newsgroups considering legal and ethical issues include <comp.admin.policy> and <misc.legal.computing>. In general, newsgroups tend to attract a wider range of responses and from outside strict disciplinary and professional interests. Thus, if you want to know what a broader spectrum of people are thinking, and you do not mind frequent flaming and off-topic noise (and subject headings like "Another CancelPrick NetCop Found" and "You Are a Neutered Wienie Dog"), check out the newsgroups. However, recognize that newsgroup activity is often inflammatory and predominantly male (by some estimates 90% or more of USENET activity is by men).

EFF, CNI, and CPSR (Computer Professionals for Social Responsibility) maintain large and comprehensive collections of online documents on their respective web sites. EFF, in particular, keeps up-to-date information about pending legislation (including records of testimony), publishes relevant editorials from a variety of newspaper, and stores samples of acceptable use policies. Perhaps the most comprehensive resource for legal and legislative material related to copyright and fair use is Stanford University's Copyright and Fair Use web site.

ONLINE DISCUSSION GROUPS (AUGUST 1996)

Alliance for Computers and Writing
    ACW-L@unicorn.acs.ttu.edu   listproc@unicorn.acs.ttu.edu
CCCC-IP (Intellectual Property List for
Conference on College Composition
and Communication)
    CCCC-IP@tc.umn.edu   listserv@ tc.umn.edu
Coalition for Networked Information
(CNI)—Copyright and Intellectual
Property Forum
    CNI-COPYRIGHT@cni.org   listproc@cni.org
Digital Future Coalition
    DFC-L@american.edu   listserv@american.edu
Discussion of Ethics in Computing
    ETHICS-L@vm.marist.edu   listserv@ vm.marist.edu
Infotech-Ethics
    INFOTECH-ETHICS@ethics.ubc.ca   majordomo@ethics.ubc.ca
Interpersonal Computing and Technology
    IPCT-L@guvm.georgetown.edu   listserv@guvm.georgetown.edu
MegaByte University/Computers
& Composition Digest
    MBU-L@unicorn.acs.ttu.edu   listserv@unicorn.acs.ttu.edu
Netiquette
    NETIQUETTE@albion.com   listserv@albion.com

NEWSGROUPS (AUGUST 1996)

alt.comp.acad-freedom.news (*Computers and Academic Freedom News*)
alt.comp.acad-freedom.talk
comp.admin.policy
comp.org.cpsr.talk
comp.org.eff.news (*EFFector*)
comp.org.eff.talk
misc.legal.computing
news.admin.censorship

WORLD-WIDE WEB SITES (AUGUST 1996)

American Civil Liberties Union Cyber-Liberties
  http://www.aclu.org/issues/cyber/hmcl.html
Center for Democracy and Technology
  http://www.cdt.org
Computers and Academic Freedom Archive
  http://www.eff.org/CAF/
Computer Professionals for Social Responsibility
  http://snyside.sunnyside.com/home/
Coalition for Networked Information
  http://www.cni.org/
Copyright and Fair Use Web Site (Stanford University)
  http://fairuse.stanford.edu/
Copyright Resources Online
  http://www.library.yale.edu/%7Eokerson/copyproj.html
Cyberspace Law Center
  http://www.cybersquirrel.com/clc/clcindex.html
The Copyright Website
  http://www.benedict.com/
Digital Future Coalition Web Site
  http://www.ari.net/dfc/
Electronic Frontier Foundation
  http://www.eff.org/archives.html
Intellectual Property Sites (James Porter)
  http://omni.cc.purdue.edu/~jporter/webIP
Kuester Law
  http://www.kuesterlaw.com/
The Legal Domain Network
  http://www.kentlaw.edu/lawnet/lawnet.html

The Legal Information Institute
   http://www.law.cornell.edu/
The Netiquette Home Page
   http://bookfair.com/Services/Albion/nqhome.html
Netrights
   http://www.netrights.com/
Oppedahl & Larson Patent Law Web Server
   http://www.patents.com/index.sht
   (For specific advice about Web law,
   see http://www.patents.com/weblaw.sht.)
The UCLA Online Institute for Cyberspace Law and Policy
   http://www.gse.ucla.edu/iclp/hp.html
U.S. Copyright Act
   http://www.law.cornell.edu/uscode/17/
The U.S. House of Representatives Internet Law Library (U.S. Code)
   http://law.house.gov/usc.htm
U.S. Supreme Court Decisions
   http://www.law.cornell.edu/supct/
Working Group Report (The White Paper)
   http://www.uspto.gov/web/offices/com/doc/ipnii/
WWW Multimedia Law
   http://www.batnet.com:80/oikoumene
   (For links to other intellectual property sites,
   see http://www.batnet.com:80/oikoumene/mmlinks.html.)

References

Alana Shoars v. Epson America, Inc., No. SWC112749 (L.A. Super. Ct. 1990).

Althusser, Louis. (1971). Ideology and ideological state apparatuses. In Louis Althusser, *Lenin and philosophy and other essays* (B. Brewster, Trans.). New York: Monthly Review Press.

American Library Association. (1971). *Intellectual freedom statement.* <http://www.eff.org/pub/CAF/library/int-freedom.ala>

Amiran, Eyal, Unsworth, John, & Chaski, Carole. (1992). Networked academic publishing and the rhetorics of its reception. *Centennial Review, 36,* 43–58.

Angell, David, & Heslop, Brent. (1994). *The elements of e-mail style: Communicate effectively in electronic mail.* Reading, MA: Addison-Wesley.

Aristotle. (1962). *The politics* (T. A. Sinclair, Trans.). London: Penguin.

Aristotle. (1976). *The ethics of Aristotle: The Nicomachean ethics* (J. A. K. Thomson, Trans.). New York: Penguin.

Aristotle. (1991). *On rhetoric: A theory of civic discourse* (G. A. Kennedy, Trans.). New York: Oxford University Press.

Association for Computing Machinery. (1995). ACM interim copyright policies. *Communications of the ACM, 38*(4), 104–107. <http://www.acm.org/pubs/copyright_policy>

Atwill, Janet M. (1990). *Refiguring rhetoric as an art: Aristotle's concept of techne and the humanist paradigm.* Unpublished doctoral dissertation, Purdue University, West Lafayette, IN.

Atwill, Janet, & Lauer, Janice. (1995). Refiguring rhetoric as an art: Aristotle's concept of techne. In Rosalind J. Gabin (Ed.), *Discourse studies in honor of James L. Kinneavy.* Potomac, MD: Scripta Humanistica.

Barbour, Ian G. (1993). *Ethics in an age of technology.* San Francisco, CA: Harper.

Barlow, John Perry. (1993). Jackboots on the infobahn: Clipping the wings of freedom. *Wired, 2*(4). <http://www.eff.org/pub/Publications/John_Perry_Barlow/infobahn_jackboots_barlow_eff.article>

Barlow, John Perry. (1994). *Selling wine without bottles: The economy of mind on the global net.* <http://www.eff.org/pub/Intellectual_property/idea_economy.article>

Barringer, Felicity. (1990, March 11). Free speech issues at the speed of light: Electronic bulletin boards need editing. No they don't. *New York Times*, p. E4.

Barron, Anne. (1992). Lyotard and the problem of justice. In Andrew Benjamin (Ed.), *Judging Lyotard* (pp. 26–42). London: Routledge.

Barthes, Roland. (1977). The death of the author. In Roland Barthes, *Image—music—text* (pp. 142–148). New York: Hill and Wang.

Barton, Ben F., & Barton, Marthalee S. (1993). Ideology and the map: Toward a postmodern visual design practice. In Nancy Roundy Blyler & Charlotte Thralls (Eds.), *Professional communication: The social perspective* (pp. 49–78). Newbury Park, CA: Sage.

Baudrillard, Jean. (1983). *Simulations* (Paul Foss, Paul Patton, & Philip Beitchman, Trans.). New York: Semiotext(e).

Bauman, Zygmunt. (1993). *Postmodern ethics.* Cambridge, MA: Blackwell.

Baynes, Kenneth. (1990). The liberal/communitarian controversy and communicative ethics. In David Rasmussen (Ed.), *Universalism vs. communitarianism: Contemporary debates in ethics* (pp. 61–81). Cambridge, MA: MIT Press.

Beale, Walter H. (1990). Richard M. Weaver: Philosophical rhetoric, cultural criticism, and the first rhetorical awakening. *College English, 52*, 626–640.

Beardsworth, Richard. (1992). On the critical "post": Lyotard's agitated judgement. In Andrew Benjamin (Ed.), *Judging Lyotard* (pp. 43–80). London: Routledge.

Bellah, Robert N., Madsen, Richard, Sullivan, William M., Swidler, Ann, & Tipton, Steven M. (1985). *Habits of the heart: Individualism and commitment in American life.* New York: Harper & Row.

Benhabib, Seyla, & Dallmayr, Fred (Eds.). (1990). *The communicative ethics controversy.* Cambridge, MA: MIT Press.

Benhabib, Seyla. (1992). *Situating the self: Gender, community and postmodernism in contemporary ethics.* New York: Routledge.

Bennett, Scott. (1993). Copyright and innovation in electronic publishing: A commentary. *Journal of Academic Librarianship, 19*, 87–91.

Berlin, James A. (1988). Rhetoric and ideology in the writing class. *College English, 50*, 477–494.

Berlin, James A. (1990). Postmodernism, politics, and histories of rhetoric. *PRE/TEXT, 11*, 169–187.

Berlin, James A. (1996). *Rhetorics, poetics, and cultures: Refiguring college English studies.* Urbana, IL: NCTE.

Bernauer, James E. (1987). Michael Foucault's ecstatic thinking. In James Bernauer & David Rasmussen (Eds.), *The final Foucault* (pp. 45–82). Cambridge, MA: MIT Press.

Bernstein, Richard. (1994, January 13). Guilty if charged. *The New York Review of Books*, pp. 11–14.

Berryman, Phillip. (1987). *Liberation theology: The essential facts about the revolutionary movement in Latin America and beyond.* New York: Pantheon Books.

Bill of rights and responsibilities for the community of electronic learners. (1993). <http://www.eff.org/pub/CAF/statements/bill-of-rights.aahe>

Bizzell, Patricia. (1992). The politics of teaching virtue. *ADE Bulletin, 103*, 4–7.

Blumenstyk, Goldie. (1995, January 6). Accord in the "Mosaic" war. *The Chronicle of Higher Education*, pp. A21–22.

Boff, Leonardo, & Boff, Clodovis. (1986). *Liberation theology: From confrontation to dialogue.* San Francisco: Harper and Row.

Bolter, Jay David. (1991). *Writing space: The computer, hypertext, and the history of writing.* Hillsdale, NJ: Erlbaum.

Bourdieu, Pierre. (1977). *Outline of a theory of practice* (Richard Nice, Trans.). Cambridge, UK: Cambridge University Press.

Bourdieu, Pierre. (1988). *Homo academicus* (Peter Collier, Trans.). Stanford, CA: Stanford University Press.

Branam, Judson. (1995, February 3). U-M expelling student for Internet fantasy. *The Ann Arbor News*, pp. A1, A14.

Branam, Judson, & Bridgeforth, Arthur, Jr. (1995, February 10). Internet writer arrested. *The Ann Arbor News*, pp. A1, A12.

Branscomb, Anne Wells. (1991). Common law for the electronic frontier. *Scientific American, 265*(3), 154–158.

Branscomb, Anne Wells. (1994). *Who owns information? From privacy to public access.* New York: Basic Books.

Branscum, Deborah. (1991, March). Ethics, e-mail, and the law: When legal ain't necessarily right. *Macworld*, pp. 63.

Brown, Alison Leigh. (1995). *Fear, truth, writing: From paper village to electronic community.* Albany: State University of New York Press.

Buchanan, Richard. (1989). Declaration by design: Rhetoric, argument, and demonstration in design practice. In Victor Margolin (Ed.), *Design discourse: History/theory/criticism* (pp. 91–109). Chicago: The University of Chicago Press.

Bunnin, Brad. (1990, April). Copyrights and wrongs: How to keep your work on the right side of copyright law. *Publish*, 76–82.

Burke, Kenneth. (1966). *Language as symbolic action: Essays on life, literature, and method.* Berkeley: University of California Press.

Burke, Kenneth. (1969). *A rhetoric of motives.* Berkeley: University of California Press.

Burke, Kenneth. (1970). *The rhetoric of religion: Studies in logology.* Berkeley: University of California Press.

Cahill, Lisa Sowle. (1990). Feminist ethics. *Theological Studies, 51,* 49–64.

Cain, Stephen. (1995, March 16). Grand jury sets new indictments against writer. *The Ann Arbor News*, pp. A1, A18.

Cangialosi, Charles. (1989). The electronic underground: Computer piracy and electronic bulletin boards. *Rutgers Computer & Technology Law Journal, 15,* 265–301.

Caputo, John D. (1993). *Against ethics: Contributions to a poetics of obligation with constant reference to deconstruction.* Bloomington: Indiana University Press.

Card, Claudia. (Ed.). (1991). *Feminist ethics.* Lawrence: University Press of Kansas.

Cherry, Roger D. (1988). Ethos versus persona: Self-representation in written discourse. *Written Communication, 5,* 251–276.

Cicero. (1942). *De oratore* (2 vols.). Cambridge, MA: Harvard University Press.

Clark, Gregory. (1987). Ethics in technical communication: A rhetorical perspective. *IEEE Transactions on Professional Communication, 30,* 190–195.

Clark, Gregory. (1994). Rescuing the discourse of community. *College Composition and Communication, 45,* 61–74.

Cole, Eve Browning, & Coultrap-McQuin, Susan. (1992). Toward a feminist conception of moral life. In Eve Browning Cole & Susan Coultrap-McQuin (Eds.),

Explorations in feminist ethics: Theory and practice (pp. 1–11). Bloomington: Indiana University Press.

Connolly, Frank W., Gilbert, S. W., & Lyman, P. (1991a). A bill of rights for electronic citizens, part one. *EDUCOM Review, 26*(2), 37–41.

Connolly, Frank W., Gilbert, S. W., & Lyman, P. (1991b). A bill of rights for electronic citizens, part two. *EDUCOM Review, 26*(3/4), 53–56.

Cooper, Marilyn M., & Selfe, Cynthia L. (1990). Computer conferences and learning: Authority, resistance, and internally persuasive discourse. *College English, 52*, 847–869.

Cooper, Martha. (1991). Ethical dimensions of political advocacy from a postmodern perspective. In Robert E. Denton, Jr. (Ed.), *Ethical dimensions of political communication* (pp. 23–47). New York: Praeger.

Corporation for Research and Educational Networking (CREN). (1993). *Acceptable use policy.* <http://www.eff.org/pub/CAF/policies/crenuse.txt>

Cortese, Amy, Verity, John, Mitchell, Russell, & Brandt, Richard. (1995, February 27). Cyberspace. *Business Week*, 78–86.

Cosentino, Victor J. (1994, March). Virtual legality. *Byte, 19*, 278.

Couture, Barbara. (1993). Against relativism: Restoring truth in writing. *Journal of Advanced Composition, 13*, 111–134.

Critchley, Simon. (1992). *The ethics of deconstruction: Derrida and Levinas.* Oxford, UK: Blackwell Publishers.

Crowley, Sharon. (1989). A plea for the revival of sophistry. *Rhetoric Review, 7*, 318–334.

Cushman, Ellen. (1996). The rhetorician as an agent of social change. *College Composition and Communication, 47*, 7–28.

D'Entrèves, Maurizio Passerin. (1992). Communitarianism. In Lawrence C. Becker & Charlotte B. Becker (Eds.), *Encyclopedia of ethics* (Vol. I, pp. 181–185). New York: Garland.

Davidson, Arnold I. (1986). Archaeology, genealogy, ethics. In David Couzens Hoy (Ed.), *Foucault: A critical reader* (pp. 221–233). New York: Blackwell.

de Certeau, Michel. (1984). *The practice of everyday life* (Steven Rendall, Trans.). Berkeley: University of California Press.

Deetz, Stanley. (1994). The new politics of the workplace: Ideology and other unobtrusive controls. In Herbert W. Simons & Michael Billig (Eds.), *After postmodernism: Reconstructing ideology critique* (pp. 172–199). London: Sage.

Dejoie, Roy, Fowler, George, & Paradice, David. (Eds.). (1991). *Ethical issues in information systems.* Boston: Boyd & Fraser.

DeLoughry, Thomas J. (1995, November 23). Gatekeeping on the Internet. *The Chronicle of Higher Education*, pp. A21–22.

DeLoughry, Thomas J. (1996, January 5). Banning "indecency." *The Chronicle of Higher Education*, pp. A19, A21, A23.

DeLoughry, Thomas J., & Wilson, David J. (1994, September 28). The case of computer conference at California college pits free speech against civil-rights protection. *The Chronicle of Higher Education*, p. A26.

Derrida, Jacques. (1977). Signature event context. *Glyph, 1*, 172–197.

Devine, P. E. (1992). A communitarian critic of liberalism. *New Oxford Review, 59*(2), 16–18.

Dibble, Julian. (1993, December 21). Rape in cyberspace. *Village Voice*, pp. 36–42.

DiMatteo, Anthony. (1991). Communication, writing, learning: An anti-instrumentalist view of network writing. *Computers and Composition, 8*(3), 5–19.

Doe v. University of Michigan. (Mich. Dist. Ct. 1989).

Donovan, Josephine. (1985). The new feminist moral vision. In Josephine Donovan, *Feminist theory: The intellectual traditions of American feminism* (pp. 171–186). New York: Frederick Ungar.

Duggan, Mary Kay. (1991). Copyright of electronic information: Issues and questions. *Online, 15*(3), 20–26.

Dussel, Enrique. (1988). *Ethics and community* (Robert R. Barr, Trans.). Maryknoll, NY: Orbis Books.

Eager, Bill. (1994). *Using the World Wide Web.* Indianapolis, IN: Que Publishing.

Eagleton, Terry. (1976). *Marxism and literary criticism.* Berkeley: University of California Press.

Ebert, Teresa L. (1991). The "difference" of postmodern feminism. *College English, 53,* 886–904.

Eldred, Janet Carey, & Fortune, Ron. (1992). Exploring the implications of metaphors for computer networks and hypermedia. In Gail Hawisher & Paul LeBlanc (Eds.), *Reimagining computers and composition: Teaching and research in the virtual age* (pp. 58–73). Portsmouth, NH: Boynton/Cook.

Electronic mail sends manners away. (1992, March 8). *Lafayette Journal and Courier,* p. C9.

Elkin-Koren, Niva. (1995). Copyright law and social dialogue on the information superhighway: The case against copyright liability of bulletin board operators. *Cardozo Arts & Entertainment Law Journal, 13,* 345–411.

Elmer-Dewitt, Philip. (1994, November 21). Censoring cyberspace. *Time,* 102–104.

Elmer-DeWitt, Philip. (1995, February 20). Snuff porn on the net. *Time,* 69.

Enos, Richard Leo, & Lauer, Janice M. (1992). The meaning of *heuristic* in Aristotle's *Rhetoric* and its implications for contemporary rhetorical theory. In Steven P. Witte, Neil Nakadate, & Roger D. Cherry (Eds.), *A rhetoric of doing: Essays on written discourse in honor of James L. Kinneavy* (pp. 79–87). Carbondale: Southern Illinois University Press.

Ermann, M. David, Williams, Mary B., & Gutierrez, Claudio. (Eds.). (1990). *Computers, ethics, and society.* New York: Oxford University Press.

Etzioni, Amitai. (1993). *The spirit of community: Rights, responsibilities, and the communitarian agenda.* New York: Crown.

Faigley, Lester. (1992). *Fragments of rationality: Postmodernity and the subject of composition.* Pittsburgh: University of Pittsburgh Press.

Farrell, Thomas B. (1993). *Norms of rhetorical culture.* New Haven, CT: Yale University Press.

Feenberg, Andrew. (1991). *Critical theory of technology.* New York: Oxford University Press.

Fish, Stanley. (1994). *There's no such thing as free speech, and it's a good thing, too.* New York: Oxford University Press.

Forester, Tom, & Morrison, Perry. (1994). *Computer ethics: Cautionary tales and ethical dilemmas in computing* (2nd ed.). Cambridge, MA: MIT Press.

Foucault, Michel. (1972). *The archaeology of knowledge and the discourse on language* (A. M. Sheridan Smith, Trans.). New York: Harper Torchbooks.

Foucault, Michel. (1979). *Discipline and punish: The birth of the prison* (Alan Sheridan, Trans.). New York: Vintage.

Foucault, Michel. (1983). The subject and power. In Hubert L. Dreyfus & Paul Rabinow (Eds.), *Michel Foucault: Beyond structuralism and hermeneutics* (2nd ed., pp. 208–226). Chicago: The University of Chicago Press.

Foucault, Michel. (1984a). Panopticism. In Paul Rabinow (Ed.), *The Foucault reader* (pp. 206–213). New York: Pantheon.

Foucault, Michel. (1984b). Space, knowledge, and power. In P. Rabinow (Ed.), *The Foucault reader* (pp. 239–256). New York: Pantheon.

Foucault, Michel. (1984c). On the genealogy of ethics: An overview of work in progress. In Paul Rabinow (Ed.), *The Foucault reader* (pp. 340–372). New York: Pantheon.

Foucault, Michel. (1984d). What is an author? In Paul Rabinow (Ed.), *The Foucault reader* (pp. 101–120). New York: Pantheon.

Foucault, Michel. (1984e). Politics and ethics: An interview. In Paul Rabinow (Ed.), *The Foucault Reader* (pp. 373–380). New York: Pantheon.

Foucault, Michel. (1985). *The use of pleasure: Volume 2 of the history of sexuality* (Robert Hurley, Trans.). New York: Vintage-Random.

Foucault, Michel. (1986a). *The care of the self: Volume 3 of the history of sexuality* (Robert Hurley, Trans.). New York: Vintage-Random.

Foucault, Michel. (1986b). Of other spaces. *Diacritics, 16*, 22–27.

Foucault, Michel. (1987). The ethic of care for the self as a practice of freedom (J. D. Gauthier, S. J., Trans.). In James Bernauer & David Rasmussen (Eds.), *The final Foucault* (pp. 1–20). Cambridge, MA: MIT Press.

Frazer, Elizabeth, & Lacey, Nicola. (1993). *The politics of community: A feminist critique of the liberal communitarian debate*. Toronto: University of Toronto Press.

Freire, Paulo. (1993). *Pedagogy of the oppressed* (Rev. ed., Myra Bergman Ramos, Trans.). New York: Continuum. (Original work published in 1970).

Friend, Christy. (1994). Ethics in the writing classroom: A nondistributive approach. *College English, 56*, 548–567.

Fulkerson, Richard. (1990). Composition theory in the eighties: Axiological consensus and paradigmatic diversity. *College Composition and Communication, 41*, 409–429.

Garver, Eugene. (1987). *Machiavelli and the history of prudence*. Madison: The University of Wisconsin Press.

Geertz, Clifford. (1983). *Local knowledge: Further essays in interpretive anthropology*. New York: Basic Books.

Geuss, Raymond. (1981). *The idea of a critical theory: Habermas and the Frankfurt school*. Cambridge, UK: Cambridge University Press.

Gilbert, Steven W. (1990). Information technology, intellectual property, and education. *EDUCOM Review, 25*(1), 14–20.

Gilbert, Steven W., & Lyman, Peter. (1989). Intellectual property in the information age: Issues beyond the copyright law. *Change, 21*(3), 23–28.

Gilligan, Carol. (1993). *In a different voice: Psychological theory and women's development* (2nd ed.). Cambridge, MA: Harvard University Press.

Grimaldi, William M. A., S. J. (1980). *Aristotle, Rhetoric I: A commentary*. New York: Fordham University Press.

Grimaldi, William M. A., S. J. (1988). *Aristotle, Rhetoric II: A commentary.* New York: Fordham University Press.

Gurak, Laura J. (1995). Rhetorical dynamics of corporate communication in cyberspace: The protest over Lotus MarketPlace. *IEEE Transactions on Professional Communication, 38,* 2–10.

Gurak, Laura J. (1997). *Persuasion in cyberspace: Privacy, community, and the online protests over MarketPlace and Clipper.* New Haven, CT: Yale University Press.

Gutièrrez, Gustavo. (1973). *A theology of liberation* (Caridad Inda & Jophn Eagleson, Eds., & Trans.). Maryknoll, NY: Orbis.

Habermas, Jürgen. (1990). *Moral consciousness and communicative action* (Christian Lenhardt & Shierry Weber Nicholsen, Trans.). Cambridge, MA: MIT Press.

Hahn, Harley, & Stout, Rick. (1994). *The Internet complete reference.* Berkeley: Osbourne McGraw-Hill.

Hairston, Maxine. (1992). Diversity, ideology, and teaching writing. *College Composition and Communication, 43,* 179–193.

Hansen, Kristine. (1994). Ethics in rhetoric. In Alan C. Purves (Ed.), *Encyclopedia of English studies and language arts* (pp. 461–462). New York: Scholastic Press.

Haraway, Donna. (1991). *Simians, cyborgs, and women: The reinvention of nature.* New York: Routledge.

Harkin, Patricia, & Schilb, John. (Eds.) (1991). *Contending with words: Composition and rhetoric in a postmodern age.* New York: Modern Language Association of America.

Harris, Joseph. (1995). The work of others. *College Composition and Communication, 45,* 439–441.

Hartman, Karen, Neuwirth, Christine M., Kiesler, Sara, Sproull, Lee, Cochran, Cynthia, Palmquist, Michael, & Zubrow, David. (1991). Patterns of social interaction and learning to write: Some effects of network technologies. *Written Communication, 8,* 79–113.

Hassan, Ihab. (1993). Toward a concept of postmodernism. In Joseph Natoli & Linda Hutcheon (Eds.), *A postmodern reader* (pp. 273–286). Albany: State University of New York Press.

Hawisher, Gail E., & LeBlanc, Paul. (Eds.). (1992). *Re-imagining computers and composition: Teaching and research in the virtual age.* Portsmouth, NH: Boynton/Cook Heinemann.

Hawisher, Gail, Selfe, Cynthia, Moran, Charles, & LeBlanc, Paul. (1996). *Computers and the teaching of writing in American higher education, 1979–1994: A history.* Norwood, NJ: Ablex and Computers and Composition.

Hawisher, Gail E., & Moran, Charles. (1993). Electronic mail and the writing instructor. *College English, 55,* 627–643.

Hawisher, Gail E., & Selfe, Cynthia L. (Eds.). (1989). *Critical perspectives on computers and composition studies.* New York: Teachers College Press.

Hawisher, Gail E., & Selfe, Cynthia L. (Eds.). (1991a). *Evolving perspectives on computers and composition studies: Questions for the 1990s.* Urbana, IL: NCTE and Computers and Composition.

Hawisher, Gail E., & Selfe, Cynthia L. (1991b). The rhetoric of technology and the electronic writing class. *College Composition and Communication, 42,* 55–65.

Hawisher, Gail E., & Sullivan, Patricia. (in press). Women on the networks: Searching for an e-space of their own. In Susan Jarratt & Lynn Worsham (Eds.), *Feminism and composition*. New York: Modern Language Association of America.

Hawkins, Donald T., Smith, Frank J., Dietlein, Bruce C., Joseph, Eugene J., & Rindfuss, Robert D. (1992). Forces shaping the electronic publishing industry of the 1990s. *Electronic Networking*, 2, 38–60.

Haynes-Burton, Cynthia. (1990). The ethico-political agon of other criticisms: Toward a Nietzschean counter-ethic. *PRE/TEXT, 11*, 289–308.

Heim, Michael. (1987). *Electric language: A philosophical study of word processing*. New Haven, CT: Yale University Press.

Hill, Forbes I. (1983). The rhetoric of Aristotle. In James J. Murphy (Ed.), *A synoptic history of classical rhetoric* (pp. 19–76). Davis, CA: Hermagoras Press.

hooks, bell. (1990). *Yearning: Race, gender, and cultural politics*. Boston, MA: South End Press.

Horkheimer, Max. (1972). *Critical theory: Selected essays* (Matthew J. O'Connell & others, Trans.). New York: Herder and Herder.

Howard, Tharon. (1991). E-mail manners and "netiquette." <purtopoi@vm.cc.purdue.edu/manners>

Howard, Tharon W. (1992). *The rhetoric of electronic communities*. Unpublished doctoral dissertation, Purdue University, West Lafayette, IN.

Howard, Tharon W. (1993, April). *E-mail ethics: Confessions of a listowner*. Paper presented at the Conference on College Composition and Communication, San Diego, CA.

Howard, Tharon W. (1996a). Who "owns" electronic texts? In Patricia Sullivan & Jennie Dautermann (Eds.), *Electronic literacies in the workplace: Technologies of writing* (pp. 177–198). Urbana, IL: NCTE and Computers and Composition.

Howard, Tharon W. (1996b). Mapping the minefield of electronic ethics. In Chris Edgar & Susan Wood (Eds.), *The nearness of you: Students and teachers writing online* (pp. 48–68). New York: Teachers and Writers Collaborative.

Hoy, David Couzens, & McCarthy, Thomas. (1994). *Critical theory*. Cambridge, MA: Blackwell.

Irigaray, Luce. (1993). *An ethics of sexual difference* (Carolyn Burke & Gillian C. Gill, Trans.). Ithaca, NY: Cornell University Press. (Original work published in 1984).

Isocrates. (1929). *Isocrates* (Vol. 11, George Norlin, Trans.). Cambridge, MA: Harvard University Press.

It's a man's, man's, man's world on-line. (1995, March 11). *Lafayette Journal and Courier*: p. B1.

Jacobi, Martin J. (1990). Using the enthymeme to emphasize ethics in professional writing courses. *Journal of Business Communication*, 27, 273–292.

Jacobson, Robert L. (1995, March 10). No copying. *The Chronicle of Higher Education*, pp. A17–A19.

Jaggar, Alison M. (1992). Feminist ethics. In Lawrence C. Becker & Charlotte B. Becker (Eds.), *Encyclopedia of ethics* (Vol. I, pp. 361–370). New York: Garland.

Janangelo, Joseph. (1991). Technopower and technoppression: Some abuses of power and control in computer-assisted writing environments. *Computers and Composition, 9*, 47–64.

Jarratt, Susan C. (1991). *Rereading the sophists.* Carbondale: Southern Illinois University Press.

Jobst, Jack. (1987). Word processing: Two ethical concerns. *Journal of Technical Writing and Communication, 17*(1), 1–8.

Johannesen, Richard L. (1990). *Ethics in human communication* (3rd ed.). Prospect Heights, IL: Waveland Press.

Johannesen, Richard L. (1991). Virtue ethics, character, and political communication. In Robert E. Denton, Jr. (Ed.), *Ethical dimensions of political communication* (pp. 69–90). New York: Praeger.

Johnson, Deborah G. (1991). Equal access to computing, computing expertise, and decision making about computers. In Roy Dejoie, George Fowler, & David Paradice (Eds.), *Ethical issues in information systems* (pp. 210–218). Boston: Boyd & Fraser.

Johnson, Deborah G. (1992). Computers. In Lawrence C. Becker & Charlotte B. Becker (Eds.), *Encyclopedia of ethics* (Vol. I, pp. 191–194). New York: Garland.

Johnson, Deborah G., & Snapper, John W. (1985). *Ethical issues in the use of computers.* Belmont, CA: Wadsworth.

Johnson-Eilola, Johndan. (1995, March). *Little machines: Rearticulating hypertext users.* Paper presented at Conference on College Composition and Communication, Washington, DC.

Johnson-Eilola, Johndan. (1996, March). *Out of bounds: The politics of technology.* Paper presented at Conference on College Composition and Communication, Milwaukee, WI.

Johnstone, Christopher Lyle. (1976). *Communication and morality: A study of the ethics-rhetoric relationship as conceived by Aristotle, Francis Bacon, and John Dewey.* Unpublished doctoral dissertation, University of Wisconsin-Madison, WI.

Johnstone, Christopher Lyle. (1980). An Aristotelian trilogy: Rhetoric, ethics, politics, and the search for moral truth. *Philosophy and Rhetoric, 13,* 1–24.

Jonsen, Albert R., & Toulmin, Stephen. (1988). *The abuse of casuistry: A history of moral reasoning.* Berkeley: University of California Press.

Kadie, Carl L. (1991). *Hypothetical netnews bill of rights.* <http://www.eff.org/pub/CAF/library/library-netnews-analogy>

Kahin, Brian. (1992). *Scholarly communication in the network environment: Issues of principle, policy, and practice.* <http://www.eff.org/pub/Intellectual_property/kahin_scholarly_communication>

Kahn, Victoria A. (1985). *Rhetoric, prudence, and skepticism in the Renaissance.* Ithaca, NY: Cornell University Press.

Kaplan, Nancy. (1991). Ideology, technology, and the future of writing instruction. In Gail E. Hawisher & Cynthia L. Selfe (Eds.), *Evolving perspectives on computers and composition studies: Questions for the 1990s* (pp. 11–42). Urbana, IL: NCTE and Computers and Composition.

Kapor, Mitchell. (1991). Civil liberties in cyberspace. *Scientific American, 265*(3), 158–164.

Katz, Steven B. (1992). The ethic of expediency: Classical rhetoric, technology, and the Holocaust. *College English, 54,* 255–275.

Katz, Steven B. (1993). Aristotle's rhetoric, Hitler's program, and the ideological problem of praxis, power, and professional discourse. *Journal of Business and Technical Communication, 7,* 37–62.

Kekes, John. (1993). *The morality of pluralism.* Princeton: Princeton University Press.

Kelly, Michael. (1989). The dialectical/dialogical structure of ethical reflection. *Philosophy and Rhetoric, 22,* 174–193.

Kelly, Michael. (1990). The Gadamer/Habermas debate revisited: The question of ethics. In David Rasmussen (Ed.), *Universalism vs. communitarianism: Contemporary debates in ethics* (pp. 139–159). Cambridge, MA: MIT Press.

Kerferd, G. B. (1981). *The sophistic movement.* Cambridge, UK: Cambridge University Press.

Kinkead, Joyce. (1987). Computer conversations: E-mail and writing instruction. *College Composition and Communication, 38,* 337–341.

Kinneavy, James L. (1986). *Kairos:* A neglected concept in classical rhetoric. In Jean Dietz Moss (Ed.), *Rhetoric and praxis: The contribution of classical rhetoric to practical reasoning* (pp. 79–105). Washington, DC: Catholic University of America Press.

Kinneavy, James L. (1987). *Greek rhetorical origins of Christian faith: An inquiry.* New York: Oxford University Press.

Kinross, Robin. (1989). The rhetoric of neutrality. In Victor Margolin (Ed.), *Design discourse: History/theory/criticism* (pp. 131–143). Chicago: University of Chicago Press.

Kleinman, Neil. (1995). Don't fence me in: Copyright, property, technology. *Readerly/ Writerly Texts, 3,* 9–50.

Komsky, Susan H. (1991). A profile of users of electronic mail in a university: Frequent versus occasional users. *Management Communication Quarterly, 4,* 310–340.

Krol, Ed. (1992). *The whole Internet: User's guide and catalog.* Sebastopol, CA: O'Reilly & Associates.

Krol, Ed. (1994). *The whole Internet: User's guide and catalog* (2nd ed.). Sebastopol, CA: O'Reilly & Associates.

Lang, Berel. (1991). *Writing and the moral self.* New York: Routledge.

Lanham, Richard A. (1993). *The electronic word: Democracy, technology, and the arts.* Chicago: University of Chicago Press.

Larrabee, Mary Jeanne. (Ed.). (1993). *An ethic of care: Feminist and interdisciplinary perspectives.* New York: Routledge.

Lather, Patti. (1991). *Getting smart: Feminist research and pedagogy with/in the postmodern.* New York: Routledge.

Lather, Patti. (1992). Post-critical pedagogies: A feminist reading. In Carmen Luke & Jennifer Gore (Eds.), *Feminisms and critical pedagogy* (pp. 120–137). New York: Routledge.

Lauer, Janice M. (1984). Issues in rhetorical invention. In Robert J. Connors, Lisa S. Ede, & Andrea A. Lunsford (Eds.), *Essays on classical rhetoric and modern discourse* (pp. 127–139). Carbondale, IL: Southern Illinois University Press.

LeBlanc, Paul. (1990). Competing ideologies in software design for computer-aided composition. *Computers and Composition, 7,* 7–19.

Leff, Michael C. (1978). In search of Ariadne's thread: A review of the recent literature on rhetorical theory. *Central States Speech Journal, 29,* 73–91.

Lemisch, Jesse. (1995, January 20). The first amendment is under attack in cyberspace. *The Chronicle of Higher Education*, p. A56.

Lewis, Peter H. (1995a, February 11). Writer arrested after sending violent fiction over Internet. *New York Times*, p. 10.

Lewis, Peter H. (1995b, March 1). Netscape knows fame and aspires to fortune. *New York Times*, p. D1.

Lobkowicz, Nicholas. (1967). *Theory and practice: History of a concept from Aristotle to Marx*. Notre Dame, IN: University of Notre Dame Press.

Lopez, Elizabeth Sanders. (1995). *The geography of computer writing spaces: A critical postmodern analysis*. Unpublished doctoral dissertation, Purdue University, West Lafayette, IN.

Lotus, Jean L. (1993, December 6). On campus, their name is MUD: Recreational activities blocked from Purdue's computing center. *Lafayette Journal and Courier*, p. A6.

Luke, Carmen, & Gore, Jennifer. (Eds.). (1992). *Feminisms and critical pedagogy*. New York: Routledge.

Luke, Timothy W. (1991). Touring hyperreality: Critical theory confronts informational society. In Philip Wexler (Ed.), *Critical theory now* (pp. 1–26). London: The Falmer Press.

Lunsford, Andrea A., & Ede, Lisa. (1990). *Singular texts/plural authors: Perspectives on collaborative writing*. Carbondale: Southern Illinois University Press.

Lyotard, Jean-François. (1984). *The postmodern condition: A report on knowledge* (Geoff Bennington & Brian Massumi, Trans.). Minneapolis: University of Minnesota Press.

Lyotard, Jean-François. (1988a). *Peregrinations: Law, form, event*. New York: Columbia University Press.

Lyotard, Jean-François. (1988b). *The differend: Phrases in dispute* (Georges Van Den Abbeele, Trans.). Minneapolis: University of Minnesota Press.

Lyotard, Jean-François, & Thébaud, Jean-Loup. (1985). *Just gaming* (W. Godzich, Trans.). Minneapolis: University of Minnesota Press.

Lyytinen, Kalle. (1992). Information systems and critical theory. In Mats Alvesson & Hugh Willmott (Eds.), Critical management studies (pp. 159–180). London: Sage.

MacIntyre, Alasdair. (1984). *After virtue: A study in moral theory* (2nd ed.). Notre Dame, IN: University of Notre Dame Press.

MacIntyre, Alasdair. (1988). *Whose justice? Which rationality?* Notre Dame, IN: University of Notre Dame Press.

Mackay, Wendy E. (1988). Diversity in the use of electronic mail: A preliminary inquiry. *ACM Transactions on Office Information Systems, 6*, 380–397.

MacKinnon, Catharine A. (1993). *Only words*. Cambridge, MA: Harvard University Press.

Mason, Richard O. (1991). Four ethical issues of the information age. In Roy Dejoie, George Fowler, & David Paradice (Eds.), *Ethical issues in information systems* (pp. 46–55). Boston: Boyd & Fraser.

Mason, Richard O., Mason, Florence M., & Culnan, Mary J. (1995). *Ethics of information management*. Thousand Oaks, CA: Sage.

McCance, Dawne. (1996). *Posts: Re addressing the ethical*. Albany, NY: State University of New York Press.

McGuire, Michael. (1980). The ethics of rhetoric: The morality of knowledge. *Southern Speech Communication Journal, 45,* 133–148.

Meeks, Brock N. (1994). The end of privacy. *Wired, 2*(4). <http://www.hotwired.com/Lib/Privacy/privacy.meeks.html>

Miller, Carolyn R. (1989). What's practical about technical writing? In Bertie E. Fearing & W. Keats Sparrow (Eds.), *Technical writing: Theory and practice* (pp. 14–24). New York: Modern Language Association of America.

Miller, Carolyn R. (1993). Rhetoric and community: The problem of the one and the many. In Theresa Enos & Stuart C. Brown (Eds.), *Defining the new rhetorics* (pp. 79–94). Newbury Park, CA: Sage.

Miller, Nicholas, & Blumenthal, Carol. (1986). Intellectual property issues. In Anne W. Branscomb (Ed.), *Toward a law of global communication networks* (pp. 227–237). New York: Longman.

Mirel, Barbara. (1996, March). *Writing for problem-solving aspects of computer literacy: Theories to guide practice.* Paper presented at Conference on College Composition and Communication, Milwaukee, WI.

Moran, Charles. (1990). The computer writing room: Authority and control. *Computers and Composition, 7*(2), 61–69.

Moulthrop, Stuart. (1991). The politics of hypertext. In Gail E. Hawisher & Cynthia L. Selfe (Eds.), *Evolving perspectives on computers and composition studies: Questions for the 1990s* (pp. 253–271). Urbana, IL: NCTE and Computers and Composition.

Mullett, Sheila. (1987). Only connect: The place of self-knowledge in ethics. In Marsha Hanen & Kai Nielsen (Eds.), *Science, morality, and feminist theory* (pp. 309–338). Calgary, Canada: University of Calgary Press.

Murphy, James J. (1974). *Rhetoric in the middle ages: A history of rhetorical theory from Saint Augustine to the Renaissance.* Berkeley: University of California Press.

National Science Foundation. (1992, June). Acceptable use policy (NSFNET). *Electronic Networking.*

Neel, Jasper. (1988). *Plato, Derrida, and writing.* Carbondale: Southern Illinois University Press.

Noddings, Nel. (1984). *Caring: A feminine approach to ethics and moral education.* Berkeley: University of California Press.

Nussbaum, Martha C. (1986). *The fragility of goodness: Luck and ethics in Greek tragedy and philosophy.* Cambridge, UK: Cambridge University Press.

Oakley, Robert L. (1991). Copyright issues for the creators and users of information in the electronic environment. *Electronic Networking, 1,* 23–30.

Ohmann, Richard. (1985). Literacy, technology, and monopoly capital. *College English, 47,* 675–689.

Okerson, Ann. (1996, July). Who owns digital works? *Scientific American, 275*(1), 80–84. <http://www.sciam.com/0796issue/0796okerson.html>

Olian, Jay Robert. (1965). *Ancient rhetoric and moral theory.* Unpublished doctoral dissertation, Northwestern University, Evanston, IL.

Online. (1994, October 26). *The Chronicle of Higher Education,* p. A24.

Ong, Walter J., S. J. (1982). *Orality and literacy: The technologizing of the word.* London: Methuen.

Opperdahl & Larson Law Firm. (1996). *May I freely link to the Web sites of others?* <http:/
/www.patents.com/weblaw.sht>

Orwell, George. (1956). Politics and the English language. In George Orwell, *The Orwell reader* (pp. 355–366). New York: Harcourt Brace Javanovich.

Oz, Effy. (1994). *Ethics for the information age.* New York: William C. Brown/Business and Educational Technologies.

Parent, W. A. (1985). Privacy, morality, and the law. In Deborah G. Johnson & John W. Snapper (Eds.), *Ethical issues in the use of computers* (pp. 201–215). Belmont, CA: Wadsworth.

Parker, Donn B., Swope, Susan, & Baker, Bruce N. (1990). *Ethical conflicts in information and computer science, technology, and business.* Wellesley, MA: QED Information Sciences.

Patterson, L. Ray, & Lindberg, Stanley W. (1991). *The nature of copyright: A law of users' rights.* Athens: University of Georgia Press.

Perelman, Chaim. (1982). *The realm of rhetoric* (William Kluback, Trans.). Notre Dame, IN: University of Notre Dame Press.

Perelman, Chaim, & Olbrechts-Tyteca, Lucie (1969). *The new rhetoric: A treatise on argumentation.* Notre Dame, IN: University of Notre Dame Press.

Perritt, Henry H., Jr. (1992). Tort liability, the First Amendment, equal access, and commercialization of electronic networks. *Electronic Networking, 2*(3), 29–44.

Phelps, Louise Wetherbee. (1988). *Composition as a human science: Contributions to the self-understanding of a discipline.* New York: Oxford University Press.

Phelps, Louise Wetherbee. (1992). A constrained vision of the writing classroom. *ADE Bulletin, 103,* 13–20.

Phillips, Derek L. (1993). *Looking backward: A critical appraisal of communitarian thought.* Princeton, NJ: Princeton University Press.

Piller, Charles. (1992, September). Separate realities: The creation of the technological underclass in America's public schools. *Macworld, 9,* 218–231.

Piller, Charles. (1993a, July). Bosses with x-ray eyes. *Macworld, 10,* 118–123.

Piller, Charles. (1993b, July). Privacy in peril. *Macworld, 10,* 124–130.

Plato. (1960). *Gorgias* (Walter Hamilton, Trans.). London: Penguin.

Plato. (1973). *Phaedrus and the seventh and eighth letters* (Walter Hamilton, Trans.). London: Penguin Books.

Porter, James E. (1986). Intertextuality and the discourse community. *Rhetoric Review, 5,* 34–47.

Porter, James E. (1992a). *Audience and rhetoric: An archaeological composition of the discourse community.* Englewood Cliffs, NJ: Prentice Hall.

Porter, James E. (1992b, May). *Network communities and the development of the electronic writer.* Paper presented at the Conference on Computers & Writing. Indianapolis, IN.

Porter, James E. (1993a). Developing a postmodern ethics of rhetoric and composition. In Theresa Enos & Stuart C. Brown (Eds.), *Defining the new rhetorics* (pp. 207–226). Newbury Park, CA: Sage.

Porter, James E. (1993b, April). *A theory of ethics for electronic writing/publishing.* Paper presented at the Conference on College Composition and Communication, San Diego, CA.

Porter, James E. (1993c, May). *Rhetorics of electronic writing*. Paper presented at the Conference on Computers & Writing, Ann Arbor, MI.

Porter, James E. (1993d). The role of law, policy, and ethics in corporate composing: Toward a practical ethics for professional writing. In Nancy Roundy Blyler & Charlotte Thralls (Eds.), *Professional communication: The social perspective* (pp. 128–143). Newbury Park, CA: Sage.

Porter, James E. (1994a, March). *A rhetorical ethics for the writing classroom*. Paper presented at Conference on College Composition and Communication, Nashville, TN.

Porter, James E. (1994b, May). *Freedom or constraint? Developing a rhetorical ethics for networked classrooms and communities*. Paper presented at Conference on Computers & Writing, Springfield, MO.

Porter, James E. (1994c). Electronic writing. In Alan C. Purves (Ed.), *Encyclopedia of English studies and language arts* (pp. 420–424). New York: Scholastic Press.

Porter, James E. (1994d). Ethics and computers. In Alan C. Purves (Ed.), *Encyclopedia of English studies and language arts* (pp. 456–461). New York: Scholastic Press.

Porter, James E. (1995, March). Review of *Computer Ethics*. *Technical Communication Quarterly, 4,* 96–100.

Porter, James E. (1996, February). *Professional writing as postmodern work: Toward a postmodern/critical rhetoric*. Paper presented at Business and Technical Writing Lecture, Department of English, University of Wisconsin-Milwaukee, Milwaukee, WI.

Porter, James E. (1997). Legal realities and ethical hyperrealities: A critical approach toward cyberwriting. In Stuart C. Selber (Ed.), *Computers and technical communication: Pedagogical and programmatic perspectives*. Greenwhich, CT: Ablex.

Porter, James E., & Sullivan, Patricia. (1996). Working across methodological interfaces: The study of computers and writing in the workplace. In Patricia Sullivan & Jennie Dautermann (Eds.), *Electronic literacies in the workplace: Technologies of writing* (pp. 294–322). Urbana, IL: NCTE and Computers and Composition.

Poster, Mark. (1989). *Critical theory and poststructuralism: In search of a context*. Ithaca, NY: Cornell University Press.

Poster, Mark. (1990). *The mode of information: Poststructuralism and social context*. Chicago: The University of Chicago Press.

Provenzo, Eugene F., Jr. (1992). The electronic panopticon: Censorship, control, and indoctrination in a post-typographic culture. In Myron C. Tuman (Ed.), *Literacy online: The promise (and peril) of reading and writing with computers* (pp. 167–188). Pittsburgh, PA: University of Pittsburgh Press.

Quittner, Joshua. (1996, June 24). Free speech for the net. *Time, 147,* 56–57.

Rawls, John. (1971). *A theory of justice*. Cambridge, MA: Belknap Press.

Ray, Ruth, & Barton, Ellen. (1991). Technology and authority. In Gail E. Hawisher & Cynthia L. Selfe (Eds.), *Evolving perspectives on computers and composition studies: Questions for the 1990s* (pp. 279–299). Urbana, IL: NCTE and Computers and Composition.

Raymond, James C. (1989). Rhetoric as bricolage: Theory and its limits in legal and other sorts of discourse. In Carolyn B. Matalene (Ed.), *Worlds of writing: Teaching and learning in discourse communities of work* (pp. 388–399). New York: Random.

Rezmierski, Virginia E. (1992). Ethical dilemmas in information technology use: Opportunity bumps on the road to civilization. *EDUCOM Review, 27*(4), 22–28.

Rheingold, Howard. (1991, July). The thought police on patrol. *Publish,* 46–47.

Rheingold, Howard. (1993). *The virtual community: Homesteading on the electronic frontier.* Reading, MA: Addison-Wesley.

Rheingold, Howard. (1994, April 5). Why censoring cyberspace is futile. *San Francisco Examiner,* p. 27.

Rice, Ronald E., & Shook, Douglas E. (1988). Access to, usage of, and outcomes from an electronic messaging system. *ACM Transactions on Office Information Systems, 6,* 255–276.

Riddle, Michael H. (1990). *The electronic pamphlet—computer bulletin boards and the law.* <http://www.eff.org/pub/Legal/bbs_and_law.paper>

Romano, Susan. (1993). The egalitarianism narrative: Whose story? which yardstick? *Computers and Composition, 10,* 5–28.

Rorty, Richard. (1989). *Contingency, irony, and solidarity.* Cambridge, MA: Cambridge University Press.

Rorty, Richard. (1991). Feminism and pragmatism. *Michigan Quarterly Review, 30,* 231–258.

Ross, Susan Mallon. (1994a). A feminist perspective on technical communicative action: Exploring how alternative worldviews affect environmental remediation efforts. *Technical Communication Quarterly, 3,* 325–342.

Ross, Susan Mallon. (1994b). Electronic mail: Legal and ethical concerns in the United States and Canada. *IEEE Transactions on Professional Communication, 37,* 218–225.

Rowland, Robert C., & Womack, Deanna F. (1985). Aristotle's view of ethical rhetoric. *Rhetoric Society Quarterly, 15,* 13–31.

Samuelson, Pamela. (1992). Updating the copyright look and feel lawsuits. *Communications of the ACM, 35*(9), 25–31.

Samuelson, Pamela. (1993). The ups and downs of look and feel. *Communications of the ACM, 36*(4), 29–35.

Samuelson, Pamela. (1994). Copyright's fair use doctrine and digital data. *Communications of the ACM, 37*(1), 21–27.

Samuelson, Pamela. (1995). Copyright and digital libraries. *Communications of the ACM, 38*(3), 15–21, 110.

Samuelson. Pamela. (1996). Intellectual property and the global information economy. *Communications of the ACM, 39*(1), 23–28.

Samuelson, Pamela, Davis, Randall, Kapor, Mitchell D., & Reichman, J. H. (1994). A manifesto concerning the legal protection of computer programs. *Columbia Law Review, 94* (8), 2308–2431.

Schilb, John. (1990). The role of ethos: Ethics, rhetoric, and politics in contemporary feminist theory. *PRE/TEXT, 11,* 211–234.

Schön, Donald A. (1983). *The reflective practitioner: How professionals think in action.* New York: Basic Books.

Schwartz, Helen. (1990). Ethical consideration of educational computer use. In Deborah H. Holdstein & Cynthia L. Selfe (Eds.), *Computers and writing: Theory, research, practice* (pp. 18–30). New York: Modern Language Association of America.

Scott, Charles E. (1990). *The question of ethics: Nietzsche, Foucault, Heidegger.* Bloomington: Indiana University Press.

Seabrook, John. (1994, June 6). My first flame. *The New Yorker, 70,* 70–79.

Selfe, Cynthia L. (1994). *Theorizing e-mail for the practice, instruction, and study of literacy.* Unpublished manuscript.

Selfe, Cynthia L. (1996, March). *The gendering of technology: Images of women, men, and technology.* Paper presented at Conference on College Composition and Communication, Milwaukee, WI.

Selfe, Cynthia L., & Hilligoss, Susan. (Eds.). (1994). *Literacy and computers: The complications of teaching and learning with technology.* New York: Modern Language Association of America.

Selfe, Cynthia L., & Selfe, Richard J., Jr. (1994). The politics of the interface: Power and its exercise in electronic contact zones. *College Composition and Communication, 45,* 480–504.

Shade, Leslie Regan. (1996). Is there free speech on the net? Censorship in the global information infrastructure. In Rob Shields (Ed.), *Cultures of Internet: Virtual spaces, real histories, living bodies* (pp. 11–32). London: Sage.

Sheard, Cynthia Miecznikowski. (1993). *Kairos* and Kenneth Burke's psychology of political and social communication. *College English, 55,* 291–310.

Shields, Rob. (Ed.). (1996). *Cultures of Internet: Virtual spaces, real histories, living bodies.* London: Sage.

Simons, Herbert W., & Billig, Michael. (1994). *After postmodernism: Reconstructing ideology critique.* London: Sage.

Simons, John. (1996, June 24). Free speech breaks loose in cyberspace. *U.S. News & World Report, 121,* 57.

Smith, Christian. (1991). *The emergence of liberation theology: Radical religion and social movement theory.* Chicago: University of Chicago Press.

Smith, Paul. (1988). *Discerning the subject.* Minneapolis: University of Minnesota Press.

Soja, Edward W. (1989). *Postmodern geographies: The reassertion of space in critical social theory.* London: Verso.

Spellmeyer, Kurt. (1993). Writing and truth: The decline of expertise and the rebirth of philosophy. *Journal of Advanced Composition, 13,* 97–110.

Spivak, Gayatri Chakrovorty. (1988). Can the subaltern speak? In Cary Nelson & Lawrence Grossberg (Eds.), *Marxism and the interpretation of culture* (pp. 271–313). Chicago: University of Illinois at Chicago Press.

Sproull, Lee, & Kiesler, Sara. (1991). *Connections: New ways of working in the networked organization.* Cambridge, MA: The MIT Press.

Stager, Susan F. (1992). Computer ethics violations: More questions than answers. *EDUCOM Review, 27*(4), 27–30.

Stanley, Liz. (Ed.). (1990a). *Feminist praxis: Research, theory, and epistemology in feminist sociology.* London: Routledge.

Stanley, Liz. (1990b). Feminist praxis and the academic mode of production: An editorial introduction. In Liz Stanley (Ed.), *Feminist praxis: Research, theory, and epistemology in feminist sociology* (pp. 3–19). London: Routledge.

Stanley, Liz, & Wise, Sue. (1990). Method, methodology and epistemology in feminist research processes. In Liz Stanley (Ed.), *Feminist praxis: Research, theory and epistemology in feminist sociology* (pp. 20–60). London: Routledge.

Steinfield, Charles W. (1992). Computer-mediated communications in organizational settings: Emerging conceptual frameworks and directions for research. *Management Communication Quarterly, 5,* 348–365.

Steuerman, Emilia. (1992). Habermas vs. Lyotard: Modernity vs. postmodernity? In Andrew Benjamin (Ed.), *Judging Lyotard* (pp. 99–118). London: Routledge.

Strunk, William, Jr., & White, E. B. (1979). *The elements of style* (3rd ed.). New York: Macmillan.

Stuckey, J. Elspeth. (1991). *The violence of literacy.* Portsmouth, NH: Boynton/Cook.

Suchman, Lucy A. (1987). *Plans and situated actions: The problem of human-machine communication.* Cambridge, UK: Cambridge University Press.

Sullivan, Dale L. (1990). Political-ethical implications of defining technical communication as a practice. *Journal of Advanced Composition, 10,* 375–386.

Sullivan, Patricia A. (1991). Taking control of the page: Electronic writing and word publishing. In Gail E. Hawisher & Cynthia L Selfe (Eds.), *Evolving perspectives on computers and composition studies: Questions for the 1990s* (pp. 43–64). Urbana, IL: NCTE and Computers and Composition.

Sullivan, Patricia, & Dautermann, Jennie. (Eds.). (1996). *Electronic literacies in the workplace: Technologies of writing.* Urbana, UL: NCTE and Computers and Composition.

Sullivan, Patricia A., & Porter, James E. (1993a). Remapping curricular geography: Professional writing in/and English. *Journal of Business and Technical Communication, 7,* 389-422.

Sullivan, Patricia A., & Porter, James E. (1993b). On theory, practice, and method: Toward a heuristic research methodology for professional writing. In Rachel Spilka (Ed.), *Writing in the workplace: New research perspectives* (pp. 220–237). Carbondale: Southern Illinois University Press.

Sullivan, Patricia, & Porter, James E. (1997). *Opening spaces: Writing technologies and critical research practices.* Greenwich, CT: Ablex.

Swearingen, C. Jan. (1991). *Rhetoric and irony: Western literacy and Western lies.* New York: Oxford University Press.

Takayoshi, Pamela. (1994). Building new networks from old: Women's experiences with electronic communications. *Computers and Composition, 11,* 21–35.

Thompson, Jeffery A., DeTienne, Kristen Bell, & Smart, Karl L. (1995). Privacy, e-mail, and information policy: Where ethics meets reality. *IEEE Transactions on Professional Communication, 38,* 158–164.

Toner, Lisa. (1996). *Ethical roles for the writing teacher: A rhetorical-casuistic perspective.* Unpublished doctoral dissertation, Purdue University, West Lafayette, IN.

Tovey, Janice. (1995). *A visual rhetoric for electronic-aided publishing.* Unpublished doctoral dissertation, Purdue University, West Lafayette, IN.

Trimbur, John, Wood, Robert G., Strickland, Ron, Thelin, William H., Rouster, William J., & Meister, Toni. (1993). Counterstatement: Responses to Maxine Hairston, "Diversity, ideology, and teaching writing." *College Composition and Communication, 44,* 248–257.

Van Bergen, Marilyn A. (1992). Copyright, law, fair use, and multimedia. *EDUCOM Review, 27*(4), 31–33.

Villa-Vicencio, Charles. (1992). *A theology of reconstruction: Nation-building and human rights.* Cambridge, UK: Cambridge University Press.

Vitanza, Victor J. (1990). An open letter to my "colligs": On paraethics, pararhetorics, and the hysterical turn. *PRE/TEXT, 11,* 237–287.

Vitanza, Victor J. (1991a). "Some more" notes, toward a "third" sophistic. *Argumentation, 5,* 117–139.

Vitanza, Victor J. (1991b). Three countertheses: Or, a critical in(ter)vention into composition theories and pedagogies. In Patricia Harkin & John Schilb (Eds.), *Contending with words: Composition and rhetoric in a postmodern age* (pp. 139–172). New York: Modern Language Association of America.

Vitanza, Victor J. (1994). Concerning a postclassical *ethos* as para/rhetorical ethics, the "selphs," and the excluded third. In James S. Baumlin & Tita French Baumlin (Eds.), *Ethos: New essays in rhetorical and critical theory* (pp. 380–431). Dallas: Southern Methodist University Press.

Wallace, Karl R. (1963). The substance of rhetoric: Good reasons. *Quarterly Journal of Speech, 49,* 239–249.

Walzer, Arthur E. (1989). The ethics of false *implicature* in technical and professional writing courses. *Journal of Technical Writing and Communication, 19,* 149–160.

Weaver, Richard. (1953). *The ethics of rhetoric.* Chicago: Henry Regnery.

Weaver, Richard. (1970). Ultimate terms in contemporary rhetoric. In Richard L. Johannesen, Rennard Stickland, & Ralph Eubanks. (Eds.), *Language is sermonic: Richard M. Weaver on the nature of rhetoric* (pp. 87–112). Baton Rouge: Louisiana State University Press.

Webster, Sally. (1992). Dispatches from the front line: Computer ethics war stories. *EDUCOM Review, 27*(4), 18–21.

Weis, A. H. (1992). Commercialization of the Internet. *Electronic Networking, 2,* 7–16.

West, Cornel. (1991). *The ethical dimensions of Marxist thought.* New York: Monthly Review Press.

Wilson, David L. (1995, April 7). Senate bill takes broom to Internet. *The Chronicle of Higher Education,* pp. A21–A22.

Winograd, Terry, & Flores, C. Fernando. (1986). *Understanding computers and cognition: A new foundation for design.* Norwood, NJ: Ablex.

Winograd, Terry. (1995). Heidegger and the design of computer systems. In Andrew Feenberg & Alastair Hannay (Eds.), *Technology and the politics of knowledge* (pp. 108–127). Bloomington: Indiana University Press.

Woodmansee, Martha, & Jaszi, Peter. (1995). The law of texts: Copyright in the academy. *College English, 57,* 769–787.

Working Group on Intellectual Property Rights. (1995, September). *Intellectual property and the National Information Infrastructure: The report of the working group on intellectual property rights.* Washington, DC: U.S. Department of Commerce. <http://www.uspto.gov/web/ipnii>

Wyschogrod, Edith. (1990). *Saints and postmodernism: Revisioning moral philosophy.* Chicago: University of Chicago Press.

Yang, Catherine. (1995, February 6). Flamed with a lawsuit. *Business Week,* 70–75.

Yavarkovsky, J. (1990). Coalition for networked information: A university-based electronic publishing network. *EDUCOM Review, 25*(3), 14–20.

Young, Iris Marion. (1990). *Justice and the politics of difference*. Princeton, NJ: Princeton University Press.

Zappen, James P. (1987). Rhetoric and technical communication: An argument for historical and political pluralism. *Journal of Business and Technical Communication, 1*, 29–44.

Zappen, James P. (1991). Scientific rhetoric in the nineteenth and early twentieth centuries: Herbert Spencer, Thomas H. Huxley, and John Dewey. In Charles Bazerman & James Paradis (Eds.), *Textual dynamics of the professions: Historical and contemporary studies of writing in professional communities* (pp. 145–167). Madison: University of Wisconsin Press.

Zavarzadeh, Mas'ud, & Morton, Donald. (1994). *Theory as resistance: Politics and culture after (post)structuralism*. New York: Guilford Press.

Zuboff, Shoshana. (1988). *In the age of the smart machine: The future of work and power*. New York: Basic Books.

Author Index

Subject Index

About the Author

James E. Porter is Professor of English and Director of Professional Writing at Purdue University, where he has taught professional writing and graduate rhetoric courses since 1988. He received a B.A. in English from John Carroll University in 1975, an M.A. from the University of Michigan in 1976, and a Ph.D. from the University of Detroit in 1982. His research, which examines connections between rhetoric theory, ethics, and professional writing, has been published in journals such as *Rhetoric Review, Journal of Business and Technical Communication*, and *IEEE Transactions on Professional Communication*. He has contributed chapters to numerous collections, and he has published a book examining audience theories in rhetoric/composition entitled *Audience and Rhetoric: An Archaeological Composition of the Discourse Community* (Prentice-Hall, 1992). In collaboration with Patricia Sullivan, Porter has published a series of articles developing a postmodern rhetoric of methodology, and he and Sullivan have written a book on methodology in the study of computer writing entitled *Opening Spaces: Writing Technologies and Critical Research Practices* (Ablex, 1997).